Green Wood
and
Chloroform

Green Wood *and* Chloroform

How a Young English Doctor Settled in Rural Maine

Anthony Betts, M.D.

Down East Books

The names of patients and their precise locations are fictitious, as are the names of all characters in this book, except for some of the physicians and locally well-known figures.

Text copyright © 1998 by Anthony Betts
Jacket illustration © 1998 by James Sollers
ISBN 0-89272-434-X
Book design by Eugenie S. Delaney
Printed at Capital City Press, Inc., Berlin, Vt.

2   4   5   3   1

Down East Books
P.O. Box 679
Camden, ME 04843
BOOK ORDERS: 1-800-766-1670

LIBRARY OF CONGRESS CATALOGING-IN-PUBLICATION DATA

Betts, Anthony, 1923–
    Green wood and chloroform / by Anthony Betts
        p.   cm.
    ISBN 0-89272-434-X (pbk.)
    1. Betts, Anthony, 1923–   . 2. Physicians (General practice)—
Maine—Biography. 3. Medicine, Rural—Maine.   I. Title.
R154.B5593A3   1998
610'.92—dc21
    [B]   97–51605
                                                             CIP

To Mary,
with love and gratitude.

1

LONDON to TRENTON

1

I T TAKES THE BRITISH about twelve years to settle in America. More than a lifetime is required to decipher the language. One might make a dent in understanding attitudes, humor, dress, driving, politics, law, policemen, sports, religion, the media, and the Weather Channel before shuffling off the mortal coil, but don't count on it. My wife, Mary, and I and our two infants moved to the United States in 1954 and nearly threw in the towel after three months.

Eight years previously I had returned to England from the war chock-full of enthusiasm for Britain's evolving welfare state. Five years of "backs to the wall," the Blitz, Dunkirk, rationing, Churchill, "There'll always be an England," and all the rest of it had fired up the British people with a spirit of equality. A fair share for all and love thy neighbor were our new social guideposts.

For two months I had sat in a tent beside the banks of the Suez Canal, swatting flies and waiting for a troopship to take me home. I also considered my future—where to fit in. I decided that my place in the brave new world was in medicine, as a doctor. I was twenty-three and brimful of altruism. Alone, I could not set the world right, or perhaps I'd already done that, but I could relieve individual suffering.

So, when I reached England in 1946, I went to the London Hospital Medical School.

The art of medicine was limited in the late 1940s. I suppose the primitive stage had been passed after Queen Victoria got her chloroform to produce Edward the Seventh. But penicillin had not yet been released when I entered medical school. Anesthetics were ether, trilene (trichloroethylene), and nitrous oxide; and chemotherapy didn't exist. Operations on the heart were experimental and dangerous. Dialysis machines were still being invented by backroom researchers, and transplants were a dream of the future.

On our first day in medical school we assembled in the anatomy amphitheater, eager to learn how to heal the sick.

"Gentlemen, you should bear in mind that 85 percent of patients who enter this hospital do so to *die*," said the dean, an eminent physician, in his welcoming remarks.

It was a bit deflating. He went on to say that we were to be taught the art of seeing patients comfortably on their way. Ours were to be lessons in the "medicine of mercy and without political interference under this newfangled National Health Service."

And so they were. Learning the ingredients of the "Brompton Cocktail" was but one example. This prescription for the terminally ill contained heroin and cocaine in either brandy or whisky with a smidgen of honey. Given every four hours, it was always effective; patients died happy and without pain. I wish we could use it now, but the legal profession has deemed otherwise.

At that time, the London Hospital wards were still big, open chambers with thirty to forty beds. The wards were named after breweries, such as Charrington and Watney, who were generous donors to the hospital (as George Bernard Shaw so cynically observed). Stern-faced nursing sisters, regarded as dragons in uniforms from the Florence Nightingale collection, disciplined the staff, in particular the young nurses and medical students. In turn, we revered the teaching staff with an awe suitable for royalty or some higher order. These doctors were often titled men, and vied with each other for appointments to Buckingham Palace. Once a year Her Majesty, Queen Mary, the hospital patron, would tour the wards. She was formidable and hunted for dust on top of cupboards.

We learned human anatomy in minute and useless detail, physiology (which resolutely ignored the metric system as being suspiciously European), too much biochemistry, and a touch of pharmacology. For the most part, it was a pleasant education, laced with ample time for sports, games, theatricals, humor, and love. You have to have a sense of humor to survive as a doctor and a human being.

After months of book work and some avoidable experimentation (trying to pass a naso-gastric tube on your student partner is not the best way to spend a summer afternoon or make friends), we tried to satisfy our teachers that we had absorbed this basic material. Reluctantly they let us loose on the wards to be taught at the bedside or in outpatient sessions.

We roamed around in teams of eight, assigned in rotation to surgeons, physicians, obstetricians, dermatologists, ophthalmologists, anesthetists, the V.D. clinic, psychiatrists, and other assortments. On bicycles, pedaling beside midwives through thick Dickensian fog, we journeyed around the Tower of London, Limehouse, and the London docks to deliver babies in the homes of stevedores and other formidable residents. The target was to net twenty-five babies inside the hospital and the same "on the district."

After a few years of this curriculum, there followed a series of interminable examinations—practical, oral, and written.

In London there were thirteen teaching hospitals. For fairness' sake and to avoid favoritism, the medical examiners felt it only right that students taught, for instance, in St. Bartholomew's should be questioned only by examiners from rival (and inferior) institutions such as Guy's Hospital, St. Mary's, or St. George's. It was a system that had worked admirably since the days of the Magna Charta.

Consequently, a thousand or so candidates spent three weeks crisscrossing London in a frenzied rush to be at the right place at the right time. It was a sort of bus and Underground obstacle race, involving elevators, stairways, and a mixture, in unequal parts, of running and walking. The pristine schedule that specified where and when a student should present himself invariably ended up as a sodden and illegible document.

No one who had successfully negotiated this system of "taking one's finals" felt any need for a change. "What was good enough for me, is damn well good enough for them" was a philosophy that had prevailed in medical education throughout Europe since the Middle Ages.

Fortunately custom had carved out havens of respite, comparable to the wayside inns from the days of stagecoaches. Peter's Bar, on Southampton Row, was one such medical student oasis, just around the corner from the Hospital for Neurological Diseases. Here, over a pint of mild and bitter in June 1952, I learned that I had succeeded in passing the exams (referred to as "fooling the examiners") and was to be granted a license to practice surgery, medicine, and midwifery. There was no graduation ceremony except in our own pub, The Black Bull.

I still had my little apartment in Bloomsbury with the rent frozen by the government. Here Mary, who had had the courage six months previously to marry me, and I made our first home. With the remnants of the British equivalent of a G.I. grant and the last of my savings from my R.A.F. pay we had a happy but frugal life.

Next came the essential business of getting a job as an intern at my teaching hospital. It was the only means of obtaining the vital reference for an application for a position as a practicing doctor. Any post in one's teaching hospital, even intern to the eye department, would suffice. It meant you were morally reliable and fairly sane. You accepted it regardless of whether you had any intention of ever examining an eye again. However, it was generally conceded that the ophthalmic job was close to scraping the bottom of the barrel.

None of these internships was paid. Actually, at no time was money discussed. Consequently, during all our medical student training, no instruction was given about the business of earning a living in the medical profession. No one mentioned salaries or incomes; it was bad form. No one warned us of the pitfalls of contracts with other practitioners, or the snags and snares of partnerships and assistantships.

I was lucky to get "jobs" in obstetrics, cardiology, and emergency medicine. And thus, in 1953 I was at last able to apply for a vacancy in general practice.

The National Health Scheme had been passed two years previously, and, to put it mildly, was still in its teething stage. The medical profession had been completely reshuffled from top to bottom, and (for reasons too long and tedious to put down here) there were now more than a hundred candidates clawing at the doors for every opening in general practice.

As a result, many family doctors who had managed to hang on to their practices during the medico-political upheaval of 1948–52, proceeded to have a field day. Their technique was to advertise for "an assistant with *a view to partnership* in a year." The pay would be nominal during the trial year, and the employing general practitioner kept all the fees. The assistant did most of the work.

Over the length and breadth of Britain, swarms of fledgling doctors, like homing bees, applied for these assistantships, the only way to get a start. But in 95 percent of the jobs, the "view" at the end of the year never came into sight, largely because it had never existed. Conferences at the eleventh hour would bring up charges of "incompatibility," "incompetence," "poor doctor/patient attitude," and so on. Another assistant would be enticed into the web even before his predecessor was shown the back door.

I fell into just such a trap at a time when our bank balance was at low ebb—its usual place in our personal finances. And I was saved only because an old, established doctor violated an unwritten rule of medical practice: "Thou shalt not inform on the workings of a rival practice even if they're as crooked as a corkscrew."

He had been out of town when one of his patients went into labor. Under the National Health Service, most deliveries had to be performed in the home. Word reached me that the midwife was in difficulty, and I went and helped out. Days later the rival doctor met me in the High Street and thanked me.

"Not at all," I said. "You can do the same for me one of these days."

"I'm afraid not. You won't be here."

"What do you mean?"

And he explained (looking around to make sure he wasn't over-heard) that the doctor to whom I was an assistant "with view to partnership" had already had ten or eleven assistants with the same view. In his opinion it would be wise to anticipate the inevitable ax. I should be looking for another opening now rather than waiting until I was thrown out.

It was devastating news. I had three months left in my contract. The diminishing bank balance had just had another blow in the form of an enormous garage bill. Our second-hand, pre-owned, experi-enced Singer sports car, which had already had major surgery for a pis-ton through a cylinder head, now lay dormant with its universal joint in two parts instead of one. I was making house calls (twenty-two a day) in my brother's eight-cylinder Alvis. Patients knew I was com-ing because its muffler was proclaiming to the world, like a twenty-one-gun gun salute, that it was about to perforate.

Salvation, like a Biblical prophet descending through the clouds, came in the form of that rarity, a private patient. We had three of this endangered species in our practice of 3,700 National Health patients. They could be charged fees and were therefore treated like Water-ford crystal. (Most people with middle and lower incomes welcomed the National Health Service; it meant unlimited medical attention, prescriptions, and hospital and nursing home care. But participation was not mandatory, and some of the affluent elected not to join the scheme, feeling that by paying their doctor his fees they could com-mand more attention—and indeed they could and did.) On my chief's days off, of which there were several, I was allowed, after due cautioning, to make house calls to these select patients. This particular patient was an elderly, kind lady with little more ailing her than loneliness.

A few days after my informer had given me his black prediction, she requested a house call. The chief had an early tee time, so off I went. As usual, it was more a social visit, and during our chat the subject of my future came up. When I told her that I suspected it was a trifle bleak, she nodded affirmatively, adding, "The doctor's assistants do seem to come and go very frequently."

She made a suggestion: I should follow her son, also a doctor, to the land of medical opportunity. He dwelt in the halls of plenty at Trenton State Hospital in New Jersey, and had written her glowing letters intimating that life there was close to paradise. She offered to write him on my behalf to see if there might be an opening for me.

Profuse transatlantic correspondence and forwarding of credentials ensued. Within a month I was offered a job at $6,000 a year with free accommodation for my family. It was indeed a golden opportunity. I was scrutinized, interrogated, screened, and examined in pursuit of a visa at the American embassy and was finally found suitable material for the Land of the Free.

With the last of our money I bought one ticket on the SS Liberte, and Mary and the babies and I moved into a single-room apartment with a medical friend and his family. It was a cozy but rather cramped arrangement, with bicycles and baby carriages having to be repositioned before every meal. Many other squalid details come to mind, such as who got first go at the newspaper and who finished the crossword. But we were as happy as anyone else who has endured conditions similar to the Black Hole of Calcutta.

A few days before I sailed, the superintendent of Trenton State Hospital wrote to say, "Reading between the lines of your last letter, it would seem that you are under the impression that ours is a general hospital. We are, in fact, a mental institution. That is implied in the title 'State Hospital.' If you wish to change your mind. . . ." (As I said, language can be a problem. It took me a long time to learn that when an American surgeon said, "Why don't you hold that retractor in place," he was not asking a question.)

I arrived in New York on July 3, 1954, with fifty-six dollars in my pocket. I had no idea how to get to Trenton, New Jersey. I had three bags, which a man with a red cap kindly carried. He seemed disturbed when I tipped him a quarter, considered at the time a generous amount in the Old Country, but not in this new land, nor by the redcap.

Somehow I found my way through a cavernous railway terminus and unearthed in its depths a train for Trenton. My racing heart finally calmed as the train deposited me at the Trenton platform. Innocently oblivious to the prevailing color bar, I accepted a ride from a black Trenton State Hospital attendant in his Cadillac convertible. Finally I was ready to step into my new professional role in a staff of twenty-one doctors (from a spectrum of twelve nationalities) caring for some four thousand inmates.

I reached Trenton on July 4, apparently a national holiday and a cause for celebration. New Jersey was in the midst of a heat wave, and my hospital apartment had central heating by electric baseboards. No one, including the girl on the switchboard, knew how to turn it off. The few resident doctors who were not sunning themselves on the New Jersey beaches lent me fans enough to turn the place into a wind tunnel. The walls were decorated in royal blue with giant white daisies, which in the shimmering heat appeared to approach and recede menacingly, even when viewed from a stationary armchair. The bedroom backed onto the regressed female schizophrenic wing, where the inmates screamed through the night with a vocabulary that I'd thought few ladies knew.

After a week, I went to get my paycheck. Money was tight for the family back in England, and I soon learned that it was going to get tighter. A remorseless, grim-faced, overheated, overweight lady informed me that the New Jersey Civil Service did not give out paychecks to newcomers for the first month.

My despair must have been evident to my chief, Dr. Jack Sharp, for he stopped to talk with me later that same day as I sat hunched over a mountainous volume of notes about one of our manic-depressive patients. Sharp was a bright young doctor, a graduate of Notre Dame, and had served in the U.S. Navy. He was a rarity, being one of the few succinct psychiatrists I have ever met. I feared that with all the other problems he had to face each day he had little time for the tribulations of his most junior staff member. Indeed, I could see during my first week that he barely knew I existed. I didn't think it would be either reasonable or fruitful to tell him of my personal problems. And there was the language difficulty; he might ask why I didn't get lost, and not want an answer.

The following morning, between two more mountains of patient notes, I found an envelope on my desk. It contained a short note: "Understand you're having some initial difficulties. Pay me back when you can. Jack Sharp, M.D." Attached was a check for one thousand dollars.

Dr. Sharp then decided (and hasn't changed his mind to this day) that psychiatry was not my forte, and put me in charge of the ward for the physically sick. The following week he introduced me to his fiancée, the prettiest nurse I have ever seen, and both of them urged me to bring my family over.

I bought a second shirt and sent money to England for air fares.

Mary and the two babes—Sara, aged one-and-a-half, and Ann, three months—arrived at Idlewild in August after a sixteen-hour trip via Shannon and Gander. Since the luggage limit was forty pounds, Mary had carried her fur coat by wearing it. She arrived to find that New York was enduring a heat wave.

I gave Sara a Hershey bar, which melted over her face, and we rehydrated Ann with two bottles (sterilized) of orange juice. We then steamed down the New Jersey Turnpike in an open Studebaker at more than seventy miles per hour, to be overtaken frequently by eighteen-wheeled trucks in tandem.

Northern New Jersey was at its ripest. A resident doctor (the son of my kindly British private patient) and his girl friend, a slinky model, had offered to help me meet the family. She was at the wheel, smoking a Marlboro, and turned around from time to time to point out landmarks of Newark and other exciting features to Mary, shrunk in the back seat.

The heat had been turned off in our apartment by this time, and it was a coolish ninety-two. But the wallpaper was as vibrant and menacing as ever and the regressed ladies behind our bedroom still kept up their nightly chant of ancient obscenities.

Much more happened, good and bad—a rebellion in the criminal wing, a hurricane, a reprimand for riding with a colored attendant, friends generous beyond belief, a pay day, trips to the shore, tennis—but after three months, and with the prospect of a Christmas marooned on foreign soil in a lunatic asylum, we'd had it. We had to escape.

The choices were tough: go home, back to the dreary dead end of National Health; try another country; or find a way to practice general medicine in America. I had no license. Was there a state that would allow me to apply for one?

We pored over the American Journal of Medicine, where there was a chart listing the requirements for foreign graduates. U.S. citizenship, internship in the U.S.A., military service, basic science, a license in another state, and half a dozen other conditions were essential. After an hour we had narrowed it down. Two states would allow me to sit their examination: Alabama and Maine.

We knew where Alabama was. We borrowed an atlas and found Maine. With nothing to lose, I wrote to the secretary of the Maine Board of Medical Examiners to ask if I might be allowed to sit the examination coming up in six months.

To my surprise, a letter with an imposing embossed heading came back by return mail: "Come and take the examination next week."

I replied: "I cannot get my credentials together in time."

Back came: "Forget the credentials until after the examination. Be in Portland next Monday at 9 A.M., City Hall."

CHAPTER

I N 1954 IT WAS POSSIBLE to travel by train from Trenton, New Jersey, to Portland, Maine, in relative safety and comfort. To the neophyte, some confusion could arise in not knowing that you had to change at Boston, and that Boston had both a North and a South Station. But this could be sorted out easily for a nominal amount by any Irish cab driver, who would also ensure that you toured most of the outskirts of the city during your ride.

And so, on a coolish evening in November, I found myself deposited at the far end of Congress Street in Portland, at the flagship terminal of the Boston and Maine Line. (This structure, a pleasing piece of architecture replicated in many major cities in northern New England, was of course flattened a few years later and replaced by a parking lot, a fast-food restaurant, a liquor store, a discount automotive parts store, and other sundry pieces of mercantile artistry.)

I was to sit the license examination the following morning at 9:00 A.M. I was dressed for the occasion in my formal business suit and carried a light case and an umbrella. I needed a hotel, and having learned the price of advice from the average cab driver, I decided to walk up Congress Street and see for myself what was available.

I suppose I could go to the library and find an accurate description of the local layout in that year, but I like to hark back in my own mind to that day when I plodded up beside The Sportsman's Grill. On the opposite side, where now stands a hideous parking garage, an improvised ski slope ran down from the red-brick hospital up on the hill above Charles Street.

Next came a square with a statue of Longfellow seated deep in thought and copper green about the waist. Then I remember coming beside an imposing building of granite, the public library, next door to a resplendent movie house. Close by, the voice of Rosemary Clooney sang "Hey There!" from *Pajama Game*.

There was an attractive-looking hotel, the Lafayette, somewhere opposite, but I suspected it was beyond my budget, and I felt the same about the Eastland, which I saw as I crossed High Street.

By now I was walking past expensive shops. A pharmacy occupied the ground floor of the curious looking Hay Building. Triangular, like a wedge of cake, it headed the point dividing Congress Street from Free Street. Then came smaller establishments with windows already decorated for Christmas. These must have included Springer's, Bernie's, Cartier, and many others. And of course there was the opulent Porteous, Mitchell and Braun department store, with its regiment of twinkling Christmas trees and windows dressed with reindeer, sleds, and snow. I also passed Emery Brown's emporium, then Loring, Short and Harmon's book and stationery store, all ablaze with light, and I realized Portland was a dignified, prosperous city.

I couldn't resist looking at all the gleaming gadgets in Day's Jewelers, and I was astonished to find myself facing Longfellow's house. And then, suddenly, I was in front of City Hall. I had arrived. I ventured up the broad steps.

No doubt about it, this was the place for tomorrow's tryst. So I needed a nearby hotel, and to my delight found a modest establishment by wandering down a side street. I registered, and for three dollars was given a key about the size suitable for a maximum-security cell in San Quentin.

An elevator not designed to inspire confidence took me in its own good time to the fifth floor, where I faced what seemed to be an infinite number of identical doors. When I eventually found mine, it was like winning the lottery. I was able to insert my pound of key (it had a steel billiard ball attached by heavy chain) and let myself into what seemed to be an expanded coffin.

The window, which couldn't be opened without a chisel and mallet, gave on to a brick wall obscured periodically by belching steam. The bed would not have been endorsed by any orthopedic authority unless a considerable sum of money changed hands. The chair, which even then should have had a sticker warning of the dangers of sitting on it, would today fetch a good price at a flea market.

But in spite of these limitations I was not downhearted. I had no books to study and the evening was just beginning. I decided to explore, and minus umbrella and overcoat, I set out with the key and ball for the foyer.

Everyone was friendly and business was brisk at the front desk. Most customers seemed to avoid the creaky elevator and took the stairs.

Somewhere nearby I managed to find some food. No fast-food chains had as yet erupted like mushrooms on a midsummer night. Some of the shops around Monument Square had lunch counters that served a hamburger and accessories. Things were pretty quiet in that neighborhood in the mid-1950s. It had become neither the rallying point for the homeless nor the quick drug mart. There were no high-rise banks, yuppie civilization had not chintzed-up Exchange Street, Middle Street, or the docks, and everything was shrouded in peaceful, foggy gloom.

I retreated to my hotel and sat in the foyer. I couldn't help noticing the various permutations of the couples who seemed familiar with the stairway route, and I began to suspect the nature of the establishment. This was confirmed throughout the night by the extraordinary amount of traffic in the corridor on my floor. Snatches of song and bursts of wild laughter continued into the early hours. I began to worry about how fresh I would be for my examination in the morning.

Next day I discovered that in Maine, November can freshen nearly anything that moves. I entered City Hall and stood beneath its echoing vaults with weeping eyes and cheeks like a pair of McIntosh apples.

Quite a mob of candidates, speaking in a multitude of tongues, had assembled and were thawing out. Some had taken the exam two or three times before and were dressed for the weather if not the event. The ability to speak or read English was not a requirement to sit the examination, although it was helpful. I directed one or two Asiatics to the cloakroom, and personally conducted by sign language a perplexed Chinese man who was staring uncomprehendingly at the words "Rest Room."

As the clock boomed out the hour, we were ushered into a large room and each shown to a desk. The head examiner, Dr. Adam Leighton, an impressive figure in a dark suit, greeted us and ran over the rules.

It was to be a written test, for a couple of days. We were not going to be asked to look at patients, nor be handed bottled surgical specimens to guess their origin. Nor was any surgeon going to pass out a tool of his trade and ask how it might be used. In other words this was not going to be a replica of that trial by fire I had experienced in London.

A ream or two of foolscap paper was set before us, and we were allowed to read the question paper.

Time has a natural way of dimming the memory of pain and suffering, as every mother knows. Offhand, I can't think of a male equivalent to the pangs of childbirth, but I do recall the shock of reading the endless list of convoluted questions that was presented to us. I remember counting their number and dividing it into the available time. It came out to about four minutes for each answer.

That wouldn't have been too bad if the answer could have been a simple yes or no with a brief comment. But there were many extraordinarily complex questions. The prize, in my book, went to

"Describe the symptoms, signs, etiology, treatment, complications, and prognosis of typhoid."

Volumes that have been recycled into immovable doorstops have been devoted to that subject alone. Typhoid! What on earth could one do with it in four minutes? My pen flew across the pages in a frenzied scrawl. I wrote like a reporter facing an impossible deadline. For an instant my eye caught that of the Chinaman, who, with a Buddha-like calm, was placidly nodding his head, his pen quietly in repose.

So the first morning proceeded. Like a demented sorcerer's apprentice, I valiantly wrote who knows what answer to those multifaceted questions. Refueled with a hot dog and milkshake, I scribbled on through the afternoon. Balzac would have been left on the starting line, Dickens with him.

In the evening I staggered back to my fifth-floor box and sank onto the bed as though it were made of foam rubber and goose feathers. No screams of delight from the adjacent clientele disturbed me; there may have been a brass band in the corridor for all I knew. I slept.

The second day was a repeat of the first, with a few gaps in the ranks where some had fallen to the initial onslaught. Dr. Leighton passed between our desks like General Washington at Valley Forge. The weather outside City Hall matched that setting.

At one point I managed to have a word with Dr. Leighton about my credentials. I thanked him for letting me be present, because, as I said, I might have been a Fuller Brush salesman for all he knew. He looked at me with what I can only describe as a Maine look and made some comment about my accent possibly being a disadvantage even to the Fuller Brush company. He explained that already data had been acquired about my background, and a copy of my British license, a look at my passport, and a few references would be all that was necessary.

I checked out of my hotel (cash) and made my way back to Trenton, this time walking between Boston North and Boston South.

CHAPTER

3

N O FRESH DISASTERS had overtaken Trenton State Hospital
in my absence, and I settled back into work on the medical ward.
I anticipated waiting a couple of months for my examination
results.

Dr. Sharp, who had transferred me to the medical ward, seldom
visited that area; outside consultants made regular rounds to give me
help and advice. However, he was in receipt of a steady flow of comments and complaints from the nurses about "that new Britisher
you've wished on us." Chief among these gripes was the stream of
comparisons I made between how we did things better in the Old
Country than they did them over here. The pharmacist's blood pressure was sustained at a pretty high level as he read the components of
prescriptions I wrote. "Unna's Paste" had never before been requested
during his career. (He was on the point of retirement, and showed
me his twenty-five-year pin.) Codeine was a Schedule 1 narcotic. He
wasn't interested in hearing that a British housewife could buy it off
the shelf. "We don't chew 'em like aspirin in *this* state," he told me.

Soon Dr. Sharp exhibited his bedside manner, his ability to mix a
formidable manhattan, and a latent talent for international diplomacy.
He invited me to dinner. In a mellow atmosphere with soft lights
and against a selection from *The King and I*, with our wives quietly
discussing the intricacies of knitting little things, he brought up the
issues that had come to his ears. He managed to gracefully word it as
if the recent medical contretemps at Trenton State Hospital were of
his own making and allowed me to advise him how to mend his ways.

Among other gems, I went so far as to suggest that he adopt a
more lenient attitude toward some of his own young mental patients.
As resident in training I had to go on teaching rounds. I was particu-

larly concerned with a group of boys who had been diagnosed as amoral and put in isolation. I had talked with two of them, and with brown, boyish, innocent eyes, they had pleaded with me from behind bars for intercession. Dr. Sharp said they were too dangerous to be let loose on the open wards. I disagreed. I had worked with them. He thought a bit, refilled my glass, and agreed to let two of them out for the day. He suggested I watch their progress.

Two days later on my medical ward, I found one patient who had been hit on the head with a urine bottle and another whose bathrobe had been set on fire. The two boys were back in isolation, and on rounds Dr. Sharp was gentlemanly enough to avoid comment.

Two weeks later I received an official letter from the Maine Board of Medical Examiners. It was brief:

"You've passed! Come and practice in Maine. Adam Leighton, M.D."

I was overwhelmed, not only by the result but by the speed of the decision. From what I remembered of my scrawled output, a world record for speed reading, deciphering, and decoding must have been broken when my exam was graded. But that was a passing thought; the great thing was that I'd actually been invited to practice family medicine. Somebody up there wanted me.

But then Mary and I began to think about money. To set up a practice or buy one would be too expensive. Reality cooled our ardor. I wrote back to Dr. Leighton, thanking him and explaining my difficulty. I was tied to my Trenton paycheck.

Dr. Leighton wrote again: "You won't need anything but a medical bag, if you're prepared to go to any one of the towns listed here." And down the side of the paper were the names of about thirty towns in need of a doctor. In a postscript he added: "If you go to Eagle Lake, you'll do very well. They need help badly. They have a forty-bed hospital. Their only doctor has had to go to Florida for the winter because of ill health. Contact a Mr. John Martin."

Our spirits rose, and again we borrowed the atlas to find Eagle

Lake. It wasn't there. Someone found us a Rand McNally road atlas, and by turning to the one-inch-to-the-mile segment for Maine, we located our target. Eagle Lake was on Route 11, about twenty miles south of Fort Kent on the Canadian border. The map showed a lot of water and a large expanse of white labeled Allagash Wilderness.

Keats's ode came to mind: "Like stout Cortez when with eagle eyes he star'd at the Pacific." I hadn't realized Maine was such a huge state. It seemed about five hundred miles long and looked as if it could encompass most of Scotland or a large chunk of England, yet its population of 900,000 was less than that of a small English city. More than half of its inhabitants lived in the south. Above Bangor, in the county of Aroostook, even with heavy coaching from the Catholic diocese, there was no danger of overcrowding.

I got in touch with Mr. John Martin in Eagle Lake. He was encouraging, and told me that I would have no trouble making a living with a practice in his town. The forty hospital beds were always full, and the state paid three dollars a day for the doctor to look after those patients. In addition to that, I'd be busy because, apart from the six or seven physicians in Fort Kent, there wasn't another doctor for a hundred miles in any direction. He added that the Fort Kent road was usually impassable for a few days after a storm.

He advised me to come up for an immediate interview with the medical committee: the priest, the owner of the variety store, and himself. "We all speak English," he added. The import of that remark was soon to be revealed.

I went to the Trenton State Hospital superintendent, Dr. Magee, to ask for leave and tell him of my plans. He was very understanding and told me he had found remote parts of Canada beautiful. Of course the Rockies didn't impinge on Maine, and he'd never traveled that far north. He'd been to North Dakota, though, which might be similar. And he wished me luck.

As this was to be an important interview, I selected my best London wardrobe: a dark suit, white shirt with my college tie, dress shoes, and a top coat. I never liked wearing hats and didn't possess one. I carried my umbrella and a suitcase.

Once more, five days before Christmas, I ventured on the railroad. Getting to Portland was a snap. The snow-encrusted landscape through Rhode Island and beyond looked superb. For the first time I saw part of a bay iced over. And a fellow passenger in a fur cap, looking like a trapper from *White Fang*, told me, "It has been a mite cold. Quite a snap."

This I could confirm when I changed trains at Portland. The cold was even more intense at 2:00 A.M. in Bangor, where I was faced with a two-hour wait. For some reason, which I can only attribute to childhood abuse, an unfortunate marriage, or a general bitterness toward mankind, he who had devised the railway timetable had arranged that the next train out of Bangor for Houlton would not depart until 4:00 A.M.

Bangor ceased its revelry quite early in those days, maybe about nine. Even the Christmas decorations were timed to go out at midnight. Thereafter everything slept or hibernated. The railroad station was closed, its lights dimmed, and there was nothing to do but walk in circles to keep warm. My drawing room shoes were not the best footwear for the slush left from the last storm. Then it started to snow, and my fellow passengers in their multicolored snow jackets and assorted headgear seemed to find my umbrella fascinating. It was even a subject for conversation, which up until then had been limited to incoherent monosyllables.

Our train eventually turned up. To subdue our enthusiasm, it shunted up and down a few times before it brought its solitary coach alongside our platform. For a train at that hour it was crowded and mercifully warm, and the air was thick with smoke. I found a seat on an armrest. By now the snowfall was turning itself into a blizzard. I think I slept in fits and starts until I woke abruptly to the cries of "Houlton!"

Worried that I might not quit the train before it took off again, I seized my suitcase in one hand and my umbrella in the other and stepped out onto the platform. Actually the platform was about five feet down; I stood for about two seconds on a snowdrift and then disappeared.

Assistance was immediately forthcoming, and I was hauled out and dusted off to cries of "Mon Dieu! Quel blaque!" Then I was led to a room and given coffee and a doughnut.

In a mixture of pidgin English and school French I explained where I was trying to get to. "Eagle Lake! Ah man, c'est difficile, non?" A long conference followed. I needed to get to Ashland, a timber center, and from there a forty-mile bus ride would land me in the heart of Eagle Lake.

I have no recollection of how I got to Ashland. For all I know I may have taken the Concorde. But I do remember the journey from Ashland to Eagle Lake as though it had taken place yesterday.

The vehicle was a yellow school bus. I was the only passenger, and the driver was a young monolingual man whose ambition seemed to be to find out whether the bus would plane when it exceeded sixty miles per hour. That is to say, whether it would lift its front end in the air like a high-speed motorboat. He had already shown that it could corner on two wheels.

The road surface was ice. The blizzard had ceased and plows had been through, adding more to the twenty-foot snowbanks on each side. It was as if we were traveling down an endless ravine. The tips of telephone poles were barely visible against an unending forest of spruce and fir trees. There was nothing else to see until we tobogganed into the town of Portage (population approximately fifty). Here we paused for a full thirty seconds, but there were no takers, and we were off again, the back end of the bus slithering like a giant fishtail as we approached Mach 1. Again, trees to the end of the earth, but eventually the monotonous scene began to be punctuated by an occasional snow-covered house glimpsed at the end of a trenchlike driveway.

Finally some larger buildings emerged through the blanket of snow. First was a gray Gothic church, clothed in ice and dripping spears of icicles like a granite fortress, then a great, square building with a giant wooden cross, and finally another road, the first and only intersection, where rows of wooden houses met at the general store of Eagle Lake.

I weaved my way to the front of the bus and made my way cautiously down the steps—and ended up sitting down in the road. The surface was indeed ice. Even getting up was difficult. Meanwhile the bus swished off down the side road to the post office. I made my way into the store.

It was a variety store in the cracker-barrel category, and packed to the eyebrows. It was almost impossible to approach the counter for all the fishing tackle, axes, barrels, electrical appliances, tools, spades, shovels, kindling, guns, rope, boxes, tins, shoes, hats, jackets, pants, boots, and packaged food of every sort. Five or six burly customers, all speaking French, filled in the gaps. My entrance didn't cause a ripple.

It was only when someone wanted to get out and found me blocking the entrance that my presence was noticed. The negotiations under way at the counter were suspended as one heavy figure bent forward over the counter and gazed at me. He was wearing a thick woolen red-and-black plaid jacket and a baseball hat.

"Ah! C'est le docteur, n'est-ce pas?"

"Oui," I called back.

He gave a torrent of explanation to the customers. He then disappeared, and after a clatter of bottles and some spontaneous rap French, by an extraordinary feat emerged at my side. He introduced himself as Monsieur Belanger.

"Enchanté," I said, relying heavily on the few months I had spent walking in France as a medical student, where the natives occasionally allowed me to maul their language. "Je suis Dr. Betts."

"Ah! C'est bon. Je donne le téléphone à Monsieur Martin."

Or something to that effect. I got the gist. No one else moved, all eyed me with cautious suspicion. They were a bulky bunch, each around the two-hundred- to three-hundred-pound mark. All listened while M. Belanger spoke volubly on the telephone in a mixture of French and English.

It seemed that he had reached Mr. Martin, and Mr. Martin was doing most of the talking. M. Belanger got in a succession of, "Oui! Mais oui! Ah, oui!" each interjection having an increasing penultimate tone, and at last there came the ding of the replaced telephone receiver. He reappeared to report to the group, and me, that Mr. Martin would be driving up immediately.

Almost as soon as he had stopped speaking, a black Cadillac the size of a deluxe hearse drew up beside the variety store. I was led to its side, edging at an awkward angle between a six-foot snowbank and the somber limousine. I used a door handle as a mooring. Mr. Martin let down his electric window and introduced himself, inviting me in. From the far side of the snow M. Belanger said something and waved.

It was not a time to linger; the outside temperature was minus thirty-four degrees. I clambered around and let myself in.

Mr. Martin—a well-known figure in the Maine legislature, as I was to learn later—seemed to be a more sophisticated, city man than the patrons of Belanger's variety store. Dark, thick overcoat, fur collar, expensive leather gloves—I was impressed, but I don't remember much more except that the car was warm and glided silently down the road.

John Martin said he was glad I had offered to come, and he would show me the house where I would be able to live and set up my practice. The limousine purred gently through the snow-laden side street toward a vast lake bounded by giant mounds of plowed snow. There were about twenty wooden houses on each side of the street, including a post office and another, smaller general store. At the end of the road, before a towering white bank, we stopped outside a little deserted house. Mr. Martin said this would be where I would live and see patients. The rent would be twenty-five dollars a month, "and there's a good supply of green and white." I nodded as if I knew what he meant. Neither of us made any attempt to get out of the car.

As he turned the car around, he pointed to a ramshackle building on the edge of the lake. A long wooden walkway led up to its door, looking like the bridge over the River Kwai (before it was blown up). This was Eagle Lake's entertainment center. During the winter season the entertainment was restricted to a monthly dance, or sometimes some bingo. The small rickety building nearby was a factory for producing skittles. It usually employed three or four people, but business had not been brisk and it was now idle. Most men were working in the woods.

We headed back to the main road, Route 11. The Cadillac was remarkably steady, and with Mr. Martin at the wheel, we cornered without a hint of a skid. There were a few more buildings on the main street. Like decayed and broken teeth, the remnants of two recently burned structures made gaps in the rows of white houses. Fire was not unusual, Mr. Martin explained with an air of acceptance. "Three or four a year. They make their stoves too hot," he murmured.

We scrunched to a halt at the gaunt, square building I had seen from the bus. I noticed that the cold snow and ice on the road squeaked under the pressure of the tires. Mr. Martin explained that this was the hospital. He thought the priest, Anthony Blais, might be within. I ought to meet him. Also I ought to meet the mother superior.

Gingerly I followed Mr. Martin up the icy pathway and steps. He trod confidently in thick rubber overshoes. My shoe leather slid on the frozen surface as efficiently as waxed skis.

The entrance hall of the hospital was dominated by Catholic emblems. Gold crosses, tinted prints of the Savior, admonitions, texts, and carved, colored crucifixes abounded on the whitewashed walls. To one side, seated in a cubbyhole something like a theater box office, a nun with a thin face, thin lips, and rimless spectacles wrote on a ledger. Hat in hand and adopting a reverent attitude, Mr. Martin spoke to her softly in French.

I looked about. The floor was black-and-white checked linoleum. A large cross of gold dominated the wall at one end of the hall. It was flanked on one side by a colored print of a blond, bearded Jesus, and on the other by a photograph of equal size showing a middle-aged man in collar and tie.

Mr. Martin came to stand beside me. "That's the man you will be replacing." He pointed to the photograph of the man minus the halo. "Doctor Kirk. He's been here for over twenty-five years. The people worship him. He's delivered half the population of the town." He raised his eyebrows and gave a shrug.

An elderly nun in full regalia, followed by a younger member of the order, descended into the hall.

Some years later, my limited knowledge about nuns and convents received a boost from *The Sound of Music,* but in 1954 that musical had not yet been produced. *Black Narcissus* and *Going My Way* had been useful Hollywood texts, however, and I did know a mother superior when I saw one. Mr. Martin greeted her in French and explained who I was. She smiled and inclined her head to me. "Docteur Betts."

I smiled back. The mother superior gestured to the other nun, a tall young woman in her twenties. Her eyes sparkled, and her face had a simple, happy radiance. There was something infectiously friendly about her. I was reminded of the young Ingrid Bergman.

"I am Sister Euloge, Doctor," she said in English with a trace of accent. "I hope you will be coming here. I am a nurse." She offered me her hand and smiled. As I shook it I little realized that I was meeting someone who was going to save my skin and sanity a hundred times or more in the very near future.

I was not shown any more of the hospital, nor did I meet Father Blais, who had been called away. I went back to the car with Mr. Mar-

tin, and he gave me a few more details about the extent of the work.
I told him my greatest worry was whether I'd be able to make a living. I would be stepping out into the unknown. He gave a laugh.
Dr. Kirk had made enough to buy the parking lot surrounding the
biggest post office in Miami, and a lot more besides. It was absurd
to think I wouldn't do well. The community was desperate. Would
I come?

Perhaps if I had returned to Trenton to think it over, I might have
hesitated. But this was a challenge and an opportunity. Mary had given
me carte blanche. I agreed to take the job.

Right away?

I'd be back ready to start work on January first.

The deal was sealed with a handshake, and Mr. Martin said I just
had time to catch the bus back to Ashland.

CHAPTER

WITHIN A MINUTE of stepping inside the door at Trenton I
broke the news. I had accepted the job at Eagle Lake. I told
Mary it was a bit off the beaten track and that we might warm up
by trips to the North Pole on our days off. But she was game; she always was and still is. If I'd suggested we move to the outer Galapagos, she'd have backed me up and started to iron a shirt or two.

I gave my news to Dr. Magee. He was very encouraging and told
me I should do well in Canada. He'd be willing to release me from
my contract as a resident-in-training in psychiatry. He was certain that,
though he'd "heard good things," Dr. Sharp could probably manage
to get along without me.

Jack Sharp was more practical. I'd need a car, and he had just the one. A two-year-old, top of the line Oldsmobile had come into his hands from a family member. I could have it for a thousand dollars. Pay when it was convenient.

Here was an embarrassing situation: gratitude versus the desire for security. I'd had my fill of second-hand cars in the Old Country. Admittedly most of them had been around for fifteen or more years and the most I'd paid for any of them was forty-five dollars; still, a second-hand car was not a thing to rely on. I explained all this to him with apologies. He said he fully understood. It was just that this Oldsmobile had been driven by his uncle and only had fifteen thousand miles on it. Still, if I wanted a new car, I'd better get one.

I told him I fancied a Pontiac sedan, and he offered to come and help me with the dealer. He had himself bought several cars in his time.

We went down to a dealership in Trenton and kicked a few tires before a helpful salesman took us in hand. I rather fancied a green two-door model. In fact I told him I thought it was a great car. He let me sit in it and he opened the hood. Jack Sharp stood aside and watched, his face expressionless.

The salesman and I began to discuss prices. He told me I couldn't do better anywhere else in the county. I was willing to accept his word. And it was at this point that Jack stepped in.

"This the only car you've got on the lot?"

The salesman confessed that there were more models.

"Let's drive a few."

The poor salesman became very active, bearing number plates from one car to another as we came and went from the lot. They were all excellent, but I was still in favor of my first love, the green Pontiac. Papers were prepared and prices discussed. This way and that, Jack made the total smaller and smaller. It was embarrassing to see how he was treating the salesman. I was about to tell him that we didn't behave this way in the Old Country, when to my astonishment Jack said he thought we would do better at the Chevy dealer around the corner and started with me toward the door. I can only say the effect was dramatic—the price on the Pontiac dropped another three hundred.

We arranged to pick up the car as soon as possible. I explained that I was going to Maine.

"You'll need snow tires," said the salesman, obviously trying to add an unnecessary extra to make up for what he had lost.

I told him the tires on the car were quite satisfactory and glanced at Jack to see that he appreciated my stand.

"You'll need snow tires," he said.

We had the car in front of our quarters on Christmas Eve and tried a trial packing. Of course we had not accumulated any furniture, appliances, or kitchen utensils. Our biggest item was a phonograph and three or four gramophone records. And we had some bedding, blankets, pillows, and sheets. Ann still lived most of the time in a carry cot—a sort of elongated box with a small hood. We had a few suitcases for our belongings. I had increased my wardrobe with a pair of overshoes. Mary had leather boots and, of course, her fur coat. Sara was bundled up in innumerable layers but was able to move her arms and legs.

The packing practice revealed that we could move everyone and everything by having the family in the back. The snow tires had been put on, and the two other tires they'd replaced were propped up against the front seats. The trunk was filled to the brim with suitcases and linen, and any overflow was put on the front seat.

We drove around the grounds to see whether the space was tolerable and returned to our apartment. Christmas Day was going to be frugal. We didn't know anyone socially apart from one or two doctors, and they had departed for their homes. It was cold and dry, no snow, and the place looked barren. Some of the houses had Christmas lights on their roofs and on trees in the garden, but the gray-stone barrack buildings housing the mental patients were grim and undecorated.

We had managed to buy a stroller for Ann, though credit was not easy in those "pre-plastic" days. We took a short walk and tried not to think of our old home in England. We wondered whether we were doing the right thing. Perhaps we should have emigrated to Australia, Rhodesia, or Malaya, but we'd had that discussion a thousand times. Eagle Lake it was to be.

It's a paradox how risk-taking and fearlessness are inversely proportional to age. In our mid-twenties, Mary and I had no hesitation about setting out for the wilderness of Maine in midwinter with two babies. In the same way we had emigrated to America with fifty-six dollars and nothing in the bank. Our families couldn't have bailed us out.

When I was eighteen and in the R.A.F., I would undertake flights into dangerous areas that I wouldn't have dared to do at twenty-five. And it's not a question of courage or ignorance. The older one gets, the more fear holds one back from anything new or adventurous. The years induce caution and cowardice. It isn't a matter of experience teaching prudence. It is an evolution of attitude toward action.

I am not trying to make out that our journey to Eagle Lake was an epic saga. I'm not trying to dress it up as though we were undertaking opening the West or blazing the Oregon Trail. But in recalling our trip, I now realize that we were taking a risk in driving ourselves up into the Allagash with no experience of what could happen to us in a moderate blizzard—if, for instance, the car went into a ditch.

We set off on December 27. Mary and Sara occupied part of the back seat, Ann was at Mary's feet. There was a strong smell of tire rubber. I was squeezed into the driver's seat, and every inch of space seemed to be filled with goods of some kind. In this way we went up the New Jersey Turnpike, crossed into New England, and somewhere in Massachusetts found a ten-dollar motel room.

In those days the empire of Howard Johnson was far-flung, and each outpost was excellent, with a cheerful, mature atmosphere. Its decline and replacement by the fast-food chains is a loss to those who enjoy traveling. H.J. was our constant source of food and drink to the borders of Maine.

Most of Interstate 95 was still in the planning stage in late 1954, and there was no Maine or New Hampshire Turnpike. We went up Route 1 in stages. Traffic was light; the era of the trucker had not dawned. The road was reasonable and plowed, and at the end of the second day we reached Houlton.

From there, we seemed to bid farewell to the world as we had come to know it. As we turned toward Ashland, the road narrowed and it began to snow. A new driving experience for us was the behavior of the rear wheels on the icy surface. We made some spectacular skids that were well up to stock car racing standards.

In Ashland the snowflakes were large and heavy, the lumberyards were shrouded in blankets of white, and it was difficult to see the edge of the road. On we went along Route 11, which I had seen before from the back of a bus. The road was still an icy chasm. The banks of snow on each side of the road rose higher than twenty feet, and beyond was a sea of fir trees.

It was warm inside our new car, the only drawback being the increasing smell of rubber from the tires stashed in front. By now I appreciated that snow tires were not a luxury even though they didn't prevent us from tobogganing down hills or slithering sideways up them. Our most hair-raising event was a skid that turned us around one-and-a-half times and left us facing back the way we had come. I don't know how it happened. Perhaps I touched the brakes— something no driver does in that area even when coming to a halt at his house.

I managed to get the car to face Eagle Lake again without slipping into the ditches and gingerly stopped so we could deal with another urgent problem. After three days on the road in that era before the invention of disposable diapers, we were having a difficult time with baby Ann. She, in turn, was having her troubles with teething and was giving vent with a constant bout of crying.

The customary teething mixture in those days contained chloral hydrate. It was often effective; however, we didn't have any. But I did remember a family doctor in England telling me that he found that a little alcohol, sugar, and water mixed with a minute amount of aspirin never failed. The hardest part of the treatment, he'd said, was to persuade the mother that you weren't turning her child into a chronic alcoholic.

I had no trouble. A teaspoonful of gin, lots of sugar, a quarter of an aspirin, and a drop or two of milk had an astonishing effect. One minute we had a bellowing, wet, twisting infant; five minutes later, a slightly pink, blissful babe.

And it must have been an omen, because we drove the next thirty miles through the blizzard without an incident. At Portage we found a store, had some lunch, and made the last fifteen miles into Eagle Lake.

2

*E*AGLE
LAKE

CHAPTER

5

I PULLED UP AT Belanger's variety store and this time reached the counter without anything resembling a third down and goal line. Actually, and I can't vouch for this after forty years, but if you are going to Belanger's at Eagle Lake, between three and four in the afternoon is a good time. It's less crowded, often empty.

M. Belanger greeted me in undiluted French from which I gathered he was going to conduct us to our new house. We went outside, and he indicated for me to turn down the side road and to follow his car. I watched him carefully; it was to be my first lesson in northern Maine winter driving technique. Belanger revved up his monstrous Chrysler and backed out at full boost for five yards, then took his foot off everything and turned the wheel slightly. The car skidded gracefully over the summit at the edge of the road, and, in a controlled curve, landed bang in the center of the street—a performance that would merit 5.9 for artistry and technique.

We followed him to the bottom of the road and drew up at the little house that Mr. Martin had said would be ours. The outside temperature was minus thirty. Belanger scrunched his way up to the front door. I left the family in the warm car and followed him into the house. It was like the inside of a giant refrigerator and rather dark.

There was a front room done in French style. The furniture comprised a large sofa with wooden arms and covered with a bright floral material, three rocking armchairs similarly draped, small tables occupied with figurines, ashtrays, and framed photographs, and a glass-topped coffee table. The walls were covered with a floral paper and numerous pictures, some done on velvet, others of sea scenes. Framed crocheted biblical quotations and homilies were mounted around a crowded mantelpiece, and there were at least two crucifixes. My first thought was to keep my elbows in for fear of damaging something. In the next instant, I became aware of the penetrating cold.

The kitchen seemed adequate. There was a wood stove and a pile of logs and a collection of old newspapers. Upstairs, a narrow landing led to two bedrooms, the furnishings of which matched the front room. There was also a bathroom with a large tub.

M. Belanger switched on the water heater. After testing the lights and telephone and showing me the fuse box, he left. I thought I had understood most of what he had to say, although it was a strain on my French. Fortunately, in northern Maine the language had been modified by the adoption of some English words.

I went to the car and restarted the engine. I needed to thaw out while I explained that the house had to warm up some before we settled in. I then went back to light the stove. It took several editions of the *Bangor Daily News* before the difference between green and white firewood dawned on me. White was definitely better, particularly the logs that had been split and were less than four feet long.

Maybe it was the result of exertion, but I was quite warm after twenty minutes, and I went out to get the family. We carefully edged our way down our driveway to the front door, taking minute steps on the icy surface.

Once inside, Mary's first words were something like: "Do you think it's as cold in Siberia?"

"I've lit the fire," I said encouragingly.

"Oh, good."

"Belanger turned on the hot water."

"Oh, good."

"Heat rises in these houses; perhaps if we took the babes upstairs they'd be warmer."

"Oh, good."

As we unloaded I told her I had indeed noticed a difference between green and white wood, but I don't think it registered. Mary decided to improvise a bed on the landing floor for Sara. Ann was submerged in about fifteen blankets in her carry cot.

In any British crisis—a heavy bombing raid on London, a mine disaster, death in the family, birth next door—the English Mother rises to the occasion by making a cup of tea. The gas kitchen range worked, and there was a kettle; however, no water came out of the kitchen tap. We tried them all, and only the bath tap obliged.

"Smells odd."

I had to agree. Boiling the water would make it safe. The kettle duly puffed steam, and the thermometer in the hallway was steadily climbing toward zero. We were making progress. Mary found some ornate cups and saucers. We elected to use dried milk, and I said I would go up to Belanger's to get some supplies.

There was a knock at the door. Our neighbors across the street were paying us a visit. They wore fur hats, huge snow jackets, and thick woolen pants and heavy boots. They were natives and spoke French. We invited them in, but they politely declined and offered us a jug of water.

The gist of their tidings was that our water was contaminated. It was in direct communication with the sewage.

We discarded the contents of our teapot. Mary gave the teapot a wash with our new water, and I went off to see M. Belanger. My complaint taxed my French vocabulary, and I was forced to make crude drawings of lavatories with pipes running to the kitchen taps and the bath water.

"Nous avons besoin de quitter la maison immédiatement," I said. Which I hoped conveyed our urgent need to find some other accommodation. Belanger got the point. For the next fifteen minutes he accumulated bread, butter, milk, cereal, and other essentials for us. Then came two huge vats of water. He piled the whole lot into his car and sped to our house.

He unloaded, poured out an apology to Mary, and explained that he would have another house ready the very next day. He then went to the stove and worked at the newspaper and white wood until it glowed like a steel mill furnace. The house began to warm up. Up on the landing, the atmosphere was almost tolerable. The front room was now hovering around twenty-five degrees Fahrenheit.

Mary set about a meal and saw to the babes, and I took the luggage into one of the bedrooms. There was a ring at the door. I heard voices, and then Mary came upstairs.

"You've got two patients waiting downstairs."

"What?"

"Two elderly ladies."

"Good heavens!"

I went down to talk to them. We exchanged smiles. One of the ladies looked slightly younger than the other. She said: "C'est ma mère."

"Your mother. Yes . . ."

"Oui. My mutter. She— 'ow you say?—Need check-up."

I led them into the frigid front room, and they sat down on the floral sofa. My private practice had begun.

The check-up is an American invention. In the National Health Service of Great Britain the process did not exist. With between fifty and sixty patients waiting to be seen without appointments, the average time spent with a patient was about two minutes. You could look at the immediate areas, hands, wrists, face, tongue, and ankle, but to get below the layer of a vest, shirt, or corset was not on the books. When a check-up was merited, you sent the patient to an outpatient clinic.

Now, in the New World, I was faced with a different standard, and I am sure that had I been at a more benign latitude and season, I would have examined the lady before me thoroughly from top to toe. However, such an undertaking in a frozen igloo festooned with knickknacks was out of range. Fortunately the patient came to my aid. "De blood presss-ure and de 'art," she murmured. I bowed and scraped like the owner of Fawlty Towers and went to get my medical bag from the car trunk.

The bag was frozen stiff, and Mary and I had to pry it open with some primitive kitchen utensils. We thawed the rubber arms of the stethoscope and warmed up the sphygmomanometer for measuring the blood pressure. The front room was now up to about twenty degrees, and the lady seemed undisturbed. A coat was removed, I took her pulse and blood pressure, and after some polite fencing managed to listen to a few areas somewhere around her heart. I felt her neck to search for any unusual lumps and to check her thyroid gland. I also checked her eyes for visual reactions and lightly squeezed her ankle to detect any swelling that might indicate retained fluid. In the frigid atmosphere the examination had to be cursory.

From time to time I threw out a question in improvised French. "Are you short of breath—avez-vous besoin de vent?" and I would mime the winner of the Boston Marathon. "Dizzy?" That beat me, so I rocked my head back and forth and swayed. My patient smiled with a "Non." I felt we had established a good working relationship, and she indicated that the visit was over by buttoning and zipping up half a dozen layers.

The younger lady smiled and reached for her handbag. "Combien, Docteur?"

I felt myself blushing. Money! An actual exchange of cash. This had never happened before in my life. I was unprepared. I held up my hand and retreated into the kitchen.

"They want to pay me!" I whispered to Mary.

"What? Not really?" she giggled. "Go ahead."

"Yes, but how much? In England we used to charge ten shillings if we ever captured a private patient. That's a dollar."

"Make it two."

"Don't you think that's rather overdoing it?"

"Try it."

"O.K., here goes. Our reputation hangs on this."

I went back to the ladies. They looked at me inquiringly. I smiled and raised my hands. "You are my first patients in Eagle Lake. Numéro un. Pour vous, c'est rien. Nothing."

"Ah non. Vous êtes très gentil." They groped into their purses and waved a five-dollar note at me.

I shrugged. "Non, non. Deux, s'il vous plaît. Two." I held up two fingers.

And with murmurs of gratitude, they made their way out. I went into the kitchen holding my two dollars aloft in triumph.

"You coward. I heard you."

The house gradually warmed up to a tolerable temperature, and we managed to sort ourselves out. I worried about the level of anti-freeze in the car, and Mary spent most of the night worrying about the state of the wood stove. We had yet to learn that it was customary to get up at 4:00 A.M. to add more wood. Meanwhile we vowed to find other accommodations immediately.

By the time we were sitting down to breakfast we had managed to get the temperature up into the eighties, and the air was so dry that sparks flew from the ends of our fingers and bits of paper glued themselves electrically onto our clothes. I left Mary to deal with the house and children—neighbors had delivered some more water—and took off for the hospital determined to negotiate for new living quarters with M. Belanger as soon as his store opened.

The car started with hesitation. The pseudo-leather seats were stiff with cold and the interior was frigid. I turned on the heater and went back into the house. The short journey up the driveway gave me my first experience of the effect of subzero air on my face and sinuses. Within two minutes my cheeks were numb and the bones beneath were aching. I am sure the low humidity contributed to this condition at thirty-four below. I realized that I wouldn't be making any house calls on foot, and that when I saw M. Belanger

I was also going to purchase some suitable headgear, long underwear, gloves, and boots.

Ten minutes later I edged my way out of the drive and drove to the hospital. The back of the car slithered around and was difficult to control, but there was no other traffic. I slid into the hospital drive and made my way to the front door, slowly enough to avoid a broken leg yet quickly enough to prevent frostbite on my nose and ears.

Inside the hospital hallway was the familiar ecclesiastic decor, and behind her box-office window sat the thin-lipped nun with her pince-nez and gleaming white wimple.

"Bonjour," I said.

She gave a faint nod, and I wondered whether I'd hit on a period of verbal retreat or just a normal bureaucratic response. However, there was no need to resolve the matter because from the stairs came the welcoming nurse, Sister Euloge. She, too, was in black robes and white wimple, but her face was alive and smiling.

"Good morning, Doctor. I saw you arrive in your car."

"Yes, I managed to get up the road without going into a snowbank."

"You must put wood in your trunk. You have none, no?"

"Wood? You mean the green and white stuff."

She laughed. "Green. Only green, Doctor," and she laughed again. This was to be the start of a few months of mutual leg-pulling. Becoming serious, although her eyes still twinkled, she continued: "It is to increase the weight on the back wheels, so you get more traction, yes? Now, shall I show you the hospital? First we go up the stairs to the operating room, the clinic, and the laboratory. Then the wards—yes?"

I walked beside her up the stairs. "I suppose red wood would do just as well?"

"Yes, just as well, but we are not in California today."

"You could have fooled me."

She stopped on the stair and gave me a look and laughed. And instinctively I knew I had a friend. The conversation may have been absurd and facetious, but how often it is that lasting empathy is conveyed in this manner.

The landing was dark, and in contrast to the entrance hall, the walls were free of decoration and religious emblems. Sister Euloge opened a door and ushered me into the operating room. It was clean and neat. The floor and wall were of white tile, and a modern adjustable operating light was suspended over an adjustable operating table. A profusion of instruments was arranged in glass cabinets. A stretcher and two or three leather seats on wheels were set about the room. In the corner was a simple anesthetic machine. I went over to it and saw that it was equipped to deliver nitrous oxide, oxygen, and ether.

"It is very old, Doctor. We do not use it. Dr. King likes us to use ether drip."

"Dr. King?"

She explained that Dr. King was a surgeon in Fort Kent who came down once a week to do any elective cases. He also would come for emergencies—when the road was open.

"And if it isn't?"

"We keep our fingers crossed. Of course, Dr. Kirk, whose place you are taking, could do many different operations, and he has only been gone a month. So far we have been lucky, and now we have you."

I swallowed. "Sister Euloge, I think you should know that I am not a surgeon. I'm able to deal with common fractures, sew up cuts, and do forceps deliveries. But that's where my training stops. Abdominal surgery, even a simple appendectomy, would not be possible. Nor can I do a caesarean section. But I can handle anesthetics."

As I made this little speech, I thanked my stars that I had done six months in the emergency department in one of the toughest areas in London, where we interns had been required to do many procedures that, at my teaching hospital, would have been passed on to a senior doctor. My experience ranged from taking foreign bodies out of eyes to extracting knives out of backs. Every day, two of us used to see a long line of patients with an assortment of such problems. Those that required performing minor surgery under anesthesia, setting a broken bone, or opening an abscess would be dealt with by the interns. One of us did the operating and the other gave the anesthetic. (One thing I had never done was to extract a tooth. Within a few weeks at Eagle Lake, I was to wish that I had learned the technique. And to any doctor who may read this before setting off for Bongo-Bongo, I recommend a quick course from your local dentist. It's all in the wrist.)

We moved next door to the labor room, similarly in orderly condition. An adjacent room was furnished with chairs and tables, and the walls were decorated with cheerful pictures. Up-to-date periodicals completed this comfortable waiting room.

"We have many deliveries in Eagle Lake, but mostly in the home."

"Do you come with me?"

She shook her head. "I keep the bag ready for you, but that is all. Here, of course, I help."

She showed me the bag and explained that Dr. Kirk had trained the population on how to prepare for a home delivery. Apparently, in his thirty or forty years in Eagle Lake, he had delivered nearly everyone of that age or younger. As there was little migration, it meant that the pattern was set for all the small towns or villages in a vast area. As soon as a pregnancy was known, the mother and family would start to save newspapers. The delivery took place on the floor (not in bed) so as to be nice and warm in front of the open fireplace. Usually the husband or a grandmother continued to administer the anesthetic during the final moments of delivery. Scissors and string were also a requirement, for tying the cord. Why Dr. Kirk insisted on this last detail remained a mystery to me; perhaps it was a back-up in case he forgot to bring his own.

Sister Euloge and I then moved on to the laboratory, which was combined with the pharmacy. Here she proudly demonstrated her repertoire in both fields. We could do simple blood tests and urinalysis. And we had a good stock of medicines all the way from morphine to aspirin, digitalis to bicarbonate of soda.

The last part of the visit was a quick walk through the wards. Many of the patients were elderly, but there were some acute cases: pneumonias, two postoperative patients who had undergone major surgery a couple of days before, head injuries under observation, fractures, and a good assortment of other medical problems. I said I would be back later in the morning for a more thorough round.

"And you'll see the outpatients at the same time?"

"Outpatients! Are there many?"

"Maybe twenty. And your own patients will come here until you have your office. I will show you the clinic when you come."

I took a breath. The last hour had been an education. As we walked down the stairs, my self-confidence was at a low level; I realized that I was going to be out of my depth within twenty-four hours.

Mother Superior stood like a black-and-white buoy in the hall, her gold crucifix gleaming at the base of her snow-white wimple.

"Bonjour, Docteur Betts. Tout va bien?"

I glanced at Sister Euloge. The corners of her mouth were twitching and her eyes were sparkling. She stood beside Mother Superior.

"Oui. Merci," I replied.

"Ah, Docteur," Sister Euloge laughed, "vous parlez français."

I looked at her. "Green wood, eh?"

As I left the two of them, Sister Euloge was explaining something to her chief.

CHAPTER

SINCE THE CAR WAS pointed south, I decided to pay my re-
spects to Father Blais. During my tour of the hospital his name
had come up several times, and it was clear that he was both
the spiritual and secular leader of the community. Eagle Lake was a
mini-theocracy. Mr. Martin, with his infrequent home visits, wielded
power in a wider and more dilute sphere from the capital in Augusta.
M. Belanger, the third member of the medical committee, was a factotum with a nonbinding vote.

The rectory was adjacent to the church and seemed but an annex to it. The church had been built on ambitious Gothic lines. Its
steeple towered high into the blue sky and its sloping gray roof and
walls were covered in thick, unsullied snow, looking like a huge ermine
robe. The wide steps had been swept clear of snow up to the portico.
The massive black doors, befitting a cathedral, had polished brass discs
and iron handles. It was the kind of church that could be seen domi-
nating any Normandy town or Quebec hamlet.

I parked behind a black Cadillac in the driveway and went onto
the porch of the annex. Both driveway and path had been meticulously
shoveled so that the asphalt showed through in patches. I rang the
bell, and a moment later a stern-faced middle-aged woman armed
with a broom opened the door. We stared at each other. I was the
first to give.

"Bonjour. Je suis Dr. Betts." I was now stuck for the appropriate
title for Father Blais.

Perhaps while I am left on the back doorstep, I had better give a
résumé of my religious upbringing. My parents had no devout affili-
ations and did not belong to any church. During my childhood in

51

England, we lived in Iver, near Windsor Castle. At about the age of five I was caught up in an evangelizing outfit that sang songs around campfires, with verses tinged with religious sentiment and supported by an infectious melody. We were encouraged to bring potatoes to cook in the fire while we sang, and we ate them hot while an adult leader gave an uplifting Christian homily. The movement was called the Crusaders, and I was an enthusiastic member for about a month.

My next encounter was with the Scriptures and came through learning to read. At my school we had to read aloud from the Bible. We sat in alphabetical order, so usually I was able to calculate which verse from the Gospel I would be asked to tackle and have a silent rehearsal. What the other verses were about seldom interested me except when violence abounded. I was horrified and haunted by the details of the crucifixion. Pontius Pilate was my introduction to corruption on the bench. After the New Testament we turned our attention to Genesis, where there were some inspiring colored pictures of Abraham about to knife his son and Elijah going into orbit through some high cloud. Until recently, I have never been able to be interested in untangling the various Middle East factions. For example, who were the Philistines? And where are they now—on the West Bank?

The remainder of my religious teaching came courtesy of the cinema—with *The Robe, Going My Way*—and books such as *The Silver Chalice*. I also attended friends' weddings; and in the R.A.F., where it was safer to be something, I put myself down as belonging to the Church of England. Very little had happened in that branch of Christianity after Bloody Mary left the throne.

I write this at length because my ignorance of the Roman Catholic faith, and my failure to embrace its beliefs or know its observations, were to be my prime source of difficulty in trying to practice medicine in Aroostook County, and Eagle Lake in particular.

The iron lady returned. "Father Blais will see you now," she said in clear English. I followed her into a hall and thence into a dining room, where Father Blais was seated at the head of the table. As I entered he stood up. He was in his thirties and wore a cassock, collar, and tie. His face was round and pale and his hair black and thinning. He had a wide nose, thick lips and wore horn-rimmed glasses. He gave me a brief smile and offered his hand.

"We are glad to have you here. I understand you have visited the hospital and met the staff."

He explained that I would find Sister Euloge especially helpful. She had her R.N. and came from Montreal. He went on to tell me where and when he held Mass, and that he would prefer me not to make my rounds on Sunday mornings. He was aware that I was not of the faith, but that should not lead to any conflict.

He paused while his housekeeper served coffee. This was done in silence with a hint of ceremony. After the door closed, he continued to give me some local information and offered to help me where he could. I tried to lighten the tone of the conversation by recounting my adventures with the wood stove, but this failed. So I told him about the sewage coming out of the bath tap, feeling that perhaps something more earthy might strike a chord of mutual sympathy. It didn't, but I was surprised to learn that he was already fully informed about these recent defects in his diocese.

He stood up, I suppose in the manner in which the Pope indicates that an audience is over. Anyway, I got the point.

"When you are settled, you and your wife must come to dinner."

"We'll have to find a baby sitter."

"You will have no difficulty. I suggest you ask Sister Euloge." Once more he offered his hand, and I had the hardest time to not retreat backward like a vassal at Hampton Court when I made my exit. As I climbed back into my car, I knew in my bones that in that interview I had been naked to mine enemy.

I decided to go back to the house before tackling M. Belanger about new living quarters. The house was now hot enough to grow tropical vegetation. Mary had cottoned on to the art of selecting white wood with the enthusiasm of an engineer on the Silver Bullet. In slacks and shirt, she was exploring the vast array of kitchenware and encountering rare implements with the joy of an archaeologist unloading an ancient tomb. The babies had been caged and were crawling and rolling around.

"I've just seen Father Blais," I said.

She held aloft a weapon that could have adorned the wall of a medieval dungeon. "Look at this. Isn't it fabulous? And this thing is for straining soup."

I told her that Father Blais was going to arrange for a new house to rent.

"Yes, we're moving into the post office. M. Belanger came to tell me," said Mary. "It's four houses up the road on the other side. We can move in tomorrow."

I was about to suggest that we take a look at it when I heard the telephone ring. After a frantic search I found the phone in the midst of a cluster of figurines beside the sofa. The call was from Sister Euloge. A patient with an injured wrist had come to the hospital. I asked her if there was any chance that it might be a fracture, and if so, would she x-ray it. (During my tour of the hospital Sister Euloge had shown me the radiological apparatus and darkroom.) I told Mary I'd be back in about an hour and went to see my first Eagle Lake injury.

Sister Euloge met me on the landing. She had donned a full-length white apron over her nun's habit, and her head was covered. The effect was to enhance her even features and the warmth of her smile. She was a beautiful young woman, and just as Shakespeare wrote of love in his sonnets, I wondered why she would deny the world her replica.

"The patient is in the clinic," she said. "I have taken and developed the X rays, and they are drying."

Seated on a chair in a red shirt and thick wool pants was a man whose size alone would have made him a first draft pick for the Dallas Cowboys' defense. His right arm was resting on a table, and one glance was sufficient to diagnose a fractured wrist. Sister Euloge introduced me and went to get the X rays while I examined him. The conversation was in French. I found that simple questions and orders were within my vocabulary.

The X rays confirmed my clinical impression. It would be necessary to set the fracture under anesthesia. Fortunately I had performed this procedure in the emergency room in England. Indeed, I had been taught to do my first reduction before an audience of a hundred by the world's orthopedic authority, Sir Reginald Watson-Jones, who had singled me out from the ranks at random. (It makes a long story, including an injunction not to join yourself to the patient with plaster of Paris.)

I asked Sister Euloge to explain the situation to the patient, that I would have to put him to sleep and put the wrist straight. He accepted the verdict, and me, without hesitation. With his left hand he signed a permission paper, and I examined his lungs and heart. He had not eaten for four hours, so it was safe to proceed. Sister Euloge went and explained matters to his wife who was now out on the landing. I went out to introduce myself and shook her hand. She had no questions and seemed to have every faith in my ability.

In England I'd had a malpractice insurance policy. As a resident at Trenton State Hospital I was also covered. But in Eagle Lake I had no such insurance. This came from sheer (blissful) ignorance and neglect on my part. But on the other hand, medical malpractice litigation was almost unheard-of in Maine in those days. Patients did not sue their doctor and drive him away. And, reflecting now, I see how that prevailing state of affairs was fortunate for the local population. With a lawyer under every stone, advertising for business, as there is now, no doctor in his right mind would have undertaken that job in Eagle Lake. No insurance company would have written a policy to embrace all the procedures a physician must undertake in that isolated area. Maybe today they have helicopters, better snowplows, and four-wheel-drive ambulances, and the Aroostook legal profession has prospered. I have not been back to see.

The patient's wife came in and helped remove his boots and shirt. We let him keep his inch-thick boiler suit on. Meanwhile Sister Euloge brought bowls of water and rolls of plaster of Paris bandage into the operating room. We led the patient to the table and gently threaded his arm through a woolen stocking.

Then came the question of the anesthetic. I went over to the little machine. Sister Euloge glided over to me.

"No, Doctor. Open ether. I have it ready," she whispered.

I took a deep breath. The last time I had used open ether was on a stevedore in London, in the hospital outpatient department. It had been part of our anesthetic training. I could recall the incident vividly: "I'll show you, gentlemen," said Dr. Robinson, in bow tie, cutaway, and white coat, "how you may use ether in an emergency. You'll need some gauze and a tea-strainer. Any of you taking up a career as a missionary in darkest Africa shouldn't leave these shores without one. And don't try smoking a fag while you're at it; the stuff's like a miniature atom bomb. Now then, Betts, let's see how you get on."

I hadn't got on. Getting a patient to inhale ether is harder than giving a pill to a reluctant cat. The patient coughs, hacks, fights, and if one's lucky enough to survive all that, he is likely to vomit.

Sister Euloge had the equipment: a vast amount of gauze and a wire mesh apparatus bigger than any tea strainer I'd ever seen. Two nuns in habits and wimples entered and sat down by the far wall, ready to assist.

"Shall I start, Doctor?" asked Sister Euloge. She was at the head of the operating table, ether can in one hand and gauze in the other. I nodded and moved to her side. She didn't know it, but this was going to be my next lesson.

The patient went to sleep like a lamb. Then one of the nuns came over and took Sister Euloge's place, and she and I went about the business of setting the fracture. This went beautifully, and together we applied the plaster of Paris. There was no way of checking the result immediately by x-kkiray, but we were able to roll the patient onto a stretcher and take him to the machine to have the wrist checked. It looked fine, and the words of Sir Reginald Watson-Jones, my orthopedic mentor, about elevating the hand to the correct angle echoed in my head.

I was ready to go home to lunch. But it was not to be. Four or five patients with minor ailments had to be seen in the clinic. Sister Euloge again was in attendance, giving penicillin injections, filling prescriptions, and making notes. When the patient was private, she asked me what my fee was. I told her I would stick to the same schedule as Dr. Kirk. In this manner I learned that fees varied between two and three dollars. Three dollars was also the fee for a house call unless it involved driving more than five miles, when it increased to five.

Still I was not free; I had to do the ward round. However, now my National Health Service experience came in useful. I had been used to seeing up to a hundred patients a day in England and had developed speed and a nose for the urgently sick. (This had only failed me once, when, looking around our packed National Health Service waiting room, I had spied a pale individual in obvious distress. I had taken him before anyone else, but once inside the office I found out he was a drug salesman. Another lesson.)

Two hours later I was ready to go. Sister Euloge accompanied me to the front hall, and I thanked her for seeing me through my first morning. In the box office the thin-lipped nun rapped on the glass. There was a message: Mrs. Parquinette was in labor in Winterville.

I 'LL GET THE delivery bag, Doctor," said Sister Euloge. I followed her upstairs to her office. From her filing cabinet she took a
folder that contained antenatal notes on Mrs. Parquinette. It was
her first pregnancy, she was young, and her medical history and physical condition were normal. I saw that for the last two months Sister
Euloge had made the check-ups.

While I studied the notes, she checked the contents of a volumi-
nous black bag reminiscent of the type we had lugged to deliveries
on the district in London.

"Everything is here, Doctor. You sterilize the instruments at the
house."

"By boiling them up in a saucepan, I suppose," I said sarcastically.

"Yes. I expect the relatives will have everything ready. They know
Dr. Kirk's methods."

There was no point in making a comment. This was Eagle Lake.
"I hope there are a couple of cans of ether in the bag, and that gauze
strainer."

Sister Euloge laughed: "The gauze is there, but not ether. They
have open fires. I have put in chloroform."

I tried to hide my alarm, but the ghost of Sniffy Robinson rose
before me like Banquo at Macbeth's dinner party. Sniffy's lecture
on chloroform had been a subsection in the fundamentals of anesthetics. "There are four stages, gentlemen," Dr. J. Arthur Robinson, the chief of anesthesia, had intoned. "The first is the *incubation,*
getting the patient just below the level of consciousness; the second
is *sleep,* the third a *coma* deep enough to allow muscle relaxation
and no reaction to pain. Keep the patient at that level, and the surgeon will remain docile and relatively civilized. Refrain, gentlemen,

from the fourth stage, as it requires a wooden box and the consoling services of a chaplain."

He had paused to allow his admonition to sink in. "That, gentlemen, was, and is, the difficulty with chloroform. Patients lap it up as a cat does cream. Patients pass into stage three in the twinkling of an eye, and then you have to watch your step, or they'll stop breathing and you'll be embarrassed. Fortunately, you will not come across chloroform today except in research. It'll knock a rabbit off in ten seconds. It also plays hell with the liver, particularly with those of your clientele who favor the better vintages."

The words echoed through the back of my mind as Sister Euloge stood up and crossed to her desk. She drew a map to show me the rough location of Winterville. It was about six miles down Route 11. She said she would telephone the family and warn them to turn on all the lights in the house and porch and watch for a green Pontiac during the next hour.

I went home to give the news to Mary, and I think she sensed my misgivings. Anyway, instinctively she made a cup of tea. After some food, I set off for my first home delivery.

Within a minute after I drove past Belanger's variety store, signs of habitation—and life on this planet as I had come to know it—vanished. Once more I was traveling on ice down the snow-banked ravine. To my left was a huge lake, although I could not see it, and on my right an endless mass of fir trees. I slithered on, never getting above twenty-five miles per hour, and was horrified when I saw another car approaching like the leader at the Indianapolis 500. I skirted the bank, and it whizzed by like a Saturday night teenager hell-bent on self-destruction. Gingerly I edged out again and kept an eye on the odometer. At the five-mile mark I saw a cluster of about ten houses all packed in with snow except for their trenchlike driveways. This had to be the hamlet of Winterville.

A man stationed at the end of one such trench waved me down. Without thinking, I touched the brake, and the car careened like a wild horse toward the opposite bank. I turned into the skid, and the next skid, and the third, and finally came to a halt about a hundred yards beyond the last house. With a thumping heart and feeling rather ashamed, I backed up and was guided into the driveway.

I stepped out and followed the man, who hadn't said a word, through the back entrance of a small wooden house. I stood on the kitchen door mat and removed my overshoes and coat. It was very warm.

"Je suis Dr. Betts."

"Ah!"

"Et vous êtes M. Parquinette?"

"Oui."

He turned and led me into a bedroom, where a young woman lay in bed. In my halting French I introduced myself and asked her a few simple questions about her labor. It would be painfully tedious to report the exchange in direct French speech. As a matter of fact, there wasn't much of an exchange. "Oui" and "non" would about cover her bit. However the patient and I seemed to establish quite a pleasant rapport as I examined her.

She was eighteen and had never been farther than Fort Kent in her life. Her husband "worked in the woods," and they had been through school together. During this halting conversation I was able to see that she was very early on in her labor. The pregnancy was mature, the baby was the right way up, and the head was in the pelvis.

At this point I was relieved to see an older woman enter the bedroom, introduced as the girl's mother. She had the confident air of one who had experience in these matters. Again, after some tricky French exchanges and a small amount of pantomime, I was able to get her to help me examine the patient more extensively. I had to know the stage of the labor more precisely so I could have some idea of when I would need to return. Getting to and from Eagle Lake would have to be factored in. It wasn't going to be as easy as zipping down Whitechapel High Street on a bicycle, and there was no midwife to hold the fort as there had been during my general practice in England.

They had a telephone, so with another vigorous bout of pidgin French to the mother, accompanied by an extraordinary mime of labor pains while pointing to my wristwatch, I was able to convey when I was to be called from my home. The old lady was greatly entertained by the performance, and I found I was picking up the language faster than I would have from any Berlitz speed course.

It was now early evening, and dark. In less than ten minutes I had turned the car around and was retreating toward Eagle Lake. Indeed, I could see the lights of Belanger's store on the horizon when the engine spluttered and stopped.

After numerous futile attempts to start it, I felt the only course was to walk. I had yet to buy appropriate clothing for my arctic life, and that half mile became the equivalent of being shut in a refrigerator for a week. Every sinus instantly underwent a dry freeze. After the initial sharp ache in the bones of my face, my head felt as if it had been shrunk to the size of a New Guinea war trophy. There was nothing to do but to keep on, but walking was like making your way across a newly swept ice rink, each step a challenge to providence and gravity. I found it more secure to hug the edge of the road and trudge through some fresh snow. Each step produced a squeak. I couldn't feel my ears and was prepared to see the lobes black along the margins when next I looked in the shaving mirror.

Finally I made it into Belanger's store. It was like entering warmup heaven. Belanger finished serving a couple of customers, which gave me time to thaw. I then explained the problem. Without a word he reached for what looked like a can of beer and led the way to his car. We tore up the ice rink, and within seconds arrived at my stalled Pontiac. He hopped out, poured the beer into the gas tank, and returned. We waited inside his warm car for a few minutes.

"Try now," he said.

I let myself out into the frigid night and tugged open the frozen car door. To my amazement, the Pontiac burst into life with an apologetic cough. M. Belanger didn't wait. He swept his car around in a distant driveway and came back and led me to town.

I left the car running and went into the store. He was back behind his counter, and for the first time I saw him grinning. He had out-witted the witch doctor. The spell of Dr. Kirk had been broken.

Even his English became more fluent: "Dry Gas. You must always put it in de tank." He went to the shelf and handed me two more of the "beer" cans. I told him I'd never heard of the stuff, and he was even more delighted. We shook hands, and I thanked him with a great show of English and French gratitude. I then examined some boots, a snow jacket, and wool pants. He nodded approval repeatedly and disappeared into the back to emerge with a set of thermal under-wear. He pressed the garments on me. It would not be a cash trans-action, he explained, laughing. Since he had written my hospital contract, he knew my credit was good.

By now more customers had come in, and Belanger was enjoy-ing himself, explaining in a torrent of French how I came to be stand-ing at his counter under several pounds of new winter garb. I caught the words "Dry Gas" several times. They gazed at me with barely suppressed laughter, and I decided it was best to go along with good humor. I modeled my blue-and-red snow outfit to a chorus of ap-proval, similarly the pants and underwear. By now everyone was smiling. Apparently the new English doctor was human after all. One of them reached up and took down a fur hat with earmuffs and passed it to me. He held my new clothes while I pulled it on. General noises of appreciation. It was to be the last time I wore anything else on my head until the ice went out from Eagle Lake.

With another round of thanks, I made for the door. It was opened for me, and I was shepherded to the purring Pontiac, now beauti-fully warm. The clothes were piled on the back seat, and with a wave I made my way to our house.

As I struggled through the back door with my new clothes, a gust of hot air and the smell of food welcomed me home. Mary had worked on her temporary nest and had somehow transformed a Siberian antique shop into a cozy little house. Both babes were asleep in a sort of cage formed by the landing banisters and an improvised door. Our water-supplying neighbor had lent a cot for Sarah, and Ann was submerged in blankets. The wood stove was emitting heat like the mainstay of a steel factory, and saucepans were bubbling away in the kitchen.

I gave a summary of my adventures and then dressed up in my new acquisitions. Mary carefully steered a course between admiration and fits of giggles. Rejecting her entreaties, I refused to be viewed in my long underwear, which I donned in the knickknack room. But I accepted the compliments on my green woodsman's trousers, red-wool shirt, and sky blue snow jacket. However, my new headdress with ear mufflers was too much, and I was forced to eject her from the kitchen until she stopped laughing her head off.

We tackled dinner with me in shirt sleeves (and still perspiring). Our little thermometer was nudging eighty degrees and threatening to go higher. The wood stove had taken over.

In my absence our move to the old post office had been confirmed; we could move there whenever it suited us. Father Blais had invited us to dinner the following week, and there was to be a grand reception for us at the Grange Hall on Saturday night, with a gala supper, music, and a dance.

The telephone rang and I answered it: "Ah! Oui. Deux minutes. J'arriverai maintenant."

"Your French is improving by the hour," observed Mary. "Even I understood that."

I put on my boots and snow jacket.

"Aren't you going to wear your hat?"

"Not until I get outside."

"I'll get used to it. Put it on now."

The car started like a charm, and with the beginnings of confidence I managed to arrive at the Parquinette house in ten minutes.

The labor was proceeding normally, and if there were no difficulties I thought we might have a baby within a couple of hours. I
examined her and tried to chat between pains, and I gave her an
injection to ease them. Meanwhile, just as I had been told, the
mother had spread several layers of the *Bangor Daily News* on the
carpet in front of the fire in preparation for the delivery. On a side
table lay a ball of string and a pair of scissors, the legacy of Dr.
Kirk's routine instructions.

I settled into a chair beside the fire and took up a couple of sheets
of newspaper to see what was happening in Bangor. The Red Sox were
not doing well for the opening of the season. M. Parquinette then
came in with an up-to-date edition and an offer of coffee. He was remarkably calm as a prospective father for the first time, and was prepared to assist with the delivery and help with the anesthetic, a sense
of fatherly duty I would encounter again in many subsequent home
deliveries.

In time the patient was transferred to the carpet. I had sterilized
my instruments in a saucepan of boiling water. By using local anesthetic and a mere whiff of chloroform, I was able to help in the final
stages of the birth. I used my own scissors and sterile tape for the
cord and handed up a beautiful baby girl to an exhausted but happy
new mother.

She gazed at the baby in wonder, and her own mother cleaned the
infant. The last stage of the birth was completed, and we helped
mother and child back to her bed.

"Comment vous appelez-vous, Docteur?" she asked me.

"Dr. Betts."

"Non, votre autre nom?"

"Anthony."

Her husband was on the other side of the bed. She looked at
him and they both smiled and he bent down and kissed her.

The mother turned her baby toward me.

"Ici, Antoinette, oui?"

I smiled. So much that was new had happened to me since I had left England. But even there, no patient had named her baby after me.

I left the room, telling the patient I would be back tomorrow but to call if there was any difficulty. M. Parquinette saw me to the door.

"How much, Doctor?" He spoke English.

I had no idea what to ask. "The same as Dr. Kirk?"

He took out his wallet and gave me twenty-five dollars.

As I went back to our new home I found myself singing.

CHAPTER

WE MOVED INTO THE old post office the next day. It was halfway down the only side street in Eagle Lake and opposite the new post office.

The first floor front was a large space with a partition of plywood to make two equal-size rooms, with a centrally placed communicating door. We made the one with the wood stove and the outside entrance into the waiting room, and the other into my office. Behind, through another door, were a kitchen and a small sitting room, with stairs leading up to the bedrooms.

The living quarters had been furnished with a less enthusiastic Acadian influence than our last abode, and there was a noticeable absence of ceramic dwarves, angels, or shepherdesses. An occasional crucifix or religious print broke up the bare walls. There were no framed cross-stitch pieces exhorting us to love our neighbors or spelling out biblical quotations. The house was dry and warm and the water safe to drink. M. Belanger had personally drunk a glass in our presence and was still at his work the following morning.

The United States Post Office, in a spirit of generosity, had left two plain benches for seats in our waiting room, and we managed to add a couple of wooden chairs. A table with an array of outdated magazines, a rug, and possibly curtains would have to wait until the practice became more prosperous.

My office was more lavish. The kitchen table was commandeered for a desk, and we set out two of the more stable chairs, both upright and wooden, for the patient and me. A modified chaise longue, comfortable for anyone under four foot eleven, became an examining couch. We brought down two small side tables and sacrificed a vivid green rug from the babies' bedroom to coordinate the furnishings. The children also lost their curtains to the cause.

I checked into the hospital and saw one or two outpatients and explained to Sister Euloge that my office was now open for business. There was to be no appointment system, but I would be there at specific hours in the morning and afternoon.

I was now dressed in my new winter attire. It was excellent for the bitter cold outside, but the hospital was kept at a temperature where orchids would blossom, and I soon felt I was being warmed up in a pressure cooker. However, the problem was solved when Sister Euloge suggested we make a round of the wards and offered me a white coat. I peeled off my snow jacket and donned the stiff, laundered white coat over my aggressively checked wool shirt. I still would have welcomed a fan, thanks to the wool pants and thermal underwear, but there was some relief in the upper regions.

I felt diffident about going from bed to bed dressed like a lumberjack. It was the first time I had approached a patient without wearing a tie.

About half the patients were elderly and were there for nursing care. But the other beds presented an array of medical and surgical problems. Postoperative wounds had to be inspected and dressed.

Stitches needed to be removed from patients operated on in Fort Kent. There were some chest and cardiac problems, and a girl with diabetes and a severe kidney problem.

It all took time. Sister Euloge was invaluable, taking notes, supplying instruments, giving me the background histories, and telling me what medications were available. She could also perform a spectrum of laboratory tests when necessary.

The major difficulty of the round came at the end when we returned to the outpatient room and found a man with an ancient cast on his leg. He was a young giant from the woods and had broken his ankle six weeks ago. Sister Euloge brought in the most recent X rays. The fracture had healed. It was time to remove the cast.

Although I had put several casts on, I had never taken one off. At the emergency room where I had worked in England, a muscular technician armed with an orthopedic saw had removed the plaster of Paris, sounding like a lumberjack felling a California redwood with a chainsaw. He then removed the remnants with a thing resembling a crowbar.

As I was to find during the next few months in Eagle Lake, there was no escape from the immediate problem: patients assumed a doctor could do anything. Within two weeks of my arrival I would diagnose an acute gall bladder and be asked when I would be taking it out.

So it was up to me to free this massive leg from its bricklike case. Sister Euloge wheeled over a trolley with an array of tools resembling the armory of an ambitious gardener preparing to limb his oak trees. I decided to at least appear to be familiar with the apparatus and took up a pair of clippers with a short bite and levers about three feet long. I eased it into the gap between his foot and the plaster and pressed the arms together. To my delight, the plaster cut through like butter and his foot was still there. Thus inch by inch we proceeded.

To any doctor reading this, the episode may seem ridiculous, but if you're alone and need to establish confidence among your patients, you have to appear to know your job. Referring this patient to Fort Kent would have resulted in a community vote of no confidence that would lead to a lame duck resignation. Soon there were to be much more serious situations, particularly in obstetrics, when the road to Fort Kent was closed and I had no choice but to proceed.

Anyway, after what seemed an age, I had cut the cast open. As if she knew I knew what it was, Sister Euloge now handed me another enormous tool. However, the London qualifying examinations, where mean-spirited surgical examiners handed instruments to you and asked their purpose, had not been for nothing. At that time I had deduced that an instrument that looked as if it had hung in the Tower of London was a bladder stone crusher, and another, a urethra bougie. So in a flash I guessed the purpose of the menacing tool offered to me by Sister Euloge. It was a spreader; you put it between the cut edges of the cast and expanded them. Within minutes the patient's leg saw the light of day.

Moments later, cleaned up, I was free to tell Sister Euloge of my successful delivery and give her the delivery bag for refueling.

"Antoinette? C'est charmant."

"The next one I'll get them to call Euloge-Marie."

"Ah! But that is not my real name."

I asked her what it was, but she only smiled. For an instant there was a barrier between us. She had changed from nurse to nun like a character in a Grimm fairy tale. I thanked her for her help.

"Now you English doctors want your cup of tea, non?"

I told her that we from the British Empire restricted tea to four o'clock in the afternoon with bread and butter, biscuits (cookies), and cakes. Now was the hour for coffee, but I would get it in my office at home. She told me that two patients were coming to see me and she would direct any more to my new workplace. She added that I had some house calls and described where these were.

I put on my snow jacket and headed home.

There were three cars parked against the six-foot wall of snow limiting my driveway. Two had occupants, and when I stepped out they trooped behind me into my office waiting room, where already the benches were filling up. I greeted them generally in both languages and continued on into the kitchen, where Mary was tending to Ann and Sara was at work with some crayons.

"When did this lot arrive?" I asked.

"Off and on over the last half hour." She handed me a cup of coffee and began building a sandwich. "I telephoned the hospital, but they said you were operating. At least that's what it sounded like."

"I was taking off a cast. The patient will live."

"We really must get a dictionary."

"We'll have to get one in Fort Kent. Meanwhile, if in doubt ask for Sister Euloge."

I changed into some shoes.

"You're not going to see patients dressed like that," Mary protested. "In that shirt, and without a tie, you look like a character in a Western."

I smiled and went toward the waiting room. "I may need a chaperon. If so, I'll pop my head round the door." I invited the first patient to step into my office.

His was a straightforward case of a chronic cough, and we managed a friendly interrogation in French. I examined his chest, listened to his heart, and, much to his approval, took his blood pressure. I assured him he would be relieved of his symptoms and wrote a prescription. Sister Euloge had said that she would act as pharmacist for me until I could get a supply of medicines for myself.

Once again there was the embarrassing question of a fee. But the formula of saying "same as the old doctor" was the key to success, and I was handed two dollars. I asked him to return in a week if he did not improve. I let him out and summoned the next patient, who turned out to have some joint pain. A glance at the lumps on his fingers and a knowledge of his age made a diagnosis of osteoarthritis—

the "rheumatism" that most people get in later years—a reasonable conclusion. I wrote a note for some aspirin to be taken regularly together with local application of heat. The French for "hot-water bottle" was beyond my scope and range of acting, but I managed to draw a lopsided bag with a distended spout and steaming water pouring from a kettle into it. "Ah! Un 'ot water botelle," exclaimed my patient after studying the back of my envelope. Another two dollars went into the kitty.

To my surprise, more people were entering the waiting room. It wasn't approaching the waiting room crowds that had turned up routinely in my National Health Service days, but it was a promising start. And it was a relief not to have patients demanding certificates to be off work, or requesting another two dozen sleeping pills, or resisting my decision to refer them to an outpatient clinic. Practice had become a pleasure.

The only snag of the day came when a young lady seated herself at my desk. She was shy, but compensated by speaking in rather a loud voice, almost as if she thought I was slightly deaf. I didn't object to that, but the contents of her complaint were delicate, exclusive to the female sex, and were being conveyed through the thin plywood partition to a fair-sized segment of the population of Eagle Lake.

I raised my hands in a gentle gesture of suppression, asked her to wait, and retreated into the kitchen where I explained the problem to Mary. She had been trying to keep the babes from being noisy by some intense but simple diversion. She had the solution in a second.

Our one extravagance at Trenton State Hospital had been to buy a small Columbia hi-fi phonograph. Its acoustics were first class, and we had managed to accumulate three classic recordings: Beethoven's Fifth with Toscanini, the overture to *Romeo and Juliet* by Tchaikovsky, and selections from *Sleeping Beauty* and *Swan Lake*. It took less than a minute to move the machine up against the waiting room wall, also of plywood.

I returned to my patient. How many months had she missed?

"C'est trois, monsieur." Now to the strains of *Romeo and Juliet,* this seemed almost appropriate. I asked a couple more questions while the New York Philharmonic brass and strings vigorously tackled the courtyard duel scene.

Mary appeared from the kitchen to report. "I've been in the waiting room. It works like a charm. The patients seem to like it, and you can't hear a word."

From then on our office, like the hills of Austria, was filled with the sound of music, but of limited repertoire until we managed to get a fresh supply of records. We didn't play music all the time; we established a warning system, and Mary controlled it. It was interesting that the male confidences were accompanied by Beethoven's forceful phrasing, while the ladies were favored by the more romantic Tchaikovsky.

CHAPTER

FOR THE NEXT FEW DAYS the practice continued smoothly, and we established a pattern of living in our post office home. The weather continued intensely cold and dry, and a trip to collect our mail from just across the road would freeze the nose and sinuses within a dozen steps. Getting logs into the house from the shed was a joint operation, with me tossing them to Mary in the kitchen doorway. But we kept the house beautifully warm even though it meant a routine refueling of the wood stove every morning around 4:00 A.M.

One day an agitated and imminent new father from the far side of the lake arrived to say that I was wanted at once. It was snowing heavily, and for the first time General Motors let me down when the Pontiac wouldn't even give a cough. (Actually, the corporation probably helped me save face, for I was very reluctant to drive two miles on ice in blinding snow, trying to dodge fishing huts and oncoming traffic. Incidentally, that day I realized for the first time why some cars had magnetic compasses.) It looked as if I'd have to walk.

As I collected an extra couple of scarves for my face, I found my apprehension had been anticipated. I had just taken up the obstetric bag when two horses attached to a sledge trundled down the street, looking like a commercial for Budweiser beer. The sledge was the property of one of the relatives on the distant shore and was the customary method of getting around in blizzards. I clambered on board like someone setting out for a party in Moscow, and off we went. We chugged by ice-fishing huts, which loomed up through the driving snow, and arrived at the patient's house. Everything ended happily with the delivery of a healthy baby, precipitated gently onto the *Bangor Daily News*. The fame of my predecessor had spread far and wide.

Meanwhile our social life had advanced. For our dinner with Father Anthony Blais, Mary and I decided to dress more formally and reverted to London clothes—dress, suit coat, etc.—with an infrastructure of heavy wool in multiple forms. Looking ten pounds heavier, I managed to sport a tie. We felt suitably attired for the occasion, but I don't think we impressed our priest host, who was probably wearing three or four sweaters and thick long johns under his plebeian robe.

On the other hand, we noted that there was nothing frugal about the father's style of living. The food was excellent, served with abundant wine by the iron-faced lady I had met previously at the back door. I noticed that conversation was limited to my and Mary's curricula vitae. I could sense that any approaching theological or secular subjects would be diverted or rebuffed. Nevertheless, I am quite sure that Father Blais soon became aware of my near-pagan background and upbringing, and he knew he was not going to control me directly by his church customs or edicts or effect a conversion. Nor, if he had expected it (which I doubt), was he to find a cultured acquaintance with whom he could have cozy theological evenings over a glass of port in front of the fire.

I came away with the impression that Eagle Lake was but a station for him on his way to higher appointments, via Portland and Boston to Rome. Meanwhile I was going to be under his watchful anti-satanic eye.

Our next social event was a welcoming dinner by the town. This was held in a grange hall down at the lake edge. About a hundred people had organized it, and when the time arrived Mary and I were escorted to the head table and seated between Monsieur and Madame Belanger. Everyone watched us intently and the buzz of conversation was low, as though the multitude were waiting for an ominous sign.

Fortunately the ice was broken by their serving us lobsters. Of course, in Maine the lobster is a delicious but not expensive commodity. In London it is the food of the elite and wealthy. Piccadilly sports a famous restaurant with a lobster in its mullioned window, red-clawed and shining in a gold bowl with a flower arrangement at each end. Neither Mary nor I had ever been near such a rare gourmet delight. Now there were lobsters to the left and right of us.

But nobody was going to start eating until we tackled ours. It was an embarrassing situation. For a beginner, dismantling a lobster is like taking a sparkplug out of a Japanese supercar. Where did one start? I picked up my crustacean. It looked impregnable as a mediaeval fort. Mary gazed at me with less than a trace of hope. Very gradually a trickle of laughter spread down the tables as people realized our difficulty. I glanced at Belanger. He was trying to keep a straight face but his eyes gave him away. I took the bull by the horns—or, rather, the lobster by the body—and passed it to him. There was a roar of approval as Belanger gave a demonstration of how to dissect the animal. And another roar when Mary handed me hers to see if I had learned the technique.

The evening was a success, and we moved among our new neighbors to meet them informally. There was going to be a dance, but apparently the band (a single violin) had not been able to make it.

We crunched our way back to our home, rewarded our baby sitter with a quarter, and went to bed with the sense that we had been accepted. Whether this was so proved too difficult to determine. Contrary to popular conception, the life of a rural doctor and his wife is a solitary and often lonely one. This is because, like the priest, the doctor is privy to everyone's intimate manner of living, their problems, secrets, and heartaches. Consequently, in contrast to other citizens, he is forbidden the common pleasure of gossip. No one engages him in close friendship for fear of being labeled a seeker of a neighbor's business. In public places the doctor is greeted with bonhomie; opinions about sport, maybe even superficial politics, are expressed or sought, but no one ventures any further. And the women adopt the same attitude toward the doctor's wife.

In urban practice, the family doctor finds his social life and friendship with his colleagues or at the golf club, the Rotary, and so on. But even there he senses caution among his fellows. As far as Eagle Lake went, even after the welcoming dinner, everyone, though pleasant, kept his distance. Fortunately the practice became so busy that any social life became out of the question.

In the middle of the week following the grange hall social, Dr. King came from Fort Kent to remove an acute appendix. In the little operating room, with Sister Euloge taking over the anesthetic, I assisted in the procedure. Afterward I asked him to look at one or two problems, and he planned to return another day to explore a patient for a lump in the abdomen. I began to see the scope of my practice widening.

House calls were common, and involved traveling to the villages scattered along Route 11 for distances of twenty miles or more. The nearest other doctor was to be found either in Fort Kent or over in Presque Isle, about fifty miles away.

Pregnancies were common, together with their complications. I made deliveries and attended miscarriages (spontaneous abortions) every week. It was on one of these occasions that the first clash with Father Blais occurred.

I had visited a young lady who was two months pregnant. She had all the signs and symptoms of a miscarriage and was losing blood. I admitted her to the hospital and told Sister Euloge that if she did not stop bleeding, I would have to operate. Meanwhile we measured the level of her blood to see how much she had lost and checked her blood group in case she should need a transfusion.

By evening the patient had changed for the worse, and I asked Sister Euloge to get the operating room ready for five o'clock for a dilatation and curettage. Until the remnants of the pregnancy were removed, the bleeding would continue and the patient might expire. I had managed several such cases as a resident-in-training in London.

By now it was snowing heavily, and at five o'clock three inches of wet snow covered the icy surface of the road. I made my way into the hospital and sought out Sister Euloge.

"Is the patient ready? Premedicated?"

Sister Euloge shook her head.

"Why not?"

"Father Blais has been here."

"What has that to do with it?"

"He has ordered us not to proceed."

I stared at her in amazement. Then I felt my anger rising. "You must get her into the operating room. You're a nurse. You know what might happen if we don't stop that bleeding."

She didn't answer.

"How does he feel about transfusing her?" I asked.

She nodded.

"Then call in her relatives and find a donor. Meanwhile I'm going to see Father Blais."

I telephoned his house and was told that he was on his way to the hospital. I decided to intercept him and ran down the stairs and out into the snow. At the end of the driveway I saw his black Cadillac edging in. I went over to it. He kept the motor running and leaned over to open the far-side door. I entered and faced him.

"Did you countermand my orders to operate on the patient with the miscarriage?"

He looked at me for a minute without answering. "You mean the pregnant woman on whom you propose to do an abortion?"

"Not an abortion. The fetus is dead, and she's bleeding badly."

"How do you know the fetus is dead?"

"With her amount of pain and this blood loss, of course it's dead."

"What proof have you? Have you seen the dead fetus?"

"No. She probably passed it at her house before I arrived. At two months it would be less than an inch."

"Then you have no proof, and you must not interfere."

"You're not licensed to practice medicine, Father, are you?"

"And you think you have right over life and death?"

We stared at each other. "Is the mother's life in danger?" he asked finally.

"Not yet."

"Then you must wait." He stopped the engine and we both got out of the car. With a great show of courtesy, I held the hospital door open for him and then went ahead swiftly to the ward.

"Did you get the blood donors in?" I asked Sister Euloge

"Yes."

"Right. We'll need two pints. I'll be there to help after I've called Fort Kent."

I took up the telephone and asked for Dr. King and explained the problem to him. What was his advice? He told me the situation was nothing new. There was no point in transferring the patient to Fort Kent. They had similar difficulties, and anyway, perhaps I hadn't noticed it, but the road was closing with the blizzard. He said the best plan was to transfuse the patient and ship her to Presque Isle in the morning. There was a Protestant hospital there, and they could handle the case.

I went to the laboratory. Here there were six or seven family members who were being blood grouped. Three of them, one of whom was the mother, matched the patient. Sister Euloge had already explained the need for blood, and we proceeded to bleed the first donor. I told Sister Euloge that I was going to transfer the patient in the morning to Presque Isle, if she and her husband agreed. Would it be transgressing Sister's faith and allegiance to explain this to them, as my French was not up to it?

This was to be our first and only clash. It was not verbalized, but her eyes glittered with anger. Later I wondered how she resolved her dilemma. Silence or confession? Meanwhile she followed my instructions. The look of relief on the faces of the young husband and wife as they listened to the explanation surely must have strengthened the conscience of Sister Euloge.

And that is what happened. That young woman was the first miscarriage patient I sent to Presque Isle via an "underground railroad" of sorts. I wondered how Dr. Kirk had managed these incidents, for they were not uncommon. I never found out, but I suspect that Dr. Kirk did a little operating in his own office, because as I encountered more miscarriages, patients begged me not to take them to the hospital. Couldn't I do something?

No woman in Eagle Lake ever asked me outright to do an abortion. Perhaps if I had remained there longer and the people had grown to know me better, I might have been approached to terminate a pregnancy. If they were practicing effective birth control, I knew nothing about it and was never asked for advice. However, it seemed to me that for a Catholic community Eagle Lake had relatively few large families. Two or three children seemed to be the norm. Perhaps the Church was preaching abstinence or advocating the "rhythm method," which I've always regarded as a variation of Russian roulette. Maybe the ladies of Eagle Lake were lucky, but I doubt it. The miscarriages I saw were too numerous for them all to have been spontaneous.

CHAPTER

NOT EVERYTHING WENT WELL in my practice at Eagle Lake. When you're isolated, lacking experience and training, there are times when nature delivers a knockout to both patient and doctor.

Two instances are engraved in my mind. One was a young girl we admitted in labor during a storm. Throughout the night we tried to help her, and the three of us—the patient, Sister Euloge, and I— were exhausted. Around 4:00 A.M. we were certain we were dealing with twins, but they were "locked." Although both babies were normal, their arms or legs and heads had intertwined and it was impossible to effect a delivery.

Today a caesarean section would easily solve the problem. At that time, because of the weather we could neither bring in a surgeon to Eagle Lake nor get her to another doctor.

It would have been possible to stop the labor with morphine if the mother became endangered further. That was what I had in mind as a last resort when, with the patient under deep anesthesia, I was at last able to untangle the two babes (and not rupture the womb in the process—one of the great dangers). But it meant that I had to deliver one normally and the other as a breech. Ironically, the breech baby survived, and with heavy heart I had to watch Sister Euloge baptize the stillborn. I waited several hours before I could bring myself to tell the mother. The father was not around, nor did we know who he was.

The second event occurred one evening just after I had seen the last office patient. Supper was ready; I was tired and hungry. I had seen seventeen patients that afternoon and one girl in labor. I had just thrown a couple of logs into the wood stove and settled at the table when there was a knock at the door.

Mary answered it, and I heard the voices of two men. They were speaking French, and I gathered there was an emergency. I went into the waiting room. The older of the two men came forward, scattering fresh snow from his heavy boots onto the floor. His face was raw with cold.

"It's old man Saucier. Real bad. Can't get his breath. Can you come?"

Mary interjected: "Doctor's eating his dinner. Let him get some food."

"He's real bad."

I said I'd be there and went back into the kitchen/living room to take a swig of coffee and swallow a couple of mouthfuls of food. Mary hurriedly gave me a packet of cookies.

"I'll follow you. How far?" I asked as I came back out to the waiting room.

"Deux ou trois kilomètres."

I told Mary I'd make it quick, to keep dinner hot, and to tell the hospital that I'd be at Saucier's and would telephone from there.

I followed the men outdoors, the cold hitting my face like a whip. They were driving a pickup with four snow treads. They edged onto the road and waited for me. The night was crystal clear; icicles hanging from the roofs glistened in the moonlight. We moved at a good clip. By now I was getting the ice-driving technique.

Just when the heater began to respond, the truck swung into a driveway. I brought the car to a slow halt beside the snowbank. The house faced the lake. I could see the frozen surface as I crunched over the protesting, squeaking snow and climbed up to a porch caked with snow and ice. I followed the men into the house.

A blast of hot air met me as I entered the kitchen. The living room, typical of that part of the world, was crowded. Two rockers flanked the fireplace, covered with embroidered afghans and occupied with cushions done in petit point. Circular braided rugs in multicolor lay on the polished linoleum. Knickknacks, ashtrays, vases, and figurines filled the tables, together with glossy photographs of relatives in bright gold frames. Scenes of mountains and lakes on colored velvet decorated the walls between the heavy floral curtains.

The family, the women in black with shawls, stood silently around the room. The men in thick woolen shirts and jackets waited with hands in pockets. They watched me in silence.

I put my bag on the sofa and took off my hat. "Where is he?"
The family stared.

"Où est Monsieur Saucier?" I repeated in my schoolboy French.
One of my guides stepped from behind me and inclined his head

toward a doorway, and I went over. In a bedroom on a big oak bed lay the patient. Above his head was a picture of Christ as a carpenter. On an adjacent wall was a crucifix and a print of *The Light of the World*. A Bible, rosary beads, and more photographs of the family covered a chest of drawers. The largest gold-framed photo was of an overweight youth being ordained.

The bedroom was like a blast furnace. A space heater and its blower made a clicking sound. The only other noise was the wheezing of the patient, fast and punctuated by an occasional grunt.

M. Saucier was around fifty-five, with pinched features and thin gray hair splayed across his forehead, anchored by sweat. His lips were purple and his eyes bloodshot. He was sitting forward in striped flannel pajamas. His chest was heaving; clearly it was an effort to breathe. He looked at me for a second, then half closed his eyes in his fight for air.

"Here's your bag, Doc," said my guide. He helped me off with my coat. Meanwhile the family filtered into the bedroom and formed a circle against the wall. A big woman moved to the far side of the patient and placed her hand on the blanket. Was she his wife?

"How long has he been like this?" I asked her in French. She seemed to understand.

"Two days—eh?" she looked around at the family.

"Has he been this way before?"

"Ah, yes. He has the asthma, says the other doctor." Again, in French.

"Asthma!"

"Oui, c'est le ragweed."

"But not in midwinter," I said in English, and then reverted to their speech: "Mais c'est l'hiver. I'l n'y a pas de fleurs."

There was no answer.

I tried again. Had he become suddenly ill? Had he had pain in the chest, down the arms? I mimed a heart attack. "Mal au coeur?" No, that wasn't the French for it, or was it? When they gave you a

Maine medical license, why didn't they throw in a phrase book for those destined to practice in the sticks?

I turned to my guide. "Do you know anything about it?"

He shrugged: "I live down the road a ways. They call me last night."

"Ask her," I indicated the woman I assumed was the wife, "whether he had bad pain in the chest."

A mixture of guttural American interspersed with Canadian French followed. The woman's eyes widened as she listened. She took a deep breath through her nose, then gushed out an answer.

"She says he doesn't complain much."

"Oh! For God's sake—" I checked myself. It would get me nowhere to vent my frustration. Their stubborn dumbness was hard enough without adding hostility. I had a lot to learn. But at the moment, the patient's history was vital. I had to distinguish between heart failure and asthma, a recurrent problem in medical practice.

I examined him. His pulse was fast and regular. His blood pressure was elevated. He had no signs of retained fluid. His chest sounded like a pipe organ—high-pitched tones emanated from bronchial tubes half-obstructed by mucus. There was so much noise that I could barely hear his heartbeat, or discern whether there were any sounds to suggest damage to the heart muscle or valves.

I was no further along, and something had to be done. I couldn't take him to the hospital. If he was having an attack of asthma, a small injection of adrenaline would relieve him at once. If, on the other hand, he'd had a silent heart attack and was in heart failure, adrenaline would be dangerous, perhaps fatal. As I listened with my stethoscope I remembered a lecture demonstration in the autopsy room. A patient suffering from severe chest disease had been given morphine because the doctor had thought he was in heart failure and had "cardiac asthma." (The chest can sometimes sound exactly the same with lung asthma as it can in severe heart failure.) It had been the wrong diagnosis.

There were little purple vessels coursing over M. Saucier's nose and cheeks. His ears were blue, as were his fingernails. I felt for his heart. It was not enlarged. I didn't think he was in heart failure.

Asthma? But why should he suffer an asthma attack in mid-winter—unless, of course, he had a chest infection?

"Has he had a cough?" I turned to the guide. "Ask him if he's had a cough."

"Vous avez la grande toux? C'est le bronchitis?" my guide asked. The patient looked blankly at him and continued to struggle for breath.

I turned to him. "Have you a cough? Avez-vous la toux?" I shouted.

He wheezed on. He wouldn't even look at me.

"What about pain? Have you had pain here? Or here? Mal au coeur?" God knows, he must be getting some of this. I looked around at the family. They stared back. His wife was fingering her rosary.

We stood in frustrated silence.

"Very well. I shall give him an injection. Can I boil some water?"

One of the women in curlers, a sister perhaps, muttered something to the guide. "The kitchen is this way, Doctor," he said.

In the kitchen I said, "I shall need a pan to boil a syringe and needle."

They gave me a small saucepan, and as I watched the water come to the boil, I went over it again. Give morphine, and if I'm wrong, he'll stop breathing altogether. Give adrenaline, and if I'm wrong, he may have another heart attack. Do nothing, and he'll die. Take him to the hospital for an x-ray of his chest? Out of the question. He was too ill to move; the trip would kill him.

I poured off the water. If only he could speak to me. Just a couple of words in English to answer my questions.

I fixed the needle on the syringe and took out the adrenaline. The teachers used to make us memorize a saying: "Give a minim a minute *and no more.*"

I went back into the bedroom. They were still hovering around the foot of the bed: three children, the wife, sisters, the guides.

I cleaned the patient's arm, found a vein, and put the needle in. I taped the syringe along the forearm.

"You'll feel better in a minute. You'll breathe better," I shouted. Deaf, he wheezed on.

One minim. I waited. No change.

Two minims. I thought his breathing was easier. I looked at my watch. Four minutes. Two more minims. Yes, he was definitely breathing better. He was even leaning back on the pillows.

I looked round at the family, smiling to encourage them. There was no response.

I glanced at my watch again. Another minim from the syringe.

Suddenly he sat up erect. His eyes were wide open, and he turned to me. Through his dense blue lips he said, *in clear English:*

"My God, Doctor, what have you given me?"

The syringe swayed as his arm fell toward the floor. He fell back as dead as anything I've ever seen.

CHAPTER

11

THERE WERE NO OTHER catastrophes of that nature as the weeks went by. Instead there were one or two minor medical triumphs. I discovered that one old man with the cough had active tuberculosis. I remembered my advice from my London teachers and visited the family and found two more cases in the grandchildren. They went up to Fort Kent and then on to the sanitarium.

I also sensed that a young girl who was constantly crying had symptoms and behavior that were similar to those of a girl at Trenton State Hospital. I had her parents take her to a psychiatrist in Portland, and she was diagnosed as a schizophrenic. Not that that helped her much in those days.

Meanwhile the practice continued relentlessly night and day, and slowly Mary and I accumulated some capital. As there were no banks in Eagle Lake and everyone paid us in cash, we had to find a hiding place. For most of the time we used to stuff our dollar bills into the back of an old Kodak box camera.

Our fees were not excessive: two dollars for an office call, three dollars for a house call, and thirty-five dollars for antenatal, delivery, and postnatal care. Everyone paid us, and it was, and is, the only practice where we had no bad debts. But we worked for it, and obstetrics was the killer. At one point I went three days and nights without sleep, and I was forced to close shop for a couple of hours to think straight.

On one occasion I came down in pajamas at 4:00 A.M. to stock up the stove and found two men seated in the waiting room. They wanted a check-up. Going back to bed with them waiting below was pointless; any more sleep was out of the question. This was the only time in my career when I did a couple of routine physicals at four-thirty in the morning. They were as fit as a couple of young oxen and went off to cut trees as soon as they were reassured that they were fit for it.

Night house calls could be difficult. One evening, around midnight, I received a telephone call that a man was seriously ill at his home about five miles south. I asked the caller to put on all the house lights so that I would not miss the place, and set off.

It was a clear night, cold as the North Pole, the roads sheer ice. By sticking to the center of the road I could get up to thirty-five miles per hour with moderate confidence. I had to keep reminding myself to keep my foot off the brake and to anticipate the slightest skid by turning into it.

I was moving along nicely when I caught the brilliant headlights of a car behind me. It was approaching at a good speed and seemed determined to pass me. I stuck grimly to the center but the fellow behind was actually tailgating me. His high-beam headlights reflected off the road and snowbanks beyond, dazzling me.

I cursed him and edged my way to the side. In a flash he tore by, and I recognized the black Cadillac of Father Anthony Blais. At the same time I saw him make a skidding turn off the road. By then I had gone beyond his exit, with only a second to see a house with every light blazing. I took about a quarter mile to stop, and then, with multiple cautious movements, turned my car around. I made my way to the house and parked behind the priest's car. The car was empty and the engine running. I thought about switching it off, as a good neighbor, but I was in no mood for friendly gestures. I had already made several hostile ones when he overtook me.

I tramped up the drive, onto the front porch, and banged on the door. I had to wait two minutes before it was opened. I was let in without a word by a black-shrouded crone.

The reason was immediately apparent. The caller had said that the patient was very ill and in pain, but I was unprepared for the scene that met my eyes. It was the first time I had ever arrived at a house where the last rites were ahead of me. In a bedroom straight ahead lay an old man. Father Blais was lighting the two candles he had just placed on either side of the bed. From a black bag he took out a black book, a length of silk, and some other paraphernalia. He then began to speak in Latin at the foot of the bed. Some members of the family were kneeling, and two women stood back clutching handkerchiefs and touching their eyes between genuflections.

The last rites took a few minutes. Then Father Blais spoke briefly to the family. He came to me.

"You may examine him now." He removed the candles, and I went forward to look at the patient. I had seen him before and knew he was terminally sick with cancer.

In French I asked him if he was in pain. He frowned and looked at Father Blais who repeated my question in a long, colloquial sentence.

"He says the pain is severe down the back of his right leg."

"I will give him an injection." I had some ampoules of morphine and had learned to carry a supply of sterilized needles and syringes. I injected a dose into a vein to give the old man quick relief.

We all waited in silence. In a minute he spoke in a whisper to Father Blais. He felt better but very tired.

I stood back, and after Father Blais had packed his bag, he approached me.

"How long?"

"Before morning," I replied. "But you never can be sure. I'll come back then."

Father Blais went over to the family, who gathered around him like a flock of disciples. I returned alone to the sitting room. It was dark, with only one lamp lit. I could hear a murmur of questions and the deep authoritative voice of Father Blais replying. They fell silent.

I took up my bag and moved toward the door. I felt absurdly out of place, an interloper. A man came over to me and spoke rapidly in French. I couldn't catch what he had to say. "Pardon," I said. "Mais—"

Father Blais turned. In English he said, "He wants to know how much they owe you."

It was difficult to face Father Blais.

"What is your usual fee for a night call?" he asked.

"Five dollars."

"Not enough, Doctor."

He turned to the man. I couldn't catch what he said, but the man came toward me with his wallet open, peeling off dollar bills. He gave me seven. I handed back two.

"Father Blais, would you tell the family that I will return in the morning whatever happens—and there will be no fee for that visit."

He shrugged and spoke to the family. I think he gave my message but suspect it may have been modified.

I stepped out of the door into the raw early morning and reached my car. As I did I heard the footsteps of Father Blais behind me. "One moment, Doctor." He opened the door of his car and beckoned me over.

Inside, with the engine running, it was cozily warm. We faced each other. We had not met since the standoff over the abortion.

"Doctor, we do not see eye-to-eye on many matters. Let that rest for the time being."

I nodded.

"However, while you are here, we may be called to cases like this where I have to administer the sacrament and you try to treat the patient. I shall always try to get there first, but if you happen to be before me, let us make this pact. The roads are icy, and to have an accident and be stranded might be dangerous."

"I agree."

He adjusted his gloves. "Then let us say that, regardless of who wins the race, the other will wait for him to complete his professional work, and we will shepherd each other home."

I smiled. "I'm not up to your speed."

He gave a laugh. "Give it time, Doctor."

"And a prayer?"

This time he really laughed, leaned over, and opened the door for me. "Good night, Doctor. By the way, never shut off your car engine in these circumstances."

I followed him down the road, and he never went over thirty-five miles per hour.

CHAPTER

12

RADUALLY THE PRACTICE FELL into a routine. Patients
came to know Mary and me, but they were reserved, careful not
to make friends. No one was interested in our background or
where we'd come from. They kept their wary distance and seemed
to offer the type of respect similar to that reserved for the highest of
the medical profession in England; and nearly equal to that for their
local priest, who ruled their lives.

The practice was busy, and I saw little of my daughters. Mary
cheerfully kept everything going without much help from me.
Every so often we used to chuck a fresh load of wood to one another from the shed to the back door, but she was the one to shovel
the driveway.

We escaped to Fort Kent once or twice and opened a bank account, taking the money from the Kodak camera to a real bank. I
found the informality of the teller unusual. In those days, to open
an account in the Old Country required two references from figures of social standing and an interview with the manager. The bank
at Fort Kent moved as expeditiously as the Maine Board of Medical
Examiners. Money first, credentials later.

Fort Kent wasn't Fifth Avenue. There were a few shops hidden
behind banks of snow, but to our disappointment, none sold any
gramophone records except "forty-fives," mainly of the new stuff
known as "rock and roll." We felt this would be out of place for our
waiting room. Eartha Kitt's "Easy Does It" was attractive but inap-
propriate, and everything by Elvis was out of bounds. We needed a few
more from the classic repertoire.

Back in Eagle Lake, it was impossible to get to know the nuns.
Except for Sister Euloge there was an impregnable barrier. Some-

times toward dawn, over long and difficult labors, she and I would talk. She had a charming sense of humor, but would avoid any talk about her background. I suppose it was natural to be curious as to why a young, attractive, intelligent woman should take vows, but I refrained from asking her. And I avoided any discussion involving religion or the nun's way of life. Over the months she saw that not only was I an agnostic, but that I had little more than a sentimental interest in the rituals, high days, and holidays of the church.

For us, Christmas and Easter were largely a matter of presents, a tree, lights, food, and chocolate, without emphasis on symbolism. In our mansion, toilet training was taking precedence over religious instruction.

Occasionally I saw some of the other nuns at close quarters. Two would be assigned to the operating room when a surgeon came down from Fort Kent or when I did something requiring an anesthetic. They would sit to one side of the room on a bench in full uniform with shimmering white wimples, looking like two large meditating penguins.

This mediaeval attire is engraved in my memory, especially by one incident, when I set a fractured ankle in a young woodsman. He was a husky man, about two hundred pounds, all muscle. For a couple of months I had gone along with Sister Euloge's tea strainer, gauze, and ether technique for anesthesia. But over in the corner of the operating room was the simple anesthetic machine, similar to one I had used in the emergency room in England. It still had its label and warranty attached to one of the taps.

Before the patient came into the room, I told Sister Euloge that I would use the machine. She was hesitant and seemed a trifle dubious, but we cleaned it and filled the container with ether and checked the nitrous oxide and oxygen cylinders. I tried it out on myself with a few whiffs from the rubber mask, and it seemed in fine shape.

We had given the patient his premedication, and as soon as he entered the room he lay down on the operating table. Sister Euloge wheeled the trolley with plaster bandages and bowls of water to the side. We were all set to go.

I sat at the patient's head and asked him to breathe normally, then gradually lowered the mask onto his face. Everything went like a charm—until he stopped breathing.

For a second I couldn't believe it, but already Sister Euloge had moved to the patient's side and was thrusting down on his chest. She was a lightweight and I was in a hurry to assist her, but first I had to establish an airway. This took a moment or two, and when I looked up I could see nothing of the patient.

He was buried beneath a heaving mass of black, as though a couple of giant crows had settled on the table. The two benched nuns had come to the rescue and were rhythmically pushing the young man's chest, their flowing black habits obscuring their considerable individual bulk. How they managed to integrate their starched wimples I'll never know, but within seconds the patient was breathing normally and remained asleep.

The nuns, a trifle pink, disengaged and returned silently to their bench. Sister Euloge moved to the head of the table, took out her tea strainer and can of ether, and resumed the anesthesia as soon as I had verified that the patient's heart and lungs were normal. We then went about fixing the man's ankle.

While he was recovering consciousness, Sister Euloge wheeled the anesthetic machine back into the corner of the room and covered it with a sheet. She said nothing; her gesture was sufficient. I thanked her colleagues, who left the scene with a gentle nodding dignity.

I was embarrassed by the event and must have looked contrite as I wrote up my notes on the case.

"Worse things happen at sea, doctor," said Sister Euloge.

"Do they?"

"His time hadn't come. Now what you need is your cup of tea to buck you up."

I explained again that tea for the British was an afternoon event.

"At four o'clock—yes. With watercress sandwiches and fruit-cake?"

"On the dot."

"Then we must give you your English tea. When will you come with Mrs. Betts and the children?"

"You mean a sort of state visit? Moving from bed to bed with a kindly nod and a touch of the hand?"

"The patients would love to see the children and Mrs. Betts."

"Well, if you insist. How about next Wednesday? It'll give us time to rehearse."

She smiled. "Very well, next Wednesday. I will tell Mother Andrea."

I went home and reported the morning's drama to Mary and told her about our invitation for tea.

"It's going to be the official visit—you know, royalty doing the wards at the London Hospital," I said. "You'll have to sport a silly hat."

"Oh dear! What shall I wear? I'll freeze before I get inside that hospital."

"The fur coat. Just the thing. Very la-de-dah. You can peel it off when we get to the hospital; they keep the place like a hothouse. How about the blue dress?"

"And long white gloves, like the Duchess of Kent at Wimbledon?"

"And I'll get my black suit and thaw it out."

"Won't the patients think there's a hearse outside?"

Wednesday rolled around without much excitement. There was the usual quota of births in between a few hair-raising house calls. Going to Soldier's Pond, a hamlet about six miles away, was one. The road had a steep icy surface and seemed to have modeled itself after the north face of Everest. It was one of the few calls where I made the terms that, if they wanted me, I'd get within a quarter mile and then they'd have to haul me up and lower me out.

And there was an incident when the barber's son was struck on the head by ice falling from his roof. He was concussed, unconscious, and under observation in the hospital. The visiting surgeon from Fort Kent said nothing more could be done in his hospital, so we kept watch with the usual head chart observations.

The barber lived next door to us and was excitable even in the quietest circumstances. His trade made him a chatterbox, and he spoke quickly, switching from subject to subject like a depressive entering a manic phase. This was fine for a quick trim round the ears and neck. But now, whenever he saw me emerging from the house, he was off and running, and listening at thirty degrees below zero was not easy.

By an act of grace and Sears, Roebuck, the fall of ice on the barber's son coincided with a strike by our water pump. Sears at that time, and perhaps even now, was not renowned for its outside service. For the price of a thirteen-mile service call, you could buy the company. The barber came to our rescue. Next to hair, his thing was pumps.

For some reason our pump was located about three feet down in the center of our living room through a trap door. We had never suspected its presence, but the barber found it and went down the hole like a homing rabbit. For the next three evenings Mary and I sat in our chairs with the head and shoulders of the barber midway between us. An unabated stream of conversation would vary in direction and intensity according to whether he was above or below ground. There were two subjects: Sears pumps and his son's head. Fortunately both recovered at about the same time.

Wednesday dawned, and after the ward round, Sister Euloge reminded me of our tea date. Promptly at 3:30 P.M. we arrived at the hospital. Mary was resplendent in her fur coat, long boots, and a fur trader's hat. Ann was in her carry-crib encased in a woolen zoot suit reinforced with innumerable blankets, and Sara was carried in more blankets, like Cleopatra brought before Caesar wrapped in carpets. I was attired in my London suit and coat. I omitted the umbrella.

We trooped into the hospital foyer and were met by Mother Superior and two lieutenants of the same order. Sister Euloge stood to one side. I glanced at her during the introductions. From her eyes I could tell something was going on.

After an exchange of pleasantries, we moved into the wards and passed between the beds. I had seen the same thing enacted by Queen Mary, General Patton, and the Shah of Iran either in person or on Pathé News. The patients were propped up, and a kindly word was given here and there. Mary had got "Comment ça va?" and "Enchantée" down pat, but Sister Euloge was at her side chatting and smiling and acting as interpreter. The babies won the day, and for Ann, who is now a nurse at Maine Medical Center, it was her first ward round and possibly her most successful.

We were then conducted into forbidden territory. During the months while I worked in the hospital, I had watched the nuns silently glide down the stairs into the basement and wondered what was down there. Single cells and bread and water? A subterranean chapel? Indoor cloisters?

The others descended ahead, and when I joined them I found we were in a large refectory. The walls were paneled. There were no windows, and the only ornaments were emblems, religious paintings, and crucifixes. At the far end the floor was raised and supported a plain table covered with a white cloth. In the center was a gold cross and to one side a lectern.

Down the center of the room was a long table covered in a starched white tablecloth. At one end stood a heavy silver tray with handles, and on this was an ornate silver tea pot, milk jug, sugar bowl, and jug of hot water. Gleaming plates, cups and saucers, and dishes piled with fresh sandwiches and cakes crowded the table. One larger plate was reserved for a splendid cake with white icing and little figures in red and green. A bowl filled with ice cream completed the offerings.

There were four place settings for our family, and a chair had been augmented with cushions for Sara. Around the refectory the nuns stood like sentries against the wall. There must have been about forty of them impassively watching us. Mother Superior stood at the door. It was like act two of *The Magic Flute*.

Sister Euloge poured the tea.

"Milk and sugar, Mrs. Betts?" she asked. "Please take a sandwich, and I will cut a piece of cake for Sara." She turned to our daughter: "And I expect you'll like some ice cream, too."

Before long we sat with our plates lavishly filled with generous helpings of everything. My own plate had a large wedge of cream cake surmounted with two scoops of strawberry ice cream topped with whipped cream.

"This is magnificent," I said. "You know, we don't have tea like this every day in England."

"Wonderful," added Mary, scraping cake from Sara's face.

I looked up. "But what about all of you? We can't eat all this alone. There's plenty for everyone." I looked at the ring of nuns standing at the periphery.

"Thank you, Doctor, but we can't," said Sister Euloge.

"Oh?"

"Yes. You see, it's Lent."

CHAPTER

13

B Y APRIL THE WEATHER was warmer, there was less snow, and we had settled into a routine. Mary and I decided, with the practice quieter, to take a trip to Presque Isle. It involved going down Route 11 for about twenty miles to Portage and then east. We would get some more music for our waiting room and throw in a house call that was outstanding on a long-distance cardiac patient.

We slid into Portage, and I went to the variety store to ask directions to the house of my patient. A stalwart man in a leather jacket was leaning against the door frame and overheard my inquiry.

He spoke with a drawl. "You're the doc making the house call on Mrs. Rancourt?"

"The very one."

"Got time to make another? We called you, but I guess you'd left the hospital."

I returned to the car to tell Mary I'd be a few minutes longer. She began to feed the baby. The man at the door hadn't moved. I told him I would see my own patient first and then perhaps he could show me the way to the other.

"Fine," he said, "that'll give me time to check whether to use skis or floats. Difficult this time of year. Have to get to a sick lady a couple of lakes in. Not sure whether the ice has broken up enough for floats, and don't want to sink with skis. Water's mighty cold."

A bit of the ice might have dropped down my back. "You mean you want me to fly?"

"Sure. No trouble—'cept landing. Hate to take a float off and be stuck out there." He eased himself off the door frame and ambled toward the dock on Portage Lake. I watched him go as if I'd had a predawn interview with mine own executioner.

A brief background will suffice to explain my state of mind: I had survived as an R.A.F. pilot for five years in World War Two largely by luck and cowardice, in a ratio of about one to three. I had volunteered for the Royal Air Force only because of the horrendous accounts of trench warfare given to me as a boy by our family gardener, and a ghastly movie about fire-stricken naval vessels sinking in mid-Atlantic. In the air, it would be a quick end. Once in the R.A.F. I saw I'd never survive the pilot training because I couldn't do math, hated learning about engines, and had a congenital inability to plot the straight lines required for navigation. It was only when I learned that failed pilots ended up as air gunners (life expectancy six hours) that I underwent a jolting metamorphosis into an academic whiz-kid. Within weeks of volunteering I found myself clambering into a training cockpit in the middle of Africa. I was shown how to land and take off and was encouraged to practice aerobatics such as slow rolls and looping the loop. Stalling and spinning made me sick. Consequently, during the practice sessions I would go off for an hour on a straight course and return to my instructor more intact than some of my colleagues.

The luck part was that wherever I was posted, the war stopped. I never heard a shot fired in anger except when I went home to London on leave and spent the night under the bed during the buzz bomb attacks. I flew for five years, and if they'd given a medal for caution, I'd have been first in line. The last time I flew was to bring a four-engine Lincoln into Khartoum in the Sudan. No one told me about the phenomenal heat and the convection currents, and the bomber floated a mile or two down the runway before touching down. That was enough. A good landing is one you can walk away from. The war had ended, and I took two vows: never to pilot anything again, and never to let any amateur fly me.

Hence I gazed in anguish at the back of this bush pilot as he went off to check the landing gear on the flimsy affair I saw anchored at Portage Lake dock. I gave the news to Mary. She asked me what I was going to do.

"Not get into that bit of string and sealing wax."

"But aircraft have improved since 1945."

"Noncommercial pilots haven't."

I crossed the street to Mrs. Rancourt's. While I checked her heart and blood pressure I tried to reconcile myself to whatever fate and the dubious-looking seaplane might have in store for me. Finally I returned to stand beside the car and wait for the pilot to return.

"Guess we'll take a chance with floats. I'll take a low run across before putting down to check," he announced, bending down to greet Mary. "Morning, ma'am. Sure is a great day for flying—crisp and clear. Lucky to catch your husband. Woman guide in there, mighty sick for two days. Husband on radio says she has pneumonia. Running a high temp and breathing hard."

Someone has said, "shame is the spur." I met Mary's eyes. A spiel about the Hippocratic oath was on the horizon. I was locked in. I took my medical bag from the car.

"Let me take that for you, sir."

He helped me into the cockpit. I put my medical bag on the floor between my legs and fastened the seat belt. Aircraft design may have advanced, but this machine wasn't much different from the Tiger Moth of my training days. It had the same smell, and a wave of miserable memories swept over me.

We taxied out between floating chunks of ice until we struck a clear patch of water, and with a roar we took off. Any fear I experienced was now replaced by the feeling I was in a gale at the North Pole. I bent double to get my head out of the wind. My chauffeur was enjoying himself. Through my helmet (another old reminder) came his humming of selections from *Oklahoma!*

"What a day! Pretty, pretty, pretty. You O.K., Doc?"

I emerged. We were at about two thousand feet. Fir trees extended to the horizon in every direction. We were heading for the Allagash, a wilderness embraced by hunters and fishermen of the

Hemingway ilk. An injunction from my R.A.F. training days came back to me: Always look for a field for a forced landing. Central Africa had been more generous with clearings than this continuous forest. Suddenly we were over another lake and losing height.

"I'll take a run across and see if enough ice is out."

We went down to about twenty feet and skimmed over the surface. There wasn't much open water. We veered off the end into a steep climbing turn, swooped down, and took another sweep. Chunks of floating ice and water flew by my eyes.

"My, my," I heard the pilot say as he seemed to stand the plane on its tail again. "O.K., this'll be it. We're going down."

A minute later we were making a glide approach. I waited for the first bump as we touched down. It was more a swish than a bump. The bumps came afterward as we taxied toward the shore and hit blocks of ice. About a hundred yards from the shore he cut the engine.

"Guess we'll have to walk the rest. O.K.?"

For those who have traversed the Knife Edge on Mount Katahdin and still feel unfulfilled, I recommend ambling with a medical bag over a hundred yards of broken ice on Fish River Lake. It does something for the soul and life expectancy. Use something better than overshoes for footwear.

A gray-haired man in a red wool jacket helped me up onto the snowbank. Without a word he led me up to a cabin, and I followed him in. It was warm and well furnished. In a bedroom lay a woman in her forties. She was having difficulty breathing, and her lips had a tinge of blue. Her temperature was 103°. One side of her chest was like a board, without a sound of air, the other was a jumble of noise. No doubt about the pneumonia.

She and the man, her husband, were owners of a series of camps. They'd come in early to get them ready. They had hiked in, being familiar with the trail, and picked up their canoe on a small river that was no longer frozen to complete their journey.

I gave her a large injection of penicillin and left another drawn up for the husband to give in a few hours. Meanwhile I explained that it was essential to get the patient to a hospital. She needed oxygen and good care. Before I left, I heard the husband calling on his radio for professional guides to come in and get her.

Then off we set on the return journey. Getting over the ice to the seaplane was more hazardous than the flight back. The whole incident had taken two hours.

"Thanks for coming, Doc. Guess we could establish a medico-air service like they do in Australia."

I nodded. "I'll work on it."

I made my way back to the car. Mary had completed about another yard of knitting on some undesignated garment.

"You were ages," she said. "Did you fly it yourself?"

I gave her a look, and she understood. We headed toward Presque Isle, quietly admiring the snowbanks and what they were beginning to reveal. There was no doubt about there being a lot of Aroostook County, and why any group should want to argue about retaining more of it (as happened in the "Aroostook War" of 1839) was beyond me.

Presque Isle, while neck-and-neck culturally with Fort Kent, had it beaten in classical repertoire. For our waiting room music, we bought the Second Rachmaninoff Piano Concerto, Mozart's greatest hits, and a melange produced by the 101 Hollywood Strings.

It was while forking out for this musical splurge that I remembered I had not been paid for my flying house call. Somehow my gratitude for survival had superseded any sordid thoughts of monetary gain. At least that's how I explained it to Mary on the way back to Eagle Lake. My father had shared the same philosophy. He used to fly on business in rather flimsy aircraft to parts of Europe before World War Two. He used to say that when he got on the aircraft he regarded it as a life investment, and when he got off he declared himself a profit.

A week later, a check for four times what I might have requested came through the mail, together with the news that the patient was doing well.

CHAPTER

14

L ENT SEEMED TO LAST beyond the usual limits specified on our refrigerator calendar, so I asked the barber, a communicant, if our information was at fault.

He took the question in his stride and said Father Blais had extended it two days this year. I refrained from comment. The only other instance I could think of where someone messed around with the calendar was Caesar Augustus, so I was impressed with Father's influence, local though it might be. However, I was not going to risk any discussion about it with him. Religion and medicine were topics to be avoided with Blais as scrupulously as politics and women had been at the Edwardian dinner table.

The Edict of Blais—the extended holiday—didn't affect my work or food intake as much as that of the hospital staff. But I could have been more judicious with nutritional advice if I had known how the current religious calendar stood. In England you knew where you were; Lent ended with rabbits and Easter eggs, the opening of the cricket season, or with some notorious horse race, and banks were closed just when you needed them. In Eagle Lake, innumerable church performances went on like a Broadway hit, and I had the impression that all the time the nuns were living on bread and water.

In our secular division, the office was humming. We saw a steady crowd in the waiting room and a pronounced increase in pregnant customers. I told Mary that perhaps the extended subzero temperatures might have something to do with it, but she said Mme. Belanger had told her that the seasonal wealth of happy events had to do with when the lumberjacks emerged from their work in the woods. It was a reasonable hypothesis and food for thought, though hardly a matter for research. But I was glad that Mary was on such chatty terms with the grocer's wife.

"Did you get all that in French?" I asked.

"We didn't have to draw pictures. Incidentally, she said the old doctor might be back in a couple of months."

That stopped me. "Was that in French or American?"

"A bit of each, but I was quite sure what she meant. 'Le docteur est down in Florida, mais il a écrit Father Blais,' is what she said, more or less."

These tidings rather dampened our Lent and opened up the next in our series of marital debates about where we'd go next. It looked as if I might be reverting to a medical nomad, a Flying Dutchman with a black bag. Over coffee, after considering Canada, South Africa, Malaya, and a dozen other improbable sites of refuge, we decided to leave our fate in the laps of the gods and have another shot at Maine.

So I wrote to Dr. Leighton to say I was an open draft for a family practice—preferably in a temperate zone, and as soon as possible.

Meanwhile I found the change of seasons from winter to spring imperceptible. Perhaps the snowbanks went down a centimeter or two and the temperature edged up a notch, but I doubt that the casual observer would have noticed. Only a well-trained, tooled-up nature watcher armed with a diary would have recorded any difference in the landscape or atmosphere from one week to the next. To me, Eagle Lake remained uniformly white and cold. A thousand miles or so south folks might be basking beneath cherry blossoms, but in the immediate neighborhood the fishing huts still dotted the ice-laden lake.

However, I did notice a thaw in the local population. I won't say we were being accepted, but I think that from the secular point of view we were now regarded as relatively harmless. One indication of this was an invitation to a prime time social event.

The "spring" dance was to be held at the lakeside barn on Saturday evening from 7:00 to 10:00 P.M., bring your own beer. Our invitation came via the barber in one of his maintenance visits to our front-room subterranean pump.

The last dance Mary and I had attended was the New Year's Eve Hospital Ball held at the Dorchester Hotel in Park Lane, London. It had been a posh affair that started at midnight. Everyone dressed to the hilt: tuxedos and off-the-shoulder gowns. Parties formed, had dinner at chic restaurants, arrived in style, danced until dawn, and ended with a stroll across Hyde Park to find breakfast.

I could swear that every bit as much thought went into what Mary was to wear for the approaching Eagle Lake hop. Could one fox-trot with any grace in snow boots, two sweaters, a goose-down jacket and long johns? Was the doctor's wife expected to grace the floor in a skirt, blouse, and high heels, and leave off the earmuffs? These were the questions. The next week was devoted to finding the answers.

"What do you think?" Mary asked for the tenth time.

"I haven't the faintest idea. We don't want another Lent fiasco, do we? Why not cover both bases and take light clothing with you? You could slip into it when you see what everyone else is wearing."

"What—change in that ice cage? I'd sooner die."

"You could be quick. Sacrifice the long johns for the sake of speed."

She gave me a look.

"Well, you could ask around," I added.

"Who, Father Blais?"

There was a pause. "I doubt if he'll be coming."

"He could wear a bearskin under his cassock and no one would notice," she added bitterly.

"I still don't think he'll be attending. I didn't get the impression that he and the grim housekeeper were the dancing types. Nor would there be any point in sounding out the nuns. How about the post-mistress?"

"No. I don't really feel close to her. She's not someone I could make a lifelong chum, if you know what I mean."

"I do indeed."

We finally concluded that I would ask the first suitable patient. Unfortunately the only female patients I encountered over the next two days had retired from the dance floor at least two decades ago. Their average girth seemed to make broaching the subject of their preference in dancing attire both impertinent and too personal. So I thought I'd have a chat with Belanger.

I stopped in on the way to the hospital. As usual his store was crowded, and I was greeted with the customary guarded courtesy. At once I found I hadn't the gall or courage to shoulder my way to the counter merely to ask Belanger what the ladies would be wearing for the Saturday night gala. I had to make the inquiry appear casual, a sort of aside. It would be tricky, for I knew conversation in the shop ceased whenever I spoke. My remarks were always fodder for fresh gossip, for a chance to appreciate my progress with French, and sometimes for a good laugh.

Under the guise of buying something, I picked up the first arti-cle at hand, a toy attached to a piece of cardboard. Only as I passed it to Belanger did I realize it was not a toy but a fishing lure, a tin guppy in turquoise and silver with artificial red feathers.

"You want this, eh, Doc?" Belanger asked.

"Sure," I replied. "And by the way, can you tell me what dress your womenfolk—?"

"Too early for casting. Ice won't be out for another two months." Belanger held up the cellophane-encased lure to the cran-ing throng.

A listener added a spiel in rapid French, to which Belanger replied with a guffaw. The matter then went to the floor and exchanges were profuse.

"You done any ice fishing before, Doc?" Belanger asked.

"No, as a matter of fact, I've never fished. There aren't any in the Thames—too polluted."

Belanger translated for the crowd. "Le Thames est à Londres. C'est plein de merde."

I knew what "merde" meant. He might have been right. "Perhaps I'll skip it," I said. "To be honest, I thought that thing was a toy fish for my kiddies."

Belanger looked at it and then at me. There were three vicious brass hooks protruding from the tin fish's mouth and another from its tail.

"I'll take a tin of Prince Albert," I said. "Sorry to be a bother."

He handed me the tobacco and I eased my way out of the store. I wondered how long news of the incident would take to circulate.

On Saturday night the weather came to our rescue. A good-sized blizzard started in the afternoon, and at seven we fought our way down to the dance hall dressed as if we were out to rescue Scott in the Antarctic. When we arrived we saw that we were no different from the rest of the community. But once inside the barn we were forced to peel off our snow jackets. Someone had jacked up the stove, and the hall was hovering between seventy-five and eighty degrees.

"Well, now you'll see whether you can tango in those boots," I said.

But there were no tangos, waltzes, rhumbas, or fox-trots that night. The band was a solo violinist. In common with most Irish fiddlers, he had a predilection for playing in open fifths, a harmony I find particularly jarring. I'm not sure I wouldn't have preferred the bagpipes. Indeed, they might have been more suitable, for we could have tried a Highland fling. Instead we got the next worse thing: an evening of square dancing.

Square dancing had never been my ballroom forte. I had had

difficulty in my only other experience of it, not only in figuring out where and when to go, but in understanding what the organizer was shouting from the podium. Now the orders were yelled in Eagle Lake French. Gamely I improvised a sort of jig, skipping from one bit of sawdust to another when anyone else changed formation. But I soon found myself panting, and my legs were like rubber.

We retired to the benches. Fortunately all this was viewed as royalty making a gesture of mucking in with hoi-polloi and then retreating in dignity. At least this was how I viewed it. "The old doc never let his hair down like that," someone told me. So at least our dancing was a popular move, and during the next few office sessions many patients asked how we had enjoyed ourselves.

But in the privacy of our home Mary said, "Never again." To which I added, "Not if you paid me."

CHAPTER

15

I HAD SPENT MOST OF A long night with Sister Euloge trying to coax a baby into the cruel world. At least that was how I felt about the world as dawn began to break. Sister had a more beatific attitude toward the event. She didn't say anything, but she had her usual serene air, as if she knew that she was doing God's work.

By now she must have assumed that my religious position was that of an agnostic—and a pretty ignorant one at that—when it came to church events, rituals, and all the rest of it. I don't think she thought I was an atheist, just anti-papal. We never discussed the matter, but of course we had been on opposite sides when Father Blais had laid down the law about the inevitable abortion and countermanded my orders for a curettage.

On occasions like this obstetric delivery, the advent of a new life, I wondered whether Sister Euloge was tempted to try to bring me to her faith. If she was, she never gave me a hint.

It had been a long, hard session, starting for Sister in the morning. Then I had come in to see the patient in the early evening. After midnight, when the poor girl needed us for the relief of pain and for moral support, we had spelled each other in order to get a short rest.

It was her first baby. She was seventeen and unmarried. When I examined her in the morning, I had found the baby the right way up but the wrong way around. She had a posterior presentation, and such deliveries could be notoriously slow and exhausting, not only for the patient but for the doctor and midwife.

"I have brought you your early morning tea, Doctor," said Sister Euloge as she entered the room with a tray. She was still immaculately dressed in her habit in spite of twelve tiring hours of busy nursing. A clean white apron was tied around her waist.

"This must be the fifth cup you've brewed for me since midnight. How about yourself?"

"I am fine, thank you. And I have brought you some biscuits."

"You mean cookies."

"Biscuits, Doctor. I was educated in Canada. We say 'biscuits,' just like the Queen. These are chocolate biscuits."

"No expense spared. Thank you. How about you?"

"No, thank you."

"It's not still Lent, is it?"

She laughed. "No, Doctor. And it will soon be time for your Easter egg."

It was 5:30, and I found myself half-asleep and daydreaming. I thought: how amazing—for the amount of time we had spent together involved with the patients, swapping opinions, giving advice—

that I knew so little of what really passed through the mind of Sister Euloge. I remembered the one time when I did venture to ask her why she had entered the order, hoping she'd open up. But she had deflected my inquiry with a smile and said it was to serve her fellow human beings, or something like that. Then she had gone into the next room.

In spite of her air of sanctity, she appeared always a woman, attractive and alive, and sometimes I felt an urge to bring her back to earth. Perhaps it was my innate desire to challenge her perfection. I was tempted to ask her why she had wanted to leave "these graces to the grave and leave the world no copy."

The girl in labor gave a groan as another wave of pain commenced. I stood up and watched her and nodded to Sister. She placed the mask with trilene anesthetic on the girl's face, and the rubber bladder shuddered in and out as our patient inhaled hungrily.

At that moment I had a feeling the girl had reached the end of the first stage of labor, and as soon as the pain had subsided I said I would re-examine her to check whether the womb was fully open. Perhaps then forceps could be used.

Once more we went through the routine sterile procedure with a thorough wash and the donning of gloves. I gently sought the head of the baby.

It was coming down. With a wave of relief I was able to tell Sister that the girl was going to deliver any minute.

But another hour went by before the head at last crowned.

Now Sister could start to administer ether to put the patient into deeper anesthesia and allow the use of forceps. I heard her murmuring words of encouragement to the exhausted girl. Five minutes later she nodded to me that I could go ahead with forceps.

My residency in obstetrics had given me plenty of experience in the forceps procedure. But delivering a baby with them after a long labor was difficult, and not without its dangers for the mother and baby.

I inserted one blade beside the head and guided it into place with my other hand. Then I inserted the other blade. They joined, and I offered up thanks. (If only Sister Euloge knew!)

Now I had to make an incision to ease the passage for both the instruments and the baby's head. There was more bleeding than I expected. And I had to apply force, pull more than I wanted. How I hated to do that. It was at such moments that I sweated blood.

Two nuns, assistant nurses, appeared from nowhere to keep the girl from moving forward. I could feel the sweat running down from my forehead behind my surgical mask.

I pulled again. There was motion. Another pull. I could feel the head emerging, and now I saw that its shape had been severely molded by the forces of labor and my efforts.

I disengaged the forceps blades. I still could not deliver the baby. The shoulders were stuck. I gave a twist this way and that, and one shoulder emerged.

I paused for a breath. The room was silent. Now the other shoulder. It slid out, and a moment later the baby was born.

I waited before cutting the umbilical cord, taking my time to clamp and tie it off and regain my own equilibrium.

The room was still silent.

The baby was dusky blue and had not breathed.

"Everything all right your end, Sister?" I asked, trying to sound casual.

"Yes, Doctor. Pulse and blood pressure normal."

I held the baby upside down by his legs and gave him a sharp slap on the buttocks. Out of the corner of my eye I could see the two nuns murmuring a prayer.

I glanced to the top of the bed, seeking the eyes of Sister Euloge. She gazed back, and at that moment I knew that everything was going to be all right.

The baby gave a cry. Then another. And another, and I was swept through and through with relief and joy. Both nuns looked up and were smiling. I blinked and turned away. Doctors are supposed to hide their emotions.

One nun took the babe from me and went to a bassinet. Then Sister Euloge asked the other nun to watch over the girl as she regained consciousness. I heard the sound of suction as Sister Euloge cleared the baby's airway.

Minutes later she and I, both relaxed and happy, were alone with the patient as we waited for the afterbirth.

The girl was still asleep. She lay on the bed naked, her thighs and body spattered with blood.

Sister Euloge bathed the girl's face. She had regular features, beautiful and young, and was now at peace. I watched as Sister wrapped her head in a tight linen cloth, concealing her hair. Now she looked as if she were an innocent novice, newly shorn.

I looked down at her, saying nothing for the moment. Then: "She looks exactly as you must have, Sister, when you took your vows," I said.

Sister Euloge stood stock-still, her hands arrested in her task. She appeared almost startled. Then her eyes filled with amusement, and she had to bite her lip—but it was useless, and she burst into laughter.

"Really, Doctor!" she said, wiping her eyes, and she nodded toward the girl.

And I saw what had caused her merriment. Our patient, with her head and face prepared as if she were ready to enter the order, was lying on the bed without a stitch of clothing, without even a blanket, and one could follow the umbilical cord to the very essence of an earthy, fecund young woman.

And once more Sister Euloge's laughter filled the room.

CHAPTER

16

O NE MORNING IN MAY I returned to the house to find a bright blue station wagon entrenched in our diminishing snowbank. As I emerged from my car, four men came toward me with a purposeful air. Preconditioned by my exposure to Cagney and Bogart films, I had a moment of panic and apprehension. Was this a contingent of the IRS or the FBI?

But as soon as their leader spoke, I realized from the absence of a New Jersey drawl that he was a Maine product, and hardly likely to pack a rod, lead me off in handcuffs, or whatever else the Feds do.

The leader said they had driven from Albion, a town a couple of hundred miles south, in the hope of catching me "before I moved." They had heard that I was about to leave Eagle Lake, and they wanted to be the first to catch me. This earnest group was a search committee seeking a doctor, for which there was a pressing need in their area.

Mentally I took a deep breath and invited them into the office. Introductions followed. Mr. Keay was the owner of a variety store. He was a rawboned, middle-aged man with penetrating blue eyes and dressed in a red-and-black snow jacket. Warren Champlin, an insurance agent—a tall, heavily-built man—had blue eyes, gold rimmed glasses, and a booming voice. The third, perhaps in his early fifties, was a farmer who spoke softly and smiled a lot. The last, and youngest, was Mickey Marden, who had an infectious grin and a hand about the size of a weekend joint of beef.

Feeling that Mary ought to be in on these proceedings, I stuck my head around the door and gave her a call. Misinterpreting the summons and thinking I had a new patient in the office, she put on a record from our new collection.

The search committee gathered around my desk and spread out a map while I went off to silence the Hollywood Strings. When I returned with Mary, and after more introductions and explanations, we were shown that the nearest city to Albion was Waterville. It acted as a center for a myriad of small towns such as Albion, Benton, Unity, China, Freedom, Thorndike, Vassalboro, Troy, and Liberty. These towns were dotted over farming country that extended eastward to Belfast, on the coast.

"So, if you was to practice in Albion, you'd do well, Doc," said Keay. "Each town's about six hundred people."

"Might do some travelin', but yer'd make out," added Marden.

I was encountering a new dialect, featuring laconic brevity. It sounded as if it had originated in northern England or maybe Devon, but at least it wasn't French.

They offered me inducements: a furnished house with heat for twenty-five dollars a month, a guaranteed minimum income. I'd be allowed to admit patients to the hospital in Waterville. They'd spoken to Dr. Hill, the hospital director, and he'd been for it: "Keen he was, wasn't 'ee?"

It sounded attractive, but I felt forced to explain that I had a commitment to Eagle Lake. I couldn't desert people who had been good to me and had come to rely on my presence.

There was an exchange of looks. Mr. Keay then took it upon himself to break the news. The reason they had driven up was that they'd been told the old Eagle Lake doctor would be back at the end of May. It wasn't their business, but nevertheless it was wise to strike while the kettle was hot—or words to that effect.

There was a longish silence devoted to contemplation of my impending decline and fall. Then someone murmured that perhaps the doc and the missus might like to visit Waterville and its environs.

Nods and murmurs of assent all around.

Meanwhile Mary had gone out and brought back Sara and Ann, and the atmosphere became lighthearted and relaxed. The foursome were family men, and our babes became the center of attention. When Mary suggested coffee, there were friendly cracks.

"Thought you folks only drank tea."

The farmer broke in: "Coffee? Just as long as it isn't made with boiled milk. Spent some time over in your country, and by gorry, that's what they gave you there." Laughter.

"Milk weren't that thick, neither."

After the proposition had been explained to her, I managed to get Mary into the kitchen to have a brief chat.

She was enthusiastic. It meant we had a place to go to where we would be welcomed and wanted. If the old doctor came back to Eagle Lake we wouldn't stand a chance. His photograph and halo were still hovering over the hospital foyer. He'd reclaim his turf. He and Father Blais were allies; we'd be outgunned before a week was out. And although the Eagle Lake folk had treated us well, it would be nice to have some friends to talk to. Albion and Waterville sounded attractive, and the men in the office were understanding and pleasant.

We rejoined them and said we'd like to visit. After looking at our delivery bookings, we fixed a date two weeks ahead.

The visitors left in high spirits.

Next day I told Sister Euloge we were going to take a couple of vacation days. When I told M. Belanger, he didn't seem surprised.

"Albion, is it?" he asked. As I hadn't told him any details, his remark was enough to show that he knew the reason for the trip. The arrival of four strangers in a blue station wagon was big news in this town, and inevitably a cause for speculation.

Within the day all of Eagle Lake knew my plans, and no one voiced dismay. Sister Euloge asked whether the news was true and said she'd be sorry to see us go. Mother Superior, who was under the impression we were departing there and then, gave Mary a pincushion as a memento.

And indeed it did seem as though the die was already cast. So, round two of the battle had been won by Father Blais by default. There would be no more debates in the Cadillac about the treatment of spontaneous miscarriages, no more secular dilemmas for the anxious nuns. No more tussles of allegiance for Sister Euloge.

On a bright day two weeks later, we left Eagle Lake full of excitement at the prospect of a potential new practice. We were armed against any sea of troubles. In the vaults at Fort Kent First Something-or-Other Bank lay our savings of six thousand dollars. We had no obligations except the monthly pound of flesh to General Motors for the Pontiac.

Once more I was impressed with the size of Maine, as we drove toward Albion. The snow and ice, the myriad of trees that I had met on the trek to Eagle Lake before Christmas, had blurred my sense of distance. But now, as I retraced its length, the state seemed vast.

After three hours we saw the dense walls of forest beside the road gradually thin out to reveal broad expanses of farmland. Fresh grass covered gently contoured hills. Red or white farmhouses and silver silos dotted the landscape. The sky was brilliant blue and the air like champagne. It was our first taste of spring in New England.

But I was not completely mesmerized by the vista. The condition of the road kept jogging me back to reality. The Turnpike and Interstate 95, the northernmost stretch of Eisenhower's highway dream, might be a gleam in the President's eye, but for now Route 2 had us in thrall.

Wounded and gashed from winter's onslaught, it stretched out like an endless Coney Island switchback. About every half mile there would be a sign saying "bump ahead." Half the time I missed it, and the car would rise and fall like a belly-flopping dolphin. Sara loved it, laughing and giggling as we sailed aloft and thumped down. Potholes were everywhere. Before long I began to pine for the smooth, icy surface of Route 11.

From the road we saw a few houses, and most were in a sorry state of repair. Some had barns leaning and crumpled as though a giant had tried to push them over. Remnants of cars—missing wheels, hoods, or doors—invariably littered the drives and front yards. While the pristine farmland looked rich and promising, the roadside inhabitants seemed poor.

We chugged by a hamlet that had adopted the noble title of Troy. Visions of ancient Greece, of Homer, Achilles, and Helen rose and then faded at the sight of five shacks and a rundown variety store. Grimly we noted from our map that it represented the northern limit of our proposed medical practice.

A few miles later we reached Unity, a town of about seven hundred which boasted a railway depot, a drugstore, a hotel, and a lake. A neat row of houses extended down its only side street, and in the town center stood a brick mansion with a walled garden. Opposite stood a gleaming white church, its steeple rising to a golden point.

Mary was all for stopping at the drugstore. We had never been in one before, and she wanted to see whether there was a soda fountain and all the trimmings, like the one in the Andy Hardy movies.

We parked in the dirt yard and got out to stretch our legs. Then we pushed open the drugstore door. A bell tinkled above our heads as we paused to appreciate the scene.

To us the drugstore was the epitome of America. It conjured up images of teenagers at the soda fountain, first dates, bobby-soxers, Norman Rockwell.

We were not disappointed. Hollywood had got it right. There stood the magazine racks and newspaper displays, cartons of Camels, Lucky Strikes, and Chesterfields, the red tins of Prince Albert and chewing tobacco, cardboard displays of corncob pipes, rows of lighters, stands of postcards, candies and chocolate bars, and jars of multicolored hard candies and licorice. Behind a counter were shelves crowded with patent medicines in boxes and bottles. And to one side were three bar stools and a soda counter with steel handles and curved spouts and jars of syrup.

"We only need Mickey Rooney and Judy Garland," murmured Mary.

Instead, we were treated to a vision of Lionel Barrymore, when a man in his sixties dressed in a brown smock emerged through a curtain. He was obviously aware of our presence, but he wasn't going to acknowledge it until he was good and ready. And this was not until he had established himself behind the soda fountain. From there he regarded us over his rimless glasses and scratched his grizzled hair. He sucked a candy, and his next move was to produce another one and offer it to Sara, who was viewing him in near terror, as if he were the Wizard of Oz.

Mary hoisted herself and baby Ann onto a stool.

"Ice creams all round, I should think," I said.

"Not too big for the children," cautioned Mary.

The old man eyed her with skepticism.

"Do you have strawberry?" Mary asked.

"Ayuh." He shuffled toward a freezer.

I felt a tug at my coat and heard an urgent appeal from Sara.

"Any mint chip?" I called.

He paused and turned his head. "Can't rightly say." He surveyed the ice cream bins with a wheeze. "How about vanilla, young lady?" Sara beat a retreat behind me. The old fellow grinned, and I nodded.

While he was scooping up the ice cream, which, judging by his breathing, was like hewing coal, I asked him the distance to Albion. He passed me the first completed cone and started on the next. It wasn't until he had delivered the last that he adjusted his spectacles and answered.

"You the new doc plans to settle in Albion?" he wheezed.

"That's me—Dr. Betts."

He looked me up and down. "Unity folks wanted you to settle

here. People were some fussed up. But Albion folk always been independent. Said we had Hanscome, the osteopath, why'd we need an M.D.?" He adjusted his glasses. "Not that I care. I'm just the pharmacist. But as long as I've been here, and that's near on fifty years, Albion's always had a doctor."

He came from behind the counter, drying his hands.

"The name's Reed. Won't shake yer hand with all this stuff on it, but if you take the job, we could be seeing each other." He smiled at Mary. "Reckon that little one's a mite small for a candy ball."

"She's Ann."

"Nice name."

We went outside and stood in the sunshine licking our ice cream cones. I had met a new character. He was no more like a native of Eagle Lake or New Jersey than a Zulu would have been.

And seeing the neat houses and the white New England church, the old elm trees casting shadows on the lawns, I felt that this was a different Maine from the one I had known.

I was about to meet a new variant of the American: not the fast-moving New Yorker, the Italian-tinged Trentonite, nor the French compulsive of Eagle Lake. I had entered the province of the "downeaster."

If I'd had an inkling, I would have revised my attitude. At that moment it was about as suitable for dealing with the farmers of Maine as my umbrella and topcoat had been for the snowbound inhabitants of Eagle Lake.

We rolled down the last eight miles toward Albion and the reception committee.

PART

3

LBION

THE EIGHT-MILE STRETCH from Unity to Albion revealed a much more prosperous landscape. The farmland looked rich; tractors were turning over dark brown soil; cattle were grazing; and huge barns were in the throes of construction in the fields on both sides of the road. All the houses were big and brightly painted in red, white, or yellow. The land undulated gently, and just before we entered Albion, the road curved gracefully over a brook where sparkling water rushed between rocks and stones.

Albion had found its place in history as the birthplace of Elijah Parish Lovejoy, born in 1802. He went to Waterville (later Colby) College and eventually became a newspaperman who wrote editorials in favor of the abolition of slavery. He was killed in Illinois in 1837 while defending his newspaper from an angry mob. The news of his death produced widespread support for his principles throughout the North.

Otherwise Albion had made little impression on the world at large or the encyclopedia. As the center of a dairy farming community it boasted three variety stores, a post office, a church, a Grange, and a three-man sawmill. If you drove at a moderate speed you were through the town in under fifty-five seconds.

This we did, and it took another four miles to reach the outskirts of China, the next village (population approximately 450), before we found room to turn around without the risk of being stuck in the mud.

Finally we arrived back at our rendezvous in Albion: the gas pumps at Keay's store, opposite the little white wooden church.

Mr. Keay was there to welcome us, nozzle in hand. His thickset build, wide jaw, and penetrating blue eyes projected a sense of stability and assurance. He was an Albion native who exuded common sense, thinking before he spoke, even when you had simply asked him the time.

After the initial greetings and before shepherding us into his store, he indicated a two-story clapboard house on the opposite side of the road. This, he told us, would be where we'd be having our office and home.

"Plenty of parking space in front of the church for all your patients." Oh yes, we'd be busy!

We went inside the store and met his plump, shy, and beaming wife standing behind the counter. And while Mr. Keay telephoned to inform the rest of the search committee of our arrival, Sara was given a candy bar and Mary and I were taken on a tour of the store.

Wheelbarrows, spades, hoes, watering cans to the right. Hammers, saws, electric drills, nails, screws, center aisle. Cornflakes, pancake mixes, bread, English muffins to the left. A freezer furnished with the precision of a Smithsonian exhibit. To the back, clothes for young men, old men, children, and women. Intimate apparel for the elderly was in a corner in the basement. Everything was laid out with an eye to space and all as clean as an operating room. I couldn't help comparing it with the Belanger setup, including the fact that English was the accepted language here.

While I was admiring an electric lawnmower I sensed that Mary was anxious to cross the road and look at what might be her new home. But Mrs. Keay, perhaps less sensitive to these unspoken signals, said we were expected as guests of Mr. and Mrs. Champlin. We trooped back to our car and followed Mr. Keay's sky blue Cadillac down the main street to the Champlin residence. For a second I had a fleeting sense of déjà vu, recalling my introductory tour of Eagle Lake in Mr. Martin's black hearse. But Mr. Keay's car was a brighter job, which was perhaps a good omen.

I noticed that we passed a red-brick school, the post office, and Robinson's Variety store. The elm leaves were turning green and gardens had early flowers in bloom. Then the road plunged downhill, and in seconds we were in the depths of the countryside. In the distance there was a glimpse of Lovejoy Pond sparkling in the sunshine.

We soon turned into the driveway of a remodeled farmhouse. As we crunched to a halt on the circular drive, five children tumbled out of the front door, followed at a gracious pace by an attractive woman in a gathered floral skirt and Tyrolean blouse. An assortment of dogs bounded about her legs, yapping and protesting, while a couple of miffed cats stalked around the periphery.

As soon as we were out of the car, the children swarmed around our babes and Mary was inundated with questions. At the same time I was the focus of four dogs and our hostess, Flora Champlin. She spoke quietly and with perfect clarity, and there was a restful beauty about her features. I was not surprised to learn later that she had been a New York actress before taking the rural veil.

Mary was rescued from the Champlin children and we proceeded indoors. Although the house retained the form of a farmhouse, it had been transformed into a modern home. It seemed to be taken for granted that we were to be the guests of the Champlins. Mr. Keay entered bearing two cases from our car, and after the eldest Champlin girl had been appointed baby sitter, Mary and I were shown to our room.

It was charmingly furnished, feminine and chintzy, with a flowered wallpaper, light floral drapes, two beds, and two small armchairs. The window offered a view of the lake and the distant hills. Immediately below, the brilliant sunshine cast dappled patterns over the lawn and drive. We were enchanted and couldn't help comparing this reception to our icy initiation into Eagle Lake. Of course we were now on the threshold of summer, with every tree in new leaf and the land bursting with fresh life. Perhaps it wasn't fair to contrast this with our January arrival in the frozen north, when the snowbanks rose to the top of the telephone poles and icicles fringed every porch.

But I was also excited by everyone's kindness, by the instant feeling that we were welcome and expected to stay. And as we crouched at the window, arms around each other, for the ceiling was as low as an English thatched cottage, we smiled and glowed, feeling we had found our place.

Much to Sara's relief we came downstairs again, and were just in time to see a blue Buick station wagon swing into the drive. In seconds, as if choreographed, the owner—a giant figure as big as a football pro—stopped the engine, threw open the door and bounded into the house. With a wide grin he thrust his hand toward me and boomed:

"Dr. Betts, Mrs. Betts—we meet again. Very glad to see you. Welcome to Albion!"

This tour de force was more than enough to explain how Warren Champlin had repeatedly won the golden goblet as one of central Maine's most successful insurance salesmen.

We migrated out to the lawn and took our places in a ring of chairs. Soon the talk was loud, jovial, and full of laughter. Flora Champlin appeared with a tray bearing delicate china cups, a teapot, and a plate of sandwiches. She gave a smile.

"I was warned I would be entertaining an English family. So I have brought both milk and lemon for your tea."

"And lump sugar," observed Mary. "Where did you find that?"

"Courtesy of Mr. Keay," said Flora. Harold Keay gave a nod of appreciation.

After all the variants of pouring, she consulted with Mary over the technicalities of bottles for Ann and food for Sara.

Meanwhile Mr. Champlin and Mr. Keay were outlining their program for me. The other two members of the search committee were due in a few minutes. We would then go over our designated house to see if it had everything for our needs. Again, no question that we were staying. After that there would be a lobster dinner at Champlin's house, followed by a reception in the Grange. People from the surrounding towns were eager to meet the new doctor.

It was overwhelming. As yet there had been no discussion about the business of the practice, indeed whether I would even settle in Albion. It had simply been assumed. And for my part, it was as if I were being swept along by a current. I felt as if I was the subject of a fait accompli—signed, sealed, and delivered.

I was still ignorant of any other practice opportunities around Maine, still suffering from being brainwashed by the prevailing conditions in England. What was happening to me now in Albion could never have occurred in the Old Country. There the class stature of the general practitioner had fallen in the eyes of the British public and was about on a par with the mailman. Under the National Health Service the family doctor was now at the beck and call of anyone at any time, and liable to a reprimand and penalty if he did not respond. The lawyer, the bank manager, the real estate broker, any businessman—all received greater respect.

During my final weeks in practice in England, I was making more than twenty house calls a day, mostly for trivia, and seeing up to a hundred patients in the office, and yet there were sixty or seventy candidates anxious to take my place the instant I vacated it. In the National Health Service, finding an opening in family practice was as difficult as auditioning for a lead on Broadway.

So it wasn't surprising that I was bowled over by the enthusiastic reception in Albion. I never realized that in the cities of Maine, in the hospitals, in other practices, there were excellent opportunities.

Following tea, with the usual references to the Revolution and Boston's method of dealing with the superfluous leaf, we went to look at our future house. As we parked beside the church, two pickup trucks joined us, and we met the remaining members of the search committee.

We trooped into the house. It had been repainted both inside and out by the people of Albion and neighboring towns. As part of the project to get a doctor, they had furnished it from their own belongings, supplied curtains, carpets, and put up fresh wallpaper. Mickey

Marden had personally supervised the furnace, while the appliances (washer, dryer, and kitchen range) had received a thorough inspection by a local salesman, Reg Clowater, who lived down the road. He gave me his card.

The kitchen was spacious and, to my eyes, fully equipped. In one direction it led onto a porch and in the other to a breakfast nook and then to the front dining room. Here volunteers had deposited an assortment of upright chairs of varying vintage together with a mahogany table and sideboard.

From the dining room we exited to a narrow hall which received a steep flight of stairs leading to three bedrooms. Mary was disturbed that there was no gate at the top of the stairway.

"The children could break their necks," she said to Mickey Marden. "And so could I."

The front bedroom was equipped with a large brass bedstead, a simple chest of drawers, and two wooden rocking chairs. Another bedroom had a single bed and mattress, while the third had a crib that by now would be a collector's item. I told Marden that I hoped the furnace in the cellar, after it had blown hot air into the first-floor rooms, had enough puff left over to warm this lot. He said I could bet on it.

Gingerly we made our way down the stairs and journeyed through the kitchen to find ourselves on the back porch. The only furniture here was a decrepit couch sagging at one end from the loss of springs, and I wondered if it had been donated or was left over from the Civil War. From the porch, through drooping rusty screens there was a view of exuberant elephant grass.

"Can you imagine the old family sitting out here on their rockers in the evening gazing at the field?" I asked Mary.

"Grandpa smoking his corncob pipe."

"Dad mending the springs and waiting for news of Bull Run, or listening to a Fireside Chat?"

"Oh, sure. Perhaps the grass was a little shorter then."

Marden found us again, and we were conducted into the massive barn alongside the kitchen. Rusted farm implements—huge scythes, rakes, bits of fence, hand plows, snowshoes, wooden skis, pitchforks, and bits of harness hung on the walls and filled the floor. In the dim light I could see at the back some broken steps leading to a loft.

"I'm not going up there. Probably chock-full of bats and more junk," declared Mary.

"Remember that little room with a view for two in Bloomsbury?" I murmured in her ear.

"Notable for the absence of bats, as I recall."

"But it had me, your very own bloodsucker."

She laughed and gave my hand a squeeze, ruefully recalling the memories of our first days together in London.

We returned to the house. In one front room, there was a door giving onto the hall and another at the rear to an annex and then the porch. I walked through and found I could make a trip from the front room to the kitchen and back again. It would be a useful line of communication in a practice.

Also, the front room had been furnished with a roll-top desk and a swivel chair with three legs on wheels. There was a gray carpet, which had either retained its color or assumed it.

"Thought this might be the office," said Mickey Marden, joining us again.

"Looks great," I said. "Needs a bit more furniture, but I expect that could be fixed."

"And you could put your medicines and tests out here," he continued, moving into the annex. I went over, and he showed me two built-in cupboards and a trestle table.

"And then 'cross here'd be the waiting room." He led us to the other front room. He was a born planner. I followed him, although we had seen it already, but now I noticed some faded magazines and an empty vase on the table. A sepia print of Colby (or Waterville) College hung on one wall and a landscape of extraordinary gloom on another.

Finally he took us into the kitchen to elaborate on the equipment—the electric stove, the supply of pots, pans, knives, forks, and culinary tools—all sufficient in quantity, variety, and age to excite a flea market buff.

Once through the house, we were given a tour of the neighborhood and a brief look at Waterville, a thriving city on the Kennebec River. On one side of the river lay Winslow, with its huge paper mill, and on the other Waterville. It was a prosperous mill town and at that time home of the Hathaway Shirt factory, Keyes Fiber, Diamond Match Company, Lockwood Mills, and other industries. Its main street was packed with fashionable stores such as Stern's, Day's, and Levine's, three movie houses (including the old opera house), and two or three good restaurants and hotels.

As a climax of the tour, we were shown Thayer Hospital. To us it resembled what we used to call a medium-sized cottage hospital in England. But we refrained from any such comment when we heard our host speaking of it in glowing terms fit for the Mayo Clinic.

And then, against the setting sun, we viewed Colby College up on Mayflower Hill, its exquisite new campus looking like a manicured and miniature Harvard.

We had been shown a typical small New England mill town, but we didn't know it. We had come from Eagle Lake, and even a medium-sized village would have impressed us. So what more could anyone want? A country practice, a welcome mat, an adjacent college and pleasant small city.

As we made our way back to the Champlins' house I asked Mary how she felt about it. She thought for a moment, certainly longer than when I asked her whether we ought to emigrate from England. Then she said it was up to me. She'd go along with whatever I decided.

CHAPTER

18

THE NEGOTIATIONS WERE BRIEF. I told the committee that we would like to accept the offer but it was vital for our peace of mind that we had a guaranteed income. There were anxious expressions all around.

"What were you thinking, Doc?" Keay asked cautiously.

My aversion to haggling tried to get the better of me, but I had to stick to my needs.

"You see, it's not as if we had any family over here to run to," I said.

"Oh, sure, Doc, we understand. What were you thinking?"

"If I were by myself, it would be a different matter."

"Of course, Doc. You just say."

"I hate to put you on the spot."

"That's what we're here for."

I took a deep breath. "I'm afraid I'll have to insist on five thousand dollars."

Silence. They all looked grave. Champlin muttered something to Marden. Keay whispered to Turner.

"Doc, my brother's an internist in Boston," said Champlin. "I don't believe he makes sixty grand *a year*. If he does, he's mighty quiet about it. It's a bit high."

"Sixty thousand a year? High? I should think it is!" I said.

"That's what I told him."

"I'm asking for $5,000 a year—about four hundred and fifty a month."

More silence, but of a different kind, with general relief and smiles. Marden slapped his knee. "Gee, Doc, you'll make more than that in the first quarter."

I was still concerned. I'd need something in writing. At this Keay took the reins and said they'd drawn up an agreement about the house rent, and the committee would be willing to add a paragraph about a guaranteed income, although he was certain I'd do far better than five thousand a year. The rent for the house would be twenty-five dollars, and it would include heat and maintenance. I would have to pay the utilities.

The atmosphere was now relaxed. There was some spirited speculation about what one could do with sixty thousand dollars in Albion, and it seemed that money was not the limiting factor. Joining in the fun, I asked whether I had to use Keay's store for groceries and Mickey Marden quickly threw in that I'd better not if I wanted a good steak.

"Send your missus to *me*," he said.

"Don't you believe him!" shot back Keay. "Tough as a boot."

Everyone laughed and stood up. Keay told me he'd bring the amended contract over to Champlin's lobster party, which would give me time to talk matters over with my wife.

The meeting broke up, and we made our way back to the Champlin house. Mary and I wandered across the lawn and again talked things over. As far as I could see the offer was ideal. We'd be secure financially. I'd be serving a community with all the traditional responsibilities of a family doctor. Thayer Hospital was about ten miles away in Waterville. I had already spoken to Champlin, who said I would be allowed to admit my patients there. His brother had looked after Albion for a few months and had been made welcome by the hospital staff. He added that two doctors from Thayer Hospital were coming to the Grange meeting after dinner.

After a couple of turns around the garden, Mary went back into the house to check the children and I wandered over to a smoldering bonfire at the edge of the lawn. Champlin was eyeing it with a satisfied air, but I thought for him to expect flames from a mass of damp seaweed was very optimistic. My own experience in bonfires had been confined to Guy Fawkes Night in England, where by tradition since

1605 we had fireworks, a bonfire, and an effigy to celebrate the failure of a bunch of minor terrorists to blow up the Houses of Parliament. I mentioned this gem of history as I stood beside Champlin. He explained to me that there was a difference between burning a traitor at the stake and cooking a bunch of lobsters. And at that point he nudged over a couple of scarlet two-pounders and rearranged a few eggs.

I felt Champlin had won that round, and I retreated to the house. Mary was feeding Ann, and Flora Champlin had Sara giggling over a game with a doll. I stood watching until Mary got the vibes that a consultation was required.

She excused herself from the company and we went up to our bedroom. Our discussion was brief. We would accept the offer; this was the place for us. Years later Mary told me that the thought of spending the rest of her life in Albion was not her American Dream, but it was better than Eagle Lake. Also, knowing my nomadic pattern, she realized that Albion might not be our final home.

So all we had to do was fix the logistics. There were a few belongings, including our new tires, left in Eagle Lake. And there was the problem of furnishing the office with medical gear—instruments, trays, basins, an examining table and lights. One source for this material was at hand, if one regarded New Jersey as being so, because before we went to Eagle Lake, Jack Sharp had offered to lend me some of his late father's equipment. (He had been a general practitioner in Camden, New Jersey.) Perhaps it would still be available. But it seemed we would need at least a couple of weeks to be ready.

By now, a small crowd had gathered on the Champlin lawn and a line had formed at the smoldering heap. Everyone had plates ready to receive the classic Maine lobster feed. I saw Mr. Keay chatting with Marden beside a flower bed and went to tell him of our decision.

We shook hands solemnly, and Keay said he'd have a simple contract drawn up. When I spoke about having to leave to clear up in

Eagle Lake and then go down to New Jersey, he told me that any one of the families would be glad to look after Mary and the children. Word of our decision spread rapidly. As we joined the food line, people came up to say how pleased they were to learn that I was to be their doctor. It did cross my mind to wonder whether they had any idea of my capabilities, but I supposed the search committee had done some homework. I couldn't imagine Father Blais endorsing me, but there had been a few successful breaks in Eagle Lake and someone might have put in a good word.

While I was mulling over these thoughts, Champlin deposited two lobsters, three eggs, and two ears of corn on my plate with the proviso that there was always more if I needed it. I moved on to receive a vat of melted butter. Mary had already been served and was seated at a table in the shade. The Champlin children had been instructed to entertain Sara, who had never had such universal attention before and was basking in it. Ann slept in a carry cot under a tree and provided food for thought for the Champlin cats, who had to be shooed away.

Two lobsters was no small meal, with each piece dipped in butter. Just one egg and an ear of corn would have filled me. Halfway through I felt I was bursting at the seams. Champlin joined me as I was fighting a fourth claw. Four bright red lobsters awaited him on his plate while he made an hors d'oeuvre of three ears of corn and a puddle of butter. Before tackling his scarlet quartet, he demonstrated his own dissecting technique. It was masterly, only requiring muscular thumbs, an exact knowledge of lobster pressure points, a head-to-toe apron, and a garbage pail within hurling distance. I watched him dismantle his four with finesse.

As I sat in the sunshine, more than replete, I reminded Mary of the day when I managed at last to land a job as an assistant to a general practitioner in England. I'd had two unsuccessful interviews beforehand. When we left the doctor's house engaged to serve him, we celebrated by getting fish and chips and some cider at the local pub.

No one knew we were coming to town, and if anyone had I doubt he or she would have cared. There were fifty more where we had come from.

Here in Albion, to our minds, our reception made the relief of Mafeking or Lindbergh's arrival in Paris mere peanuts.

CHAPTER

A NEW ENGLAND GRANGE HALL is an institution unique to these parts of America. Certainly there isn't anything like it in Olde England or Olde France. If there were, Thomas Hardy would have described one in *Tess of the d'Urbervilles* or *Far from the Madding Crowd*. The assembly rooms of Jane Austen are too foppish; Flaubert's settings for Madame Bovary too bourgeois, and Dickens's inns too roguish.

Anyway, I had no idea what to expect as I followed the lobster-laden mob up the stairs of the gloomy hall to the room above. Once inside, I saw it was part of a giant barn with a cathedral ceiling. The dark, varnished beams and rough-planked walls gave the impression of a place where one might have a band practice, rehearse a play, or store small arms.

Now the periphery was lined with chairs, and nearly all were occupied. In front of and behind seated ladies were clusters of men deep in conversation. Dress varied. Some were formal, the ladies in print dresses or skirts and blouses, and the men in light suits. But others were less prim, and scattered at intervals were men in heavy farmer's clothing: overalls and peaked caps with advertisements for seeds.

A row of chairs and a table had been arranged as a speaker's platform at one end of the hall, together with a microphone. Mary and I were led in this direction and introduced to two men who were waiting for us.

One, Dr. Frederick Hill, was a lean, angular figure in his sixties. He wore rimless glasses and his gray hair was sparse. He exuded an air of authority even in repose, but had reinforced his position by wearing a white hospital coat. The other official, Dr. Goodof, was in more relaxed dress, being attired in slacks and a tailored open-neck shirt. He was younger, and his dome-shaped head and black horn-rimmed glasses suggested energy and intelligence. I noticed, when he moved to assist a lady with a chair, that he was swift and had a gait with slightly bent knees, like Groucho Marx. Any other resemblance ended there.

During the introductions, Mr. Champlin mentioned that Dr. Hill was the director of the Thayer Hospital, and suggested that he and the hospital were the equal of Massachusetts General, Johns Hopkins, and the Mayo Clinic rolled into one. Dr. Goodof was the Thayer pathologist, but he also supervised numerous laboratories in the state.

Once more I was mentally bowled over. I tried to picture the Anglo equivalent situation, where Lord Evans, physician to the Queen, and Sir Francis Camps, pathologist to Scotland Yard, turned out to launch my general practice debut in South Swindon, U.K. Just to get near Lord Evans required about three weeks' advance warning, and Sir Francis was always too busy giving evidence in some criminal case in the Old Bailey to introduce a new family doctor in the remote countryside.

Yet Dr. Frederick Hill, who was well known in Washington and on the board of the Hillburton Committee (a body with power to dispense federal funds in large amounts for hospitals), was here to speak on my behalf.

I shook hands, and we all sat down at the table. Champlin kicked off by announcing my decision to become the local doctor. Mary and I stood up to universal applause. There followed an effusive oration with a lot of references to "these wonderful, attractive people," etc. Then the floor was turned over to Dr. Hill, who really had the touch. He talked of rural medicine, of lines of communication to the central command at Thayer Hospital. Albion's initiative today was a model for other peripheral hamlets. And everyone please note that Dr. Betts would receive the maximum backup from every source, not the least of which was provided by his colleague Dr. Goodof.

Dr. Goodof stood and in a relaxed manner said that his laboratory service was at the ready day and night to serve the people in the towns surrounding Albion that Dr. Betts was taking under his wing. They had to be thankful that the doctors' state organization, the Maine Medical Association, had responded so admirably and in such a timely fashion to local need.

It was my turn. I was unprepared and rather flustered. I had not yet absorbed the American style of overstatement and love of a wingding—as exemplified by New Year's Eve at the Waldorf, or the return of MacArthur to West Point. My background was one of understatement, never understood by Americans. I thought I might get a laugh with a reference to "perfidious Albion," a term used by the Dauphin (circa 1143) when referring to the England of King Henry the Second; but I realized it was a bit farfetched and possibly incomprehensible to the average Maine farmer. I only mention it here to show the desperate state of my mind. I think I said we were glad to be there, or something equally original, and thanked everyone in sight for being so kind. I tried to coax Mary to the microphone, but she remained glued to her chair. As I sat down there was applause, some warm laughter, and a buzz of conversation.

A reception line then formed. Dr. Hill and Dr. Goodof gracefully made an exit, and Mary and I began to shake the hands of everyone in the room. It went on for over an hour.

Mr. and Mrs. Someone smiled broadly and asked how we liked the front room wallpaper. They'd put it up. Another couple hoped the drawers of the kitchen sideboard didn't stick. It had been in their family before Mother died. A farmer from Freedom said he'd be in the office "soon as you open—my knee's something awful." They came from everywhere—Thorndike, China, Vassalboro, Unity, Benton—and everyone had a kind word. One or two asked if I came from London, and if so, had I met their cousin, brother-in-law, or adopted daughter who lived there. Several said they loved my accent, a comment I had never received in England.

Finally the line came to an end. We had met nearly everyone who had papered or painted the house or put furniture in it. And we had come to realize that we were going to be medically responsible for a vast area.

We went back to the Champlins' house and picked up the children. Once more we thanked the committee for all their help and kindness, and then we headed back to our prospective home for one more look. It was a short trip, and we were both silent. We had never dreamed of anything like the day we had just experienced.

We entered the house and turned on all the lights. We were not yet familiar with the layout. I went into my new office. It looked just right for a country doctor, and I sat down in my swivel chair and swung to and fro.

I heard a call from Mary and went out into the hall. She was at the top of the stairs on the landing.

"Look!" she laughed, pointing to a brand-new gate blocking the head of the stairs. There was a note: "Hope this is what you wanted. Don't forget to try our steak. —Mickey Marden."

I shook my head. "These people are fantastic."

"Yes. But you know what it means, don't you?"

I looked at her, puzzled.

"We'll never be able to leave."

We turned out the lights and went back to sleep at the Champlins' residence.

CHAPTER

20

URING THE NEXT TWO WEEKS we seemed to spend much of our time on the roads and our money on gas, then at twenty-one cents a gallon.

Our first trip was a return to Eagle Lake. There we learned that the old doctor had not yet arrived, so while Mary started to pack up our belongings, I continued to see patients and make a few house calls.

I was flattered that two women who had seen me for their antenatal care were upset that I was departing. One even suggested that she would be happier if she were not pregnant, but that was as far as the discussion went.

My real regret was leaving Sister Euloge-Marie. At the hospital, when asking if I might write her, I learned her full name at last. During the next two days I went through one final delivery in the hospital and managed to discharge a few chronic patients from the wards. However, still occupying a bed was a young woman with severe diabetes. She was already showing signs of kidney failure and had been in and out of coma during the last three months.

I suggested that she be transferred to Fort Kent Hospital, but the patient wouldn't hear of it. So Sister and I went over the management of her insulin dosage and the level of urine sugar. Blood sampling was not possible in the Eagle Lake laboratory, so that checking how acid her blood became and where her blood sodium stood were out of the question. It was an awesome responsibility to leave with Sister, but she accepted it with a mixture of fatalism and faith. And she said she would say a prayer for me.

"You think it might do me some good?"

"It's never too late, Doctor," she answered with a flash of a smile. And that was the last I saw of her.

I called a Fort Kent internist and Dr. King to alert them to the state of the remaining patients, and they said they would encourage Sister Euloge to telephone whenever necessary. The road to Eagle Lake was now always open and they would come if needed.

So, with some regret, modified with excitement for our new practice, we took our leave.

Hours later we turned into our drive in Albion and entered our new house. Everything was clean as could be, and when Mary opened the kitchen cupboards she found the shelves filled with staples—flour, sugar, salt, even a loaf of bread. It was difficult to know which store had made these gifts, so we went to both Keay's and Marden's to render thanks and buy a little more.

But we still had to travel to New Jersey and borrow some equipment for the practice. I had called Dr. Jack Sharp, and he had invited us to stay in Trenton. He said that Mary could get in some shopping with his wife, Martha, while we went to hire a U-Haul trailer and load his father's old office accoutrements.

Dr. Sharp had proudly insisted that I take his father's examining table. It was a solid affair that suggested it was probably built at the same time as the Brooklyn Bridge, and with the same caliber of steel. Even though its structure was covered with black leather and looked comfortable enough, we found later that some patients said they would prefer to lie on a bed of nails.

It seemed to weigh a ton as we pushed it into the trailer, which immediately tilted head-down. We attached the Pontiac with difficulty and then added boxes of medical tools and implements. Two or three pairs of obstetric forceps, long steel probes, cast cutters, scissors of all sizes, needles, ampoules of catgut and silk, dishes of steel and enamel, and even a mortar and pestle. A casual observer might have thought we were refurbishing the Inquisition. And even though I said that there were some procedures that were no longer current even in darkest Maine, Jack said I never knew when I might need something, and then I'd be sorry.

The trailer was not filled to capacity, and on a trial lap around the grounds there was a steady jingle of steel against steel.

Later we spent a pleasant evening catching up on the mental asylum gossip. The superintendent had housed the German and Austrian resident doctors in the same quarters, thinking in error that as they spoke the same language they'd be bosom friends. The extraordinarily handsome American resident with the new Lincoln, who had every student nurse panting, had turned out to be gay. And so on.

Our wives discussed their successful siege of Wanamaker's in Philadelphia. Mary had come back with a "fabulous" dress and a two-piece outfit that Martha said would have Albion on its ear. And so inexpensive!

We left the next day. Jack and I had studied the map like Lewis and Clark, and had plotted a course that skirted the Merritt Parkway (which did not allow trailers). The approach into Connecticut might be tricky.

Time has mercifully dimmed the details of the ensuing journey. We left the New Jersey Turnpike in the vicinity of Elizabeth. This turned out to be not the wisest move. Somehow we saw a lot of Newark, where all traffic lights have an affinity for red when a U-Haul comes into range. We managed to get ourselves onto the George Washington Bridge, and after paying a toll that would have ransomed Richard the Lion-Hearted, ended up being pressured by Yellow and Checker cabs into a lane that deposited us in upper Manhattan.

Fortunately there was a sign indicating an entry back onto the bridge. We found ourselves heading toward the New Jersey Turnpike with the inevitability of a barrel going over Niagara Falls. We paid another outrageous toll, took an exit, and returned to the bridge. Our second attempt was a precise repeat of the first. Only by grimly getting into a lane that said "Albany only" were we able to see the last of the Hudson.

After ten miles in a straight line for Albany, we exited into some nondescript town and recharted our course for Maine in a convenient churchyard.

We pitched up in Albion in the early hours, left everything in the car and trailer, and fell into bed. Two days later I opened my practice.

My first house call in Albion was a disturbing one, and I was unprepared for it. The Albion telephone operator had a message: would I go as soon as possible to the house five doors down the road to see Dr. Ross, the old Albion doctor. He had been ill for several weeks.

The old Albion doctor? What did she mean? Albion didn't have a doctor—at least not until yesterday.

I wanted to ask more, but I couldn't cross-examine the telephone operator, especially since I had just discovered that I'd been hooked up to a party line.

Worried and perplexed, I checked my medical bag and tried to think why no one had mentioned the fact before. Surely the search committee would have told me that I was a replacement. Instead, everyone had behaved as if no medical help at all existed in the town. I felt almost compelled to walk across the road and ask Mr. Keay what the story was. Why had I not been told?

Then I thought, could he be another sort of doctor? In any unpredictable crisis or embarrassment I was always subject to flights of fancy. Was he a doctor of divinity, a retired college professor, a bogus evangelist? It was unlikely. Absurd. No one would refer to anyone in those categories as "the old Albion doctor." Perhaps he was some local eccentric.

It was a warm June morning, but I dressed in a suit, white shirt, and tie. Calmer but still alarmed, I went into the kitchen to let Mary know where I would be.

"Just going to visit the old Albion doctor," I said casually.

"Who?"

"Tell you later."

My concern and near-panic may appear excessive. Therefore I should explain that it had been drummed into me as a student that in the medical profession it is unethical and discourteous to set up practice on a fellow doctor's turf without first communicating with him. If Dr. Ross was a medical man, I had been guilty unwittingly. In England he would have the right to report me to the licensing board, and in Maine there was probably something equally harsh. I feared for my license, my lifeline.

As I went to the car, I decided I would immediately apologize and give the doctor an explanation of my behavior, tell him how I had been led by the nose. It would be painful, but I would also have to tell him that I was committed to staying. I had signed a contract. Of course this would imply that the town had acted against him behind his back. In his place I would be furious and resentful. The least I could do, if he would forgive me and overlook my blunder, would be to ask him if I might work with him when he recovered from his illness.

I drove up the street and found the fifth house. It was a large rambling place with an unruly garden, with traces suggesting that some time ago it must have boasted neat flower beds and trim lawns. Now it proclaimed neglect. Peeling paint and a vine-tangled trellis met my gaze as I stepped onto the front porch. There was no shingle or brass plate proclaiming "Dr. Ross."

I rang the bell and waited uneasily. After two further rings I knocked briskly on the door. I was just about to walk around to the back of the house when the door was opened a fraction. A woman of middle years attired in an all-enveloping dark dress peered at me.

I said, "Dr. Betts. You sent for me, I believe."

She looked at me suspiciously, like the housekeeper in a gothic novel, then muttered "Just a minute" and pushed the door back, leaving only a crack. More than a minute passed before a man appeared. He was in his late thirties, with a prominent forehead and deep-set eyes. He also inspected me before speaking. I had to strain to hear what he had to say.

"You've come to see the doctor? Yes. Please follow me."

He walked silently ahead, and I was taken through a dim hallway and a sitting room shrouded by curtains. From its musty odor I sensed it had not been occupied for a long time.

We next passed onto an enclosed porch, which was furnished with a table, a couch, and a chair. The plank floor was bare and the curtains drawn. On the couch lay the patient, an elderly man. A blanket half covered him, leaving his arms exposed. He stared at the ceiling. As I drew closer I could clearly see he was haggard and wasted. I greeted him gently but drew no response, and I took up his wrist. The arm was quite flaccid, his hand icy cold, yet his pulse was surprisingly steady and strong.

This motion caused him to turn his head, and he tried to focus on me, but his eyes were lifeless and blank. One side of his face was as smooth as a child's and his mouth drooped and dribbled. In slow, clear tones I told him why I was there and asked him if he was in pain. He closed his eyes, dropped his head back, and I let his hand rest at his side.

My escort spoke softly and gave me the facts of the poor doctor's medical story. It was a hesitating tale of what I supposed may have been a diagnosis of cancer, followed by a stroke.

As the man rambled on I once again heard the dean of my medical school: "Remember, gentlemen, most patients come to this hospital to die." But was there a reason to move this poor man? I asked if there were in the house enough people to nurse the ill doctor. The young man nodded and explained that the family wanted to make sure the new doctor knew of this case. I wondered if I could read anything in the way he said "the new doctor"?

I told him I understood the situation and would be available to help in any way I could. Then I briefly examined the patient for any current difficulties: bed sores, distended bladder, and the like. He had been well-nursed.

I stood up and said I would look in again the following day. "Are you a relative?" I asked.

The man nodded but did not elaborate. From his back pocket he took out his wallet. I shook my head emphatically.

"This is the least I can do for a fellow physician," I said. From what he had told me, I knew that the patient was indeed a medical doctor. "I only wish I could talk with him and he to me. You see—"

But I couldn't bring myself to add anything further. Neither the man nor the woman had been present in the reception line at the Grange. Now I sensed they hadn't wanted to be. Both had withheld their names and relationship to the doctor, and I felt it was because they resented me. I was set up for paranoia, but in this instance I was not deluded.

I left the house and sat thinking in the car. Had that first house call in Albion been for myself as much as it had for him? The old Albion doctor was dying and I could do nothing for him. And I was troubled with my own problem—my need to confess, explain, apologize, and be forgiven for invading his territory without a word—and he could do nothing for me.

So we passed the torch.

I returned to the house and Mary gave me a cup of coffee. "First house call," she said gaily. "How did it go? I bet you didn't ask to be paid."

"No," I replied. "I didn't." And I went into my new office and sat in my swivel chair.

CHAPTER

21

DURING THE NEXT WEEK the office work was fairly steady. Many patients arrived on one pretext or another to find out what I was like. The usual request was to have a check-up or a chat about some chronic trouble such as rheumatism or insomnia. In this way they met me and I met the donors of the swivel chair, our double bed, the waiting room table, the picture of Colby College by the railroad tracks, and most of the chairs.

I had managed to establish office hours for afternoons and evenings by putting a placard on the front door. This in itself was productive because the Parke-Davis drug salesman brought it in to me and asked if he might make me something "more professional looking." Woodcarving was his hobby. A couple of weeks later he arrived with an impressive chunk of wood with my name and hours in fluorescent paint.

The remainder of my day was to be devoted to house calls and visits to the hospital as necessary. I also had one or two telephone calls late at night, and I handled these as I had in my other practice experience: unless the problem seemed serious or involved a child, I would ask whether they couldn't call back in the morning. This was readily accepted.

My first experience involving the hospital came when I was called to Thorndike to see Michael, a ten-year-old boy with a pain "in his stomach from eating too much ice cream and candy, Doctor. He's thrown up twice."

After I had examined him I told Michael's mother I thought her son had acute appendicitis and would require surgery.

"Where will you do it, Doctor?" she asked.

It was going to take me a little time to adjust to this blind confidence. But I explained that Michael should see a specialist, a surgeon, to make sure of the diagnosis. If she had no special preference, I would suggest Thayer Hospital in Waterville.

Until then, my only hospital contact had been the welcoming speech at the Grange by Dr. Hill. I hadn't had time to take up his invitation to tour Thayer. However, after that meeting I was confident that I would be allowed to take my patients there. I made a call to the hospital to inquire about an available bed.

It was strange not to have a nun answer my call in murmuring French. Instead I had a snappy but courteous switchboard operator, and I was transferred to the admitting nurse who asked for some information about my patient. So far the procedure was similar to the one I had used for sending patients into the hospital in England.

But then things took a different tack. On hearing my diagnosis, the nurse asked me which surgeon I would like to use. There lay the difference: in England I wasn't asked, I was told.

For a moment I was struck dumb because I didn't know the name of any local surgeon. As Michael's mother was standing expectantly beside me, I didn't want to sound as if I were making a selection from a mail order catalogue by asking "What surgeons have you got?" or "Who would you recommend?"

Then from out of the blue I was inspired to ask the nurse which surgeon was in the hospital right now. I was asked to wait while she looked at the doctors' check-in board.

I smiled confidently. "Just checking," I murmured to Michael's mother. The nurse gave me two names. I asked for the first, a Dr. Saran. Would I care to speak to him? Yes, I would.

Dr. Saran's crisp voice came through. What could he do for me? That, for me, was another first. I gave him details of the boy's illness and my conclusion. He suggested I bring in the patient right away. If I could call him when I arrived, he would meet me in the foyer.

It was about 9.30 A.M. I asked Michael's mother to take her son to the hospital and told her I would meet her there. I made a quick diversion to my home, then set off for Waterville.

There were three roads from Albion to Waterville. (There still are, but they're not the same.) At that time each route was equally long and equally perilous, with potholes, vicious bumps, and right-angled bends. All required negotiating slithery-surfaced, narrow bridges over the estuaries of the Kennebec River. But it was summer, and I would learn these snags before the snow and ice returned.

By this time I had also absorbed a few facts about Waterville. I soon learned that the residential area was divided by religion and class. The more affluent Anglo-Protestants had fanned out onto the low hills above the city, while the French Catholics, mostly descended from Acadian families, lived downtown "on the plains" around Water Street or on the other side of the river in Winslow. Colby College, on its hill, was the focal center of the WASP segment.

Waterville society had five subsets: the Colby entourage; the businessmen of Main Street; the French workers in the paper and cotton mills; the executives of Scott Paper, Keyes Fiber, Lockwood Mills, and Diamond Match; and the professional group of doctors, dentists, and lawyers. It was an interesting mix, and it integrated about as well as oil and water. It was as rare to see one of the French at a Colby function as it was to see an Anglo at midnight Mass.

Much of this was to have a bearing on my practice. Meanwhile, I was about to enter Thayer Hospital with my first referral.

It was a modern cream-colored structure built with Hillburton funds, a recipient of Washington largesse sent in this direction by Thayer's medical director Dr. Frederick Hill. As a member of that Washington committee he had voted monies to build a small (fifty-six-bed) deluxe hospital.

The entrance was impressive, and I went into the foyer to find my young patient and his mother seated on a flowered sofa in a lavish waiting area. It resembled a VIP airport lounge, with low tables, wall-to-wall carpeting, deep armchairs, and long beige drapes.

As I went over to join my patient, a white-clad nurse and a lady in a pink smock and chunky jewelry converged on us. The woman in white spoke:

"Dr. Betts, I am Miss Fisher, the administrator, and this is Mrs. Manders, one of our pink ladies."

Miss Fisher was a handsome woman of middle years who spoke quietly and with authoritative charm. "I am putting your patient, Michael, in room 112." She gave the boy a smile. "He'll like that. It has a lovely view of the college. Dr. Saran said he would meet all of you there. I'll show you the way."

While we all trooped down the corridor to the elevator, I tried to adjust to the situation. My last encounter with a general hospital (I didn't count Eagle Lake, which had a classification and rating all of its own) had been in London. There the drill for patient admissions had remained rigid and unchanged since before the Boer War: first the patient was received by a cockney hospital porter, next cross-examined by an admission clerk, and then, if deemed worthy, conveyed into an open ward similar in structure to those in the heyday of Queen Victoria. Then an eagle-eyed ward sister took over, and no doctor was allowed to see the patient until she had him trussed up in bed and had given the all clear. As for the hospital administrator, the thought of Lady Alexander, matron of the London Hospital, conducting the doctor and patient down the corridors like a *maître d'hôtel,* was beyond the wildest possibility.

We emerged from the elevator with Mrs. Manders the pink lady carrying the luggage and quietly reassuring the little boy. At the charge nurse's desk there was a hum of activity. White-coated doctors seated on high stools studied their charts and made notes. The telephone rang constantly, and messages came steadily over the intercom. Nurses came and went, wheeling trolleys laden with medicines, towels, and instruments and discussing their patients with an accompanying physician, who was often still in his green operating suit, his mask dangling around his neck.

I was familiar with the scene from the movies. It needed only Dr. Kildare to come striding down the corridor or Walter Mitty to recount his success with a brain transplant. I was impressed—and when I realized I was now part of the action, I was overawed with my own position.

A slim nurse in a tailored white uniform and slip of a cap rose from the desk when she saw us. Miss Fisher introduced me. We shook hands. It was the first time I had ever shaken a nurse's hand (on duty.) Then the nurse concentrated on Michael: "Come and see your room, Michael. You'll have your own television set, and Mrs. Manders will get you books and toys—you'll see."

The spacious room was decorated in muted pastels and had four beds. A picture window allowed a view of Colby College on the hill, with the spire of the chapel etched against the blue sky. Michael was shown the controls for adjusting his bed and instructed how to manipulate the television by a remote box.

For the next two minutes the bed went through a variety of contortions and the TV screen changed like a crazy montage under Michael's control.

Michael was very excited, and I was amazed at the patience, kindness, and enthusiasm of Miss Fisher and the nurse. Finally he was persuaded to surrender his gadgets and undress. There were no other patients in the room, but the curtains were drawn around the bed to leave Michael and his mother alone.

Dr. Saran arrived. He was a tall, thin man in his forties dressed in operating room greens and a white coat. He had sharp features and his blue eyes were magnified by his gold-rimmed glasses. Again Miss Fisher effected the introductions, and then she and Mrs. Manders withdrew.

Dr. Saran listened with rapt attention while I repeated the history of Michael and the results of my examination.

"Sounds like a hot appendix. Let's have a look at him, nurse."

Michael lay on the bed tense with anxiety as he watched Dr. Saran approach. He put his hand on the boy's shoulder and gave it a light squeeze.

"Hello, young fella, I'm another Michael. Michael Saran. I'm a doctor. So you've had some pain. Where?"

I have seldom seen a more gentle and kind surgical examination. When he had finished, Dr. Saran shepherded me out into the corridor and said it was probably an acute appendix. He'd order a couple of laboratory tests, and if they confirmed the diagnosis he'd like to operate as soon as a room was available. He thought it would be about one o'clock. Would that suit me? He'd write the orders and get the permission.

Suit me? To assist!

Dr. Saran spoke as if it were routine; to me, it was like being ordered to the front. Once more my past had caught up with me.

CHAPTER

EARLY IN MY MEDICAL TRAINING it became obvious that I was not destined to be a surgeon. I was fascinated by the process of diagnosis, but my field was medicine, not the knife. Nor the scissors, nor the clamps, forceps, snaps, catgut, or wire. Furthermore I was soon bored by the repetitious business of opening and closing the abdomen. On the way in, you had to clamp little bleeding vessels and tie them off, a process I never mastered. On the way out, you had to endure the endless sewing of one layer after another. That routine, and having to listen to the banter of the surgeon, his jibes and anecdotes, turned me off.

Actually the *coup de grâce* occurred in my final year. One of the surgical knights, Sir Humphrey Someone-or-other, was operating on a thyroid. It was my turn to assist, which largely meant wearily hanging on to a retractor or clamp for an hour or so. Observing the master were a group of residents, a few visitors from abroad, and a cluster of nurses. The operating room was crowded. At the operating table Sister was handing Sir Humphrey his tools with swift anticipation. Scrub nurses scurried around counting sponges, and the whole place was tense with precision and action.

At last we reached the final moments when the skin was to be sewn. This menial task was usually given to the surgical intern, but this time, to my horror, Sir Humphrey said, "Come on, young Betts. Let's see you take the needle and suture the skin—and don't botch it."

My heart was in my mouth. Silence reigned as Sister handed me a curved needle threaded with fine silk. All the observers were still observing. With a tremble I took the skin in my forceps and in a hesitant quiver pushed the needle through the edge of one piece of skin and then the next. Success! I then drew the silk together and twisted one thread under the other. In a flash the intern drew the two together in a knot. I felt a pull on my finger. My hand was fixed to the patient. Without knowing it I had taken the needle and thread through my rubber glove. There was a titter of laughter from the back of the operating room and an amused murmur.

I was mortified. In tones of ice Sir Humphrey said, "Jenkins, cut the suture and try not to amputate his blasted finger. Sister, resterilize. Betts, you're a bloody fool. Buzz off."

And since then I had more or less buzzed off permanently from that specialty and nursed a deep-seated resentment toward all surgeons in any form.

Another galling incident had occurred in Eagle Lake. We had few surgical emergencies, and I only once had to assist a visiting surgeon from Fort Kent. It had been a benign performance, although the overture had been traumatic to my medical pride.

Apparently one of the older nuns had a gynecological complaint and was disturbed that Dr. Kirk, the regular Eagle Lake physician, had not been available to attend her. But rather than undergo an examination by the new young doctor (me) she wanted to wait until the Fort Kent surgeon visited.

This he did. But doctors can get rather fussed up about who invades their territory, and as I had been appointed to look after the inhabitants of Eagle Lake, I had rather assumed it would include being physician to the nuns.

It became manifestly not so when the surgeon announced, after he had seen two of his old patients from before my time, that we were going to operate on Sister B— forthwith.

Now, since before surgery can begin, a patient has to be prepared, refrain from eating, and be premedicated, it was obvious that I had not been part of the initial act. This was the only time when I had to assume that Sister Euloge was not in my camp.

I was rather miffed, but wisely said nothing and washed sulkily at the operating room sink. I was helped into a white gown and gloves and took myself to the assistant side of the operating table. Apparently this was to be my only role.

Already the patient was being put to sleep under the steady drip of ether through layers of gauze and a tea strainer.

Everything went smoothly with the operation. We went down through the usual layers of skin, muscle, and peritoneum (the abdominal lining), and I managed to tie off the sutures around the small blood vessels with considerable aplomb. I was given charge of a retractor, an instrument with which I was secure, and the surgeon then brought to light a smooth, tense cyst of the ovary about the size of a baseball.

This was removed in a matter of minutes and placed, like a trophy, in a dish. From there we proceeded to sew up the various layers. There were no anecdotes about football, just a few remarks about the local snowfall.

While we were ungowning, the surgeon wrote up his notes and

postoperative orders and two nuns wheeled the patient back to a ward. On my subsequent daily rounds I was diplomatically shepherded around that particular bed, and a few days later Sister B— had disappeared back into the cluster of nuns.

So now, when I went back to Michael's mother, I was careful to explain to her that Dr. Saran would now be responsible for Michael's care. But I was pleasantly surprised when she asked that I continue to visit and said she considered me to be her doctor.

It is curious how little the patient and doctor understand the significance of each other's words. You have to be a patient yourself to appreciate the sense of security and reassurance that comes from a doctor's mere presence. And a patient would have to be a doctor to realize how much a kind word of appreciation or expression of confidence means to him.

At the nurse's desk I was handed a blank chart to write in Michael's history and physical examination. When I completed this work the charge nurse asked if I had any orders. I said I would leave them to Dr. Saran. I added that I wasn't sure when Michael's operation was to take place, and she told me the operating room had been reserved for one o'clock. She must have seen that I was worried, and I explained that my office hours started at the same time.

"Do you want to call your house?" she asked. When I nodded, she made the call for me, and I was able to tell Mary to reschedule my patients. Next the nurse inquired whether I knew where to get a snack and offered to take me to the cafeteria. As we walked there together, she asked me about my background and told me of a visit she had made to London. We filed around the serving areas, filled our trays, and joined a group of nurses and doctors at a round table.

"This is Dr. Betts, who is practicing in Albion," the charge nurse said, introducing me to everyone. There was a lot of cross-chatter and laughter, and when I wasn't being questioned I sat thinking how extraordinary it was. I was astonished at the informality and the absence of any sense of hospital hierarchy. To a born and bred

American, a physician eating a hot dog in a white coat and an open-necked lumberman's shirt may be nothing out of the ordinary. But to me it was wild. So was seeing a scrub nurse and surgeon comparing their fishing experiences at Moosehead Lake the previous weekend. And my immediate acceptance into the group, with everyone interested in my background, was a more than novel experience.

As I took my tray back to the kitchen, a nurse in a scrub suit came up and said she'd heard I'd be assisting Dr. Saran. She'd show me the way to the doctors' changing room and how to get into the operating room itself.

At the dressing room entrance I was given a green operating suit, cap, cloth boots, and a mask. Inside the room I found Dr. Saran already changed. I told him I didn't know the ropes and he'd have to make allowances for me. This confession was an inspiration, because from then on Dr. Saran shepherded me through the whole business like a mother hen. He conducted me to the wash-up area and demonstrated how he lathered his arms and hands, how he turned the water off with his elbows, pushed the operating room door open with his backside, and other minor feats. He showed me how to allow the nurse to gown him and help him get into sterile rubber gloves without emerging through the fingers. I was introduced to the anesthesiologist and the operating room supervisor and shown where to stand.

The operation went like a dream. Everyone moved into position around the table. Green drapes were clipped into position with precision. The instruments were handed to Dr. Saran without a word. The incision seemed no longer than two inches, and my-cut-and-tie technique had almost no challenge. A swollen red appendix was extracted and its attachment cauterized. Within fifteen minutes the chief nurse was applying gauze and sticking plaster to the neat wound.

Back in the dressing room Dr. Saran said he would talk to Michael's mother and make postoperative visits each day, but he hoped I would also be looking in, especially on the day of discharge. I appreciated his courtesy.

It would take a few weeks before I understood that this was the way the specialists made sure that referred patients returned to their original doctors—an important factor in a jealous profession. But there was a reciprocal touch: would I be able to assist him the following morning at 8:00 A.M.? He had to perform an abdominal exploration on one of his own patients.

For the next twenty-four hours my surgical *amour-propre* was revitalized and the memory of my ignominious expulsion by Sir Humphrey expunged from my anxiety center. For a few weeks I lived in a rosy delusion, before I learned that such invitations to assist had an accepted economic basis. In common parlance, it's expressed as, "If you scratch my back, I'll scratch yours."

Meanwhile, pleased with myself, walking on air, I went up to the ward to see my patient. He was still sleeping and looking fine. I told the mother that it had been a case of a red-hot appendix, and I made no effort to restrain her from thinking that I had played a major role in removing it.

CHAPTER

BEFORE I LEFT THE HOSPITAL I was introduced to some future colleagues. All of them were specialists and were delightfully informal both in dress and manner. They gave friendly admonitions, urging me not to hesitate to call them for assistance, day or night.

In the corridor outside the coffee shop I met Dr. Frederick Hill again. I had not seen him since his stirring speech on my behalf at the Albion Grange. Tall, with a slight stoop, he exuded a competent charm. His name was embroidered on the breast pocket of his starched white coat, and he wore a head mirror held by a strap around his head. This device, which looked something like a coal miner's lamp, was the proud and exclusive emblem of the ear, nose, and throat fraternity. Usually members discarded it outside the clinic and operating room, but Dr. Hill seemed unaware of its presence.

"Ah! Tony, welcome aboard," he said, rubbing his hands. "Assisting Dr. Saran for an appendectomy, I see. Everything went well?"

"Yes, sir. Dr. Saran did a very neat job."

"Just so. Just so." He smiled and nodded, sending flashes of reflected sunlight onto the opposite wall. "Good man, Saran. By the way, you won't forget to put a progress note on the boy's chart each day. It's one of our rules. A short note about the patient's condition. It lets anyone having to take over his care know what's going on."

I told him I would see to the matter right away, explaining that I hadn't caught up with all the regulations yet. In fact, I added, laughing apologetically, I wasn't sure I was even on the staff officially. He put a fatherly hand on my shoulder. Dr. Goodof and he had already proposed me for membership, and the application would be voted on at the next staff meeting the following Thursday.

With that, he walked me up and down the corridor and explained a few of the Thayer Hospital rules and conventions. He expounded on the principles upon which the institution had been established and sketched the history of the hospital.

Thayer Hospital was but a few years old and had been founded by five doctors who had broken away from the rival "Sisters' Hospital," an institution dominated by the Catholic order. Perhaps I was aware of such conditions? I was to understand it wasn't a question of religious bias, but a desire to meet certain medical standards that had been the basis for the local revolt.

I was tempted to recount my own experiences in that realm, but held my fire.

We turned and started back down the corridor as Dr. Hill con-

tinued his recital of principles: All thirty-eight specialists at Thayer had
to be board certified. Since there were only five general practitioners
on the staff, I would make the sixth. My hospital privileges would be
limited until I proved myself. Any minor surgery or obstetrics that I
wanted to perform would have to be witnessed the first time by the
chief of that service. He would report to the staff committee as to
whether I was competent.

"Just a precaution, you understand," Dr. Hill smiled. "Only fair
to the patient and ourselves."

"Of course."

"Last year there was a Dr. Harrali Singh—charming fellow—
trained in Bombay, so he alleged, or perhaps it was Calcutta." He
paused, and a faraway look came into his eyes. "He was a lesson to us
all. Ah, yes, indeed a lesson."

We continued our way in silence, but at the next turn he bright-
ened and went on to give me a few more pointers. If in doubt, I was
always to get a second opinion from the appropriate specialist. When
the patient was indigent, I was to tell the consultant, who was honor-
bound not to charge a fee of more than five dollars.

All histories and physical findings were to be dictated on the day
of the patient's admission and followed by a daily progress note. Any
physician was entitled to read another doctor's chart. He himself personally read them all and made a selection of the interesting cases to
present at the weekly staff meeting. "Keeps them on their toes, Tony,"
he said with a satisfied smile.

Also, any patient who was thought to be gravely ill and liable to expire had to have his case presented immediately in the staff room. Every
doctor in the hospital was required to attend these sessions and con-
tribute his advice and recommendation without charge. The code announced over the intercom for such an event was "Special meeting
immediately in the conference room." If, for example, we were to
hear the "special meeting" notice at this moment, we would cease
our discussion instantly and go to the conference room. I got the point.

By now we must have patrolled the corridor a dozen times. The discussion had been conducted with pleasant charm and pride, and I found myself eager to agree with him.

So, when he finished by telling me I would be expected to offer my services free at the outpatient medical clinic every other Thursday morning, I readily assented. I had yet to discover that it would be at those sessions that I would meet a sprinkling of my own patients seeking another (and different) opinion, much to our mutual surprise.

Dr. Hill's homily had come to an end outside the coffee shop, and when he left me I decided to get a cup of tea and a bun before going back to Albion.

The coffee shop was manned by two of the volunteer ladies in pink smocks and chunky jewelry. They worked behind a bar doing some short-order cooking and urging everyone to eat a slab of home-made pie. The place was crowded with five or six white-coated personnel seated on high stools, most of them smoking and exchanging news and gossip and reading the newspaper. The shop also served as a reservoir for gifts, stuffed animals, paperbacks, postcards, and toiletries. It was difficult to move without knocking over something.

Leaning forward between two customers, I asked for a cup of tea. I might have been announcing the start of World War Three. All talk ceased, and I was looked upon like something from outer space.

One of the pink ladies broke the silence: "A cup of tea or a pot of tea?" Her voice had a trace of mimicry, intimating that she knew what went on in English high society.

"A cup, thank you."

"With a tea bag?" She smiled and I realized my leg was being pulled. So did everyone else.

"Yes. And a bun, if you have one."

"Oh, my dear—we don't have a 'bun.' Would a danish do?" She extracted an attractive looking pastry from an assorted collection.

This, together with other minor differences, meant that by the end of the day I had been identified as "the Brit" who had settled in Albion. Questions had followed left and right. One nurse asked if I would be doing obstetrics. When I said I hoped so, provided my technique was approved, she inquired whether I delivered with the patient on their side. She'd heard that that was what they did "over there."

"You mean the Sym's position? Yes, I do. It's very convenient, especially if you're on your own and the mother's on a feather bed."

"Gee, I'd love to see it."

I noted her name and promised that, should the opportunity arise, I'd be in touch. I little realized how soon that would be. Meanwhile I had my tea. Putting milk in it produced another ripple in the crowd, and after a lot more banter I managed to escape to my car.

I tried a new route to Albion, but the road was as bad as the one I had used to come in to Waterville, with the added difficulty of no signposts. After about an hour in the wilderness, crossing the same river twice or more, I drifted into Unity, which I identified by Reed's Drugstore. At least from there I knew the direction to Albion, and after another eight miles, I was able to park next to the church.

Here, for the first time in several months, I heard live music. (I excluded the Eagle Lake lone violin.) Someone was pounding out Elgar's "Pomp and Circumstance" no. 1 on a primitive piano in the church.

As the composer once said, "It's a damn good tune." In England it had come to be known as "Land of Hope and Glory" and was sung lustily on patriotic occasions and annually in London's Albert Hall. I whistled along with the piano as I moved toward our kitchen door.

Mary was feeding Ann, and Sara was busy with a floppy doll.

"Hear the music?" I said, giving Mary a kiss.

"I'll say. It's been going on all morning. Must be some lunatic anglophile practicing. Have you looked out the back?"

"No. Why?"

I strolled onto the porch. To my astonishment I saw that an acre of our two-foot-high elephant grass had been cut and converted into a lawn. It wasn't the sort of thing you'd see on a PGA green or Lords' Cricket Ground, but a good chunk of flat greenery nevertheless.

And as I was admiring it, a massive yellow and red tractor hove into sight on the summit with Mickey Marden perched at the wheel. He seemed engrossed with tilling the ground to make a giant flower bed.

I went out and made my way toward him. He was plowing a new furrow away from me, and as the roar of the tractor diminished, I heard again the tinkly strains of "Pomp and Circumstance." In the background, some woman was shouting orders like a drill sergeant.

I waited for Marden's return. He turned off his machine and jumped down.

"Bit late in the year, Doc, but I thought you might put in some corn, beans, tomatoes, and maybe a flower or two."

"And did you mow the grass?"

"Thought I might as well. Didn't take but a minute."

I thanked him. It was another example of the kindness everyone was showing us. He grinned and clambered onto the tractor.

"By the way, who's playing the piano?" I asked.

"Aurora Smith. Always does. Plays a mean tune."

"But doesn't she know any other piece? Minuet in G or something?"

"No, Doc, not for graduation." He fired up the engine and started another furrow.

I went back to the house. Graduation? What on earth was he talking about?

CHAPTER

WHEN I RETURNED TO THE KITCHEN Mary told me that there were two patients in the waiting room and a house call in Freedom. She'd make my tea before I went.

"I'm all right, I had a danish at the hospital."

"A what?"

"A sort of bun."

By the way, Mary's use of the word "tea" might need some elaboration. In America, as far as I could see, tea appeared to be a drink wherein a thin paper bag containing a few tea leaves was placed in a cold mug and lukewarm water poured over it. This infusion was drunk without milk or sugar. Sometimes a slice of lemon was floated on its surface.

In the Old Country, tea is a ritual running a close second to making Christmas pudding or porridge. Selected tea leaves are placed into a dedicated pot in strict proportions: one teaspoonful of leaves for each drinker and "one for the pot." The pot is heated before any boiling water is added. Two to five minutes are allowed for the tea to brew. An inch of milk is then placed in a teacup and the tea is poured over it. Sugar may be added.

On the other side of the Atlantic "tea" also has a second meaning. It is a meal, and takes place at 4:00 P.M. Tea is drunk and slices of bread and butter (for the lower orders) or watercress sandwiches with the crusts cut off (in the upper classes) are consumed, followed by pieces of fruitcake or a selection of biscuits (crackers).

And, since by about 4:30 P.M. the populace is nicely stuffed, the evening meal (dinner) is not served until eight o'clock. In leaving our native shores, it was a major adjustment to face meat and two vegetables at five o'clock in the afternoon and little more until breakfast.

* * *

I went into the waiting room to call the first patient into my of-fice. He was in his seventies, a onetime farmer. Judging from the not unpleasant bucolic odor, he still was attached to his calling—and, as I was soon to discover, to his multiple layers of clothing. He kept on a hat that might have been the pride of the railroad at the turn of the century and looked at me over his rimless glasses.

He sat down wheezing noisily, and I estimated that his respiratory rate was double that of a normal man his age. His face was flushed and his eyes bloodshot.

I sat in my swivel chair and waited for him to settle before asking him some routine questions.

"You're short of breath," I said. "How long has it troubled you?"

He nodded, swallowed, took a deep breath and managed: "Long enough."

"Any pain here—or here?" I pointed to the sides of his chest.

He shook his head.

"How about here?" I placed the flat of my hand in the region of the breastbone.

Another negative.

"Never?" I found myself raising my voice as if he were deaf. "Ever have bad pain here?"

Another head shake. He searched his pockets for what I antici-pated to be a handkerchief, so I handed him a tissue. He took it and tended his eyes and nose and gave me a toothless smile.

I tried a few more questions. After ten minutes I gathered by his gestures and the aid of pencil and paper that he lived alone on the out-skirts of town. During this interrogation we established a sort of trust-ing relationship, and he managed a few words, mostly confined to the universal rural Maine affirmative "Ayuh."

But I wasn't going to get far with any more questions, so I said, "I need to take a look at you."

"Ayuh," he wheezed.

I stood up and indicated that I wanted him to undo his coat. He made a feeble attempt at a couple of buttons before I gave him a hand. After a frustrating five minutes I had reached only the second layer. Here I could see a sweater and beyond that a woolen shirt. I felt like a mountaineer viewing Everest from the foothills. It was obvious that to arrive at Mr. Browning's skin was a task for at least two independent operators.

I told him I'd be back and went to get Mary.

Fortunately she was used to random calls for clinical help and was able to see that the children were safely stowed before joining me. While we were so engaged, I outlined the problem.

The task of disrobing the poor fellow almost defies description. We must have gone through seven layers, each more resistant than the last, before we bottomed out. But Mr. Browning endured it all with good humor and a frequent toothless grin. Halfway through, I went into the waiting room to reassure the other patients that they were not forgotten.

The Browning excavation proved worthwhile. With my stethoscope I could now hear his chest crackling like a kindled fire, his heart thumping against his ribs a couple of inches beyond where it should have been, with every second beat accompanied by a whistle or murmur. His liver was enlarged and his ankles swollen.

It all confirmed heart failure. I explained this to him as best I could and said I could probably make him better with a couple of injections and some pills. I don't think he really understood, but he readily accepted the advice. Then, apparently encouraged by our interest, he indicated that while we were there it might be a good opportunity to cut his toenails.

It was still the days before plastic sterile syringes, so while Mary boiled up two of our glass ones, I had a go at his nails. Cutting them required some heavy orthopedic shears and a lot of wrist work. It almost rivaled the time when I took a tooth out of a woodsman in Eagle Lake.

Next I gave him a diuretic and started him on digitalis. Finally we dressed him. Going down the mountain was easier than going up, and we had him shipshape in less than ten minutes. I told him I would drive him home if he'd wait until I'd seen the other patients.

He shook my hand, extracted two dollars from his wallet, and placed them on my desk. I thanked him and assisted him back to the waiting room.

Thanks to Mary, who had opened the windows, a gentle breeze fluttered the curtains and the room smelled of crushed violets when I returned to my office with the next patient, a middle-aged lady.

I apologized to her for the delay and mentioned that the last man had been very short of breath and needed immediate treatment.

"I'm not surprised," she said, plumping down. "I have a touch of asthma myself. I have been told that I am allergic to dust, and that vintage carpet in your waiting room," she raised her eyebrows and gave the suggestion of a shrug of her shoulders, "might be a potent source."

"It was donated by the community, together with the house."

"I see. Well, in that case . . . " She sniffed and gave a cough and went on with some more remarks obviously fostered by her having been kept waiting. I allowed her to let off some more steam and at last steered her on to her reason for visiting me. She wanted her blood pressure taken and a "liver shot."

I soon learned that this first was a common request and that many people were worried that they had "low blood pressure." When I told them that I'd be happy if my own were so low I was regarded with suspicion. Apparently "low blood pressure" was a diagnosis commonly handed out to patients who had symptoms brought on by stress and worry. It was an easier way to deal with them than to attempt Freudian analysis.

The "liver shot" was an injection of vitamin B_{12} and usually served the same purpose as the tag of "low blood pressure." Perhaps it was more effective in that it involved the ritual of an injection. It had come into vogue through the media and lay gossip, and had assumed an undeserved reputation as a magic bullet. Fortunately it did no harm. I seldom met anyone who recanted their demand for the injection even after I had explained its dubious value. Of course there was the rare patient with a certain type of anemia for which it was a specific therapy.

By now, even with my limited general practice experience, I realized that about three-quarters of all patients only suffered from what was termed "anxiety neurosis," with its psychosomatic symptoms. Bodily pains, headaches, palpitations, dizziness, insomnia were the usual complaints. Nevertheless, I had been taught that it was dangerous to dismiss any of these symptoms without an investigation to make sure there was no underlying disease. Usually a physical examination, a mild medicine or sedative, and a follow-up visit would provide enough evidence that the symptoms arose from stress. But if I tried to explore the source of the stress, I usually found myself in deep waters that were better explored by clergy, counselors, psychologists, and psychiatrists—and even they often floundered around.

Even superficially, these cases took a lot of my time, energy, and patience. Ironically, I found that it was simpler and more satisfactory to treat a real disease like pneumonia or a gastric ulcer than a case of imaginary aches and pains.

One of my older and more cynical teachers had solved this aspect of his outpatient practice by giving every such patient a diagnosis, a label with a medical connotation. He claimed that by doing so he helped patients keep their self-respect. He would tell a healthy, anxious man with pains in the abdomen that he had a "gastric stomach" or a "stretched abdominal nerve," and give him an innocuous bottle of medicine and an appointment for two months hence. It worked well in the East End of London, where medical literature was scarce, but I did not favor that technique.

* * *

After seeing one or two more patients who had dropped in, I was ready to take Mr. Browning home. I settled him in my car and drove a mile or so out of Albion. His home was a trailer. Together we made our way up some rickety steps and inside. He headed for an old armchair like a homing pigeon.

I told him I'd drop by in a couple of hours to see how he was getting on and would bring him a newspaper. At this, his eyes lit up and he gave me another toothless grin. I left feeling anxious about his immediate future. He needed help; either someone should be living with him or he ought to be in a nursing home.

The problem nagged at me as I started to my house call in Freedom. Thinking I would talk about Mr. Browning with Mickey, I stopped to fill up with gas at Marden's pumps. As if he'd read my thoughts, Mickey came out, and while he filled the tank I told him the problem.

But as I was to learn, news spread faster in Albion in those days than by any modern internet. Mickey already knew that Browning had been to see me. A group was going to give him a hand sometime in the next hour. Apparently, every week they took a box of food to him and tidied up his trailer. I said he would need daily attention for the next few days, and Mickey said he'd get in touch with the district nurse while I was in Freedom.

"Might be a good idea to get him into Quimby's," he added.

"Who?"

"Mrs. Quimby runs a nursing home on the Benton road. Good woman. Folks like her. They say it's a firetrap, but do-good folk can always find fault."

"I'll also speak with the district nurse. Maybe we could get him there for a few days."

"Just let us know, Doc, when you need any help."

"I promised him a newspaper; take him a *Morning Sentinel*."

I journeyed toward Freedom with a lighter heart.

CHAPTER

25

O N JULY FOURTH WE AWOKE to find our front lawn covered
with more than a hundred miniature American flags. A myriad
of Stars and Stripes fluttered in the bright, clear air. It looked a
bit like Arlington Cemetery. There was no accompanying note, and
I could swear that our lawn had been bare at midnight.

Our prime suspect for this mini–Boston Tea Party was Mickey
Marden, with whom, at the gas pump only the previous week, I
had discussed the unfortunate happenings of 1776. I had made a
point of emphasizing General Washington's poor sportsmanship in
opening fire at Trenton on Christmas Day, and he informed me
that Americans always played to win.

The display of flags provided a steady conversation piece later that
day at a party at the Higgins farm, where we were invited to watch
some fireworks. The subject also came up during office visits for the
next two weeks. It seemed to be a sign of further acceptance when I
learned that our neighbors didn't mind my mentioning that the
British two or three times burned down Portland (Falmouth) and in
1812 ignited the White House. However, cracks about Benedict
Arnold selling the secrets of West Point's defense were off-limits.

Meanwhile, over the weeks, the medical practice slowly increased,
but it was different from Eagle Lake where I'd had a monopoly. Some
families had established firm relationships with doctors in Waterville
and were reluctant to change, even though they were anxious to have
a physician at hand should they have an emergency. They seemed to
feel they had a dual loyalty. Consequently, many of the office calls were
to try me out.

On the other hand, I inherited several patients with chronic conditions who were relieved that they no longer had to make the long

journey into Waterville. It was easier for them to have me make a house call. Thus I roamed far and wide, often getting lost on the numerous dirt roads in search of little rural houses. Getting instructions over the telephone about how to find a house could be frustrating. It took me a while to understand that "the four corners" meant a crossroads. "Go just a mite down the dirt road" could mean a voyage through mud for five miles. "You can't miss it" meant you'd be lucky to find it.

For a night call, I used to insist that all the house lights and porch light be turned on. "All?" Yes—upstairs and downstairs. Such landmarks as Bessey's garage, the blinking red light after the four corners, or Farwell's seed store, while assumed to be common knowledge by the patient, had to be learned by the new doctor. Flying across Arabia or Africa had been simpler. "Go up the Red Sea and turn right, and you'll see Mecca off the wing tip" or "just follow the Nile" were easier than finding the third dirt road on the left after Palermo.

The local telephone operators were a great help. Each town seemed to be governed by a different and independent telephone company, and each exchange had its own hours of operation. Albion's closed at nine in the evening, with Mrs. Bessey controlling the switchboard in her home. Freedom shut down around eight o'clock. Most telephones were on party lines, and in the morning each of the towns had what would in these days amount to a series of conference calls among ladies wishing to keep abreast of the local news and gossip.

The telephone in my office consisted of a box with a handle. It had been mounted in the kneehole of my rolltop desk and regularly attacked my left shin.

To get Mrs. Bessey I had to turn the handle briskly twice. Mrs. Bessey was very particular about that technique. She would interpret three turns as impatience, and she'd ignore a single revolution. However, she was very helpful in relaying messages and seemed to know where I was at any hour (before nine o'clock). Often, when I was at a house in another town, she'd convey a call from a house nearby and usually render a brief summary of the problem.

It was in this manner that I learned that I was needed to deliver my first baby in the new practice. I was in a house beside a railroad yard in Thorndike when I received the call.

"Mrs. Chiswell has taken herself into Waterville. She's been having pains every five minutes. Says the last ones are coming quicker," reported Mrs. Bessey, who had tracked me down.

I thanked her, completed my house call rapidly, and set off for Thayer Hospital. Now I could take a faster route and bypass Albion. Mrs. Bessey had told me she would tell Mary where I was. (Mrs. Bessey's switchboard service was every bit as efficient and convenient as today's cellular phones, and *she* did not require batteries.)

So far, my obstetric bookings had been meager, to say the least. I had inherited Mrs. Chiswell from a Waterville general practitioner of whom she was critical. I was later to learn that this was a mutual sentiment. On the doctor's part, this was due to the fact that she had not paid him for the two previous confinements. But for the time being I was ignorant of the facts and glad to have the work.

As I drove into the Thayer parking lot I wondered whether I ought to get in touch with the chief of obstetrics, who was supposed to witness my performance and pronounce on my abilities. However, Mrs. Bessey's warning that Mrs. Chiswell "came quick" overrode any thought of a pass or fail by the obstetric chief, and I headed for the obstetric floor since there was no sign of my patient in the foyer.

As I stepped out of the elevator, a nurse in a green operating gown, felt boots, cap, and mask bore down on me and asked if I was the father, Mr. Chiswell. It was a reasonable mistake, but unnerving not to be known by the staff.

It reminded me of the time when I was at medical school, learning obstetric deliveries under the supervision of midwives in the rugged neighborhood of Jack the Ripper's Whitechapel, a tough district around the Thames wharves. Although we were only medical students and the midwives ran the show, we were given the title of "doctor" to inspire confidence in the patient. One of my fellow medical students, John, had a deceptively youthful appearance, looking more like a stand-in for Lord Fauntleroy than Dr. Kildare.

"Doctor" John had completed his delivery (the second in his life) and had been exiled to the outside fire escape by the midwife while she "tidied up." As he stood there, he saw the father, a massive longshoreman, rushing up the stairs two at a time. John moved forward to greet him with a magnanimous and authoritative "Let me congratulate you, sir, on becoming a father again," when the giant eased him aside with one arm, saying, "What are *you* doing here, sonny?"

I felt somewhat in the same position on the Thayer obstetric ward. Even when I said I was Dr. Betts, I was met with an air of skepticism, and not helped by my "funny" accent. I was saved by the appearance of another green-gowned nurse, apparently of higher rank. "You're Dr. Betts. Mrs. Chiswell is in the delivery room. You'd better change at once," she urged.

Of course I had to be shown where to go, where to find clothing, hat, and mask, and be propelled to the sink to wash and be "gloved up." I found myself weakly apologizing to anybody who would listen. As I lathered my hands and arms at the sink I was able to see through the window into the delivery room, where Mrs. Chiswell was lying on an operating table, being helped by Dr. Moore. I was relieved that he was to be the anesthesiologist, since we had already met when I had assisted Dr. Saran. Seeing Dr. Moore was like recognizing a friend in court. When I entered the room he introduced me to the two scrub nurses.

The delivery setup was a far call from the floor of the average Eagle Lake home. In fact, it was different from anything I'd met before. But in delivering babies, first principles take command, whether you're assisting in a hospital, a home, or the jungle.

During those years, the fashion was for the birth experience to be kept minimal for the mother by using a considerable amount of anesthesia. The experience was nonexistent for the father, who was excluded from the room and either paced the corridor or the nearest bar.

For first babies, the mother was put to sleep and the baby gently helped into the world by low forceps. Even for more experienced mothers, fairly heavy anesthesia was the rule. The newborn would be examined and cleaned up and given an injection of Vitamin K to help the blood clotting mechanism. Often, by the time the mother woke up both she and babe had been returned to the ward. I think this procedure was probably less traumatic for the doctor, but not necessarily as satisfactory for the parents as it is today.

Mrs. Chiswell had an easy time, and so did I. This gave me a chance to learn the conventions of an American hospital birthing without appearing to be an ignoramus, because the circulating nurses had anticipated what they thought would be my routine orders.

When I emerged from the delivery suite, another doctor was at the opposite sink, preparing to deliver a patient in the opposite room.

"How did it go?" he asked through his mask.

"Fine. It was her third. No trouble," I replied.

"Good. I'm Dr. Sewall, chief of obstetrics. You must be Dr. Betts, the limey?"

I apologized for not calling him to observe me in action, explaining that I hadn't had time.

He laughed. "I saw enough through the window, and Dr. Moore said things were O.K. Done many deliveries?"

I told him of my experience. He chuckled when I mentioned Eagle Lake. As he backed away into the delivery room he said he had once hunted bear up there.

CHAPTER

26

AFTER SIX MONTHS IN ALBION, Mary and I were concerned about what is vulgarly known as cash flow. At our kitchen table on the tenth day of the month we would review our current balance. We now calculated that we had to take in a thousand dollars by that date each month just to keep afloat.

In Eagle Lake the flow had been a steady dribble into our Kodak Brownie box bank, and as there was no spending temptation apart from Belanger's store, our balance sheet showed a constant plus. The Albion practice suggested that the tide might have turned.

In Eagle Lake everything had been a cash transaction; now we had to send out bills. We soon found that some might as well have been sent to sea in a bottle. Before long the sight of a patient waving an insurance form, a guarantee of payment, warmed our hearts.

Some days I would find the waiting room empty or perhaps with only one patient. The telephone appeared to be dead, and Mary and I would spend twenty-four hours in deepening gloom.

There were also new expenses. I found I had to stock medicines, and drug salesmen were frequent visitors to our waiting room. Sometimes their multiple calls were annoying, but they had to make a living, and several representatives left quantities of useful samples, particularly antibiotics, which I could hand out to the poor patients in the area. But some salesmen were exasperating and liked to talk forever.

In Albion, our office pharmacy stocked a small range of medicines. Aspirin in three colors was a useful combination. When the white didn't seem to be doing the job, I would suggest a change to another variety. Several patients swore that the red was better than the white, while others demanded the green.

A bottle of five hundred phenobarbital half-grain tablets was a source for sedation and a relief for anxiety and stress. Combined with some estrogen, it brought relief to menopausal patients. Cough syrup I bought in gallon containers. In the evening we'd pour it into small bottles and apply labels, and I'd be reminded of my brother's advice before I left my native shore: "Don't forget to ask the patient to bring a specimen on the next visit; you'll get your bottles back."

We also had a supply of digitalis, codeine, and a couple of gallons of bicarbonate of soda. This "soda-bic." was doubly useful—to fight gastric disturbances or to soothe itches and rashes. I found I had to stock my medical bag with items I hadn't carried previously: a full range of narcotics, several packaged catheters, a set of minor surgical instruments, and a series of "starter" doses of medicines. My patients in Albion and the surrounding countryside often had to travel twenty miles or more (much of the distance on unpaved roads) to get to a pharmacy. A starter dose of medication from my supply would see the patient through the night and until a neighbor could make the journey into town.

So the bills piled up for these supplies, and even though gasoline was inexpensive, the Pontiac was drinking it up as I covered my huge territory and made daily trips to the hospital.

I always had to have the car at the ready. This led to one patient, in perfectly good health, coming in under the guise of needing a check-up. After a superficial examination by me, he managed to bring me to a halt, and with charming concern for my own and Mary's welfare suggested that I needed a second car "for the missus."

It just happened that he owned a dealership in one of the nearby towns, and he had taken the liberty of leaving one of his vehicles in my driveway for a few days. He got out of his chair and pointed through the office window to a gleaming Cadillac about the size of a battle cruiser, parked across the entrance to the church. I agreed that the car looked superb, but I said I was already well equipped and had three more years to pay off the Pontiac. Furthermore, floating around the poorer rural areas in such a luxurious colossus would not be appropriate.

"Doc, try it for a week. You'll love it."

"It's just not in the cards. Incidentally, your blood pressure is normal."

"The wife will get a kick out of it."

"Will she?" The largest thing Mary had driven in England had been our 1927 Austin Seven, an item about the size of the Cadillac's hood.

But I was conscious of the horde of patients in the waiting room, and it seemed as if my salesman-patient wouldn't budge until I gave in. Also, I must confess that my business sense had not changed from when Jack Sharp had negotiated the Pontiac deal in New Jersey. I was weak.

Weak.

So the Cadillac stayed. In its way it was a thing of beauty and moved noiselessly and smoothly like a hand over satin. I sat at the wheel as if levitated on an oriental cushion. I drove it to the hospital that very day, loving every minute. The road felt smooth, and frost heaves were like gentle ocean waves. At the hospital, with a twinge of conscience, I parked it as far out of sight as I could behind the nurses' section.

But the moment I reached the second-floor nursing station, Dr. Beckerman, a rival general practitioner, said with raised eyebrows he guessed things were looking up in Albion. Did I need a partner? The charge nurse said she adored my new car, and a smiling nurse student inquired whether there were any openings in Eagle Lake for a worn-out, old, poverty-stricken nurse to make a fortune.

At the Marden pumps, while the gas flowed into the Cadillac's tank like an Arabian oil spill, Mickey went into his store and came back to wipe the windshield ostentatiously. Could he check the oil? With a grin he inquired if I still needed that five-thousand-dollar guarantee, and he told me he had a wealthy uncle who had a similar car, only it wasn't quite as new, nor as long.

After a week of driving the sleek beast, and in spite of all the remarks, giving up that car was worse than breaking a drug habit. However, with Mary's support (she had now learned to drive the Pontiac), we took the only course. After office hours we drove both cars back to the Caddy's original home, left the keys with an assistant, and fled.

But the salesman had established a beachhead. Two weeks later he repeated the process with a two-tone, automatic shift, 1949 Pontiac coupe. He said it was a steal, without mentioning from whom.

One passenger who might have been impressed by our temporary opulent transport was Mr. Gamplin. He was in his seventies and had farmed in Freedom all his life, like his father before him. At one time he had fifty head of cattle, and as a lad had won the milking championship in Bangor three years running. Now he had one cow and kept bees.

I received a telephone call from his niece just before the Albion exchange closed. She said her uncle was in great pain. Could I come over right away? She gave directions. It was the usual rural litany, with such subtle pointers as: take a left after I saw Albert's repair shop, continue on the dirt road to the four corners, go right for a mile to Jackson's farm, turn left, and after a mite I'd see the house with a light on the porch.

I replied that I hadn't a hope of seeing anyone's repair shop in the depths of the country in the dark. Perhaps she could meet me in Freedom and lead me to her house?

There followed a long discussion about whether she could get her uncle's car to start. Mrs. Bessey, who was benignly listening in, came to the rescue by volunteering to put a call through to a neighbor to see whether he could make the Freedom rendezvous with me.

Ten minutes went by before the telephone rang again. This time it was the Gamplin neighbor, who, in a rich Maine brogue, told me he'd be at Sprague's pump in Freedom in a red Ford pickup. Mrs. Bessey intervened to ask if I knew where Sprague's pumps were. No, I didn't. She gave me directions as if instructing a three-year-old to cross the road.

Amazingly—and you should go to see Freedom after dark to appreciate it—the arrangement worked.

As I followed the Ford pickup from Sprague's pumps, I offered up a prayer of thanks to Mrs. Bessey, especially as we plunged into the depths of the countryside via narrow, twisting dirt roads. At one time I thought I saw a garage, looking like a relic from a ghost town, and it may well have been Albert's repair shop; I'll never know. We seemed to cross intersections that might have been two, three, or four corners for all I cared. Finally we slithered up a muddy drive to the door of a large white farmhouse. The red truck skidded to a halt, gouging out a splendid rut, and I pulled up behind it.

I approached to thank my guide. He sat at the wheel with the engine running. He was feeding on a toothpick. "Reckon you know your way back now. Could tell you a short cut, but guess it might confuse you a mite." I nodded, and he let out the clutch.

By the time the mud and water had settled, a young woman with blonde hair flowing over her shoulders, dressed in a white shirt and jeans, was standing in the doorway rubbing one bare foot over the other. She had a pleasant, vibrant face with regular features and no makeup. As she closed the door behind me she told me her uncle was in the far room.

"He's an independent cuss. He says I shouldn't have called you."

I glanced around and could see that I was probably in the main room. It was sparsely furnished with two rockers, a beat-up sofa, a big round table, and a couple of plain chairs. The carpet was a worn oval weave. Some old books and magazines half filled a simple bookcase.

The girl watched me take in the scene and in apologetic tones said that her uncle lived alone. She was at college but had always come down to spend summer vacation with her aunt and uncle. Her aunt had died a few months previously. Now she didn't know how he'd manage when she went back. She conducted me to a door in the corner, gave a tap, and went in.

"This is Dr. Betts, 'nunk. Come to see how you're making out."

An old man, heavily built, with sparse white hair, watery blue eyes, and partially open mouth, lay back on three pillows in his bed. Over his high cheekbones the skin was sallow and showed a weave of veins. He turned his head and surveyed me before speaking.

"You're a young 'un. Shouldn't have fetched you this time o' night."

I told him I had heard he was in pain and that I might look young but I didn't feel it.

"I wasn't going to let you suffer all night, uncle," the girl said.

I drew up a chair and gradually extracted a history from him. He told me his trouble had come on suddenly, with spasms of pain in his abdomen just under his right ribs. From his description and by his laconic answers to my leading questions, I was sure he had gall-bladder stones, with one probably stuck in a duct.

"Does the pain come and go, getting worse and then letting up?"

"Might say so."

"Yes?"

"Mebbe."

He was tender under his right ribs and had a slight temperature. Even by the poor light I was tempted to think he was slightly yellow.

I told him he'd have to go to the hospital right away. This was met with a stubborn refusal. He shook his head and stared into space. For ten minutes I argued with him to no effect. His niece begged him to take my advice and got nowhere. She and I looked at each other in mute exasperation.

"I told you he was a mule."

"Hospitals!" Gamplin muttered. "Doctors!" But fortunately at that moment Dame Nature stepped in on our side, producing another great spasm of pain. I took out a syringe and gave him an injection of narcotic. It took a few minutes to give him relief.

"Does that persuade you?" I asked.

"They won't get paid," he said. "I won't live long enough to pay your hospital, nor them doctors, nor you. Best leave me."

Then a minute later: "Let them take me up to number three." I had met this expression once before. Number three was one of the local cemeteries. But I also recognized a tone of resignation in his voice, and after another round of persuasion he gave in to our suggestion.

With an energetic and purposeful air, the girl found his slippers and stood beside the bed holding out his bathrobe.

It was hard work getting him into my car. The girl, who I now knew as Jennifer, or Jenny, sat beside him on the back seat. She had locked up the farmhouse and brought an overnight bag with her.

She knew the way, and an hour later we drew up outside the Thayer entrance. To my surprise, the night nursing staff was expecting us, and as soon as we stopped at the entrance an orderly came forward with a wheelchair.

Miss Fisher, a reassuring and authoritative figure, stood waiting in the foyer. She explained that Mrs. Bessey had called the hospital from Albion, knowing the Freedom exchange would have closed for the night.

"But how did she know we were coming here?"

Miss Fisher gave me a smile. "You'd be surprised, Dr. Betts." Turning to Mr. Gamplin, she introduced herself. "Hello, Mr. Gamplin. We've been waiting for you. We're going to take you to a nice room on the second floor."

Gamplin nodded with resignation. As we entered the elevator he said, "Shan't be able to pay you, you know."

"Don't worry about that. Let's get you better first," said Miss Fisher. She turned to me. "You'll want Dr. Saran?"

Within half an hour Mr. Gamplin had been settled in his bed

and examined by Dr. Saran. An x-ray study and laboratory tests had been ordered for the morning, and a tentative booking made for the operating room.

Just before midnight I was ready to drive back to Albion. Jennifer had been given accommodation in a side room. I was due back at the hospital at 8:00 A.M. and was of two minds about whether to find a bed in the hospital for myself, but decided to go home. I walked slowly across the parking lot. Before I could reach my car, I was captured by the night porter.

"Dr. Betts, they need you at once in obstetrics!"

I didn't go home that night. And from then on I kept a toilet kit in my locker, together with a stock of cookies.

CHAPTER

A T NINE O'CLOCK THE FOLLOWING MORNING I was hanging on to a retractor to allow Dr. Saran to get a good view of Mr. Gamplin's fiery gallbladder. After dislodging a stone from a duct, he removed the offending organ. My relief from retractor duty came at last when for a few minutes I was given a pair of scissors to cut a suture or two. I also took part in the ritual of closing the various layers leading up to the skin. I still found this process tedious, and I was not spared from anecdotes about salmon and trout in Moosehead Lake, views on the relative superiority of Harvard over Yale, or the tragic epic of the Boston Red Sox. But I did have the pleasure of seeing that I had made a correct diagnosis of Mr. Gamplin's condition.

Our patient was taken into the recovery room, and I went out to tell Jennifer that her uncle had come through the operation successfully. I tried to be upbeat, but I was tired. I had delivered a baby in the early hours and I'd only had a short sleep since then.

When I telephoned Mary to find out how things were at base she had nothing alarming to report. There were three house calls, two of which I could do on my way back to Albion before the office started at one o'clock.

I sought out the doctor for whom I had been deputized in the delivery room at 3:00 A.M. I hoped I might have earned the fee. Not so; he said he'd seen the patient while I was in the operating room. He said she hadn't been aware of my presence (by which he meant his absence), so he wasn't going to disabuse her. He was grateful, and hoped he could do the same for me sometime.

As I have mentioned, money was beginning to take a prominent place in my day-to-day thinking. The dogs of poverty seemed to be nipping at my heels. My exertions of the last twenty-four hours had brought nothing into the kitty.

Nor did the next house call, which came to resemble an improvised clinic. I arrived at a house where streptococcus had cut a swath through a family of seven like an Old Testament plague.

Strep is a dangerous and unpleasant bug for the patient and a great consumer of time for the doctor. Every infected child has to have the ears and throat examined, and the heart must be checked to spot the start of rheumatic complications. In a family of seven, with children of ages ranging from one to ten, this takes time, patience, and energy. Then everyone has to have an injection of penicillin, a fearful and tearful business in the days before oral tablets came on the market.

This visit took the best part of an hour, and I was asked to put the fee on the books, which meant that I might as well write it off. I was glad to help them, and if I hadn't done so, I wouldn't have been doing my job. But it still wasn't earning anything, and I had supplied several vials of penicillin. I told the mother I would return the following day to make sure everyone was responding to treatment.

The next call took just as much time. The patient, a young, nervous man, had nothing physically wrong with him, but was suffering crippling bouts of pain on the left side of his abdomen. His description was bizarre and fit no specific medical entity.

By now, in my short medical experience, I had come to the conclusion that pain in that area, especially in the young, was seldom serious or an emergency. The large bowel occupied that part of the body, and the list of possible troubles was usually benign and short, with constipation leading the field. But trying to reassure this patient who thought he had cancer, trying to save him the unnecessary expense of X rays and laboratory tests, was an exhausting business.

In training we had been urged to understand that such patients were suffering real pain. As one comfortable London consultant told us, "Although there is no underlying physical cause, these people are sending out distress signals. Distress signals, gentlemen, due to stress. You must root it out. Dig for it. Dig."

This exhortation is all very well in textbooks and in a medical school lecture, but out in the real world there isn't much time for a session on the family couch. Invariably you are confronted with a patient with an inadequate personality in dreary surroundings. His every day is boring, his occupation dull, and he is devoid of curiosity or interests. A glance at his partner is usually enough to suggest an unfulfilled sex life or none at all. After a fruitless hour both the patient and doctor are frustrated. The only beneficiaries in these cases are the pharmaceutical companies supplying mood modifiers such as Valium and a myriad of similar drugs.

So it was with this patient. And after a thorough examination and a long talk, I drove away as dissatisfied with myself as he was with me.

I arrived in Albion an hour late, and when I tried to park in my driveway I found the place jammed with cars and trucks. Mary greeted me, saying that the waiting room was packed. The first patients had arrived half an hour ago. She insisted I eat something and started to cook bacon and eggs. It was no good; trying to eat a meal was impossible when I knew that patients were waiting for me in the next room. Despite Mary's protests, I took myself into the office and started work.

Everyone was good-natured and took my tardiness as a natural consequence of rural practice. There was no need to apologize, and I felt better. Soon a break occurred when I had to examine a new pregnancy. Mary came into the office to help the lady get ready and I went into the kitchen to tackle my tepid eggs and bacon and say hello to the children. They hadn't seen much of me for the last few days.

I finished seeing the rest of the patients by about five o'clock. By then two more house calls had come in, and I had one left over from the morning. With the evening office starting at seven, life was getting too hectic. By the end of the day my conversation was not at its most brilliant, and I fell asleep in a kitchen chair.

We didn't need an alarm clock for the morning call. Sara reliably arrived slightly ahead of sunrise, ready for games, and at the same time it seemed as though Ann would have no difficulty if called upon to project her wakening cry to the back of Madison Square Garden. During breakfast Mrs. Bessey came through from her switchboard with some early requests.

On the whole it looked as though I was in for a reasonable day. My first job would be to see Mr. Gamplin, then I would visit my strep family. But I had barely set foot in the hospital foyer before Dr. Hill bore down on me like a destroyer coming in for the kill. He hoped I had not forgotten the medical clinic at eleven; it was my day. Sunk, I assured him it had been uppermost in my mind. He patted my shoulder and said I was a good man.

While I waited for the elevator, Jennifer Gamplin approached me from the coffee shop to ask whether I was going to see her uncle. She had sat beside him for most of the night, and he seemed free of pain. He was worried about all the expense, however, and she could understand his anxiety. The room alone was costing fourteen dollars a day. Was there anything I could do to help him?

She appeared remarkably fresh and attractive in her tomboyish way, and my defenses melted under such a charming onslaught. I suppose, to impress her, I became expansively reassuring.

"There's nothing to worry about. Not a thing. The hospital is bound to make allowances," I said.

"You see, he hasn't any savings," Jennifer explained as we rode to the second floor. "He lives on his Social Security and the little he makes from his bees."

"Bees?"

"Honey. And then there's the surgeon's bill and the anesthesiologist."

I couldn't help noticing that she'd left me off the list.

"Don't upset yourself. I'm sure everyone will realize your uncle's situation."

"He hates charity. He's always been proud of his independence."

"Not to worry," I said, for about the tenth time.

The charge nurse looked up as we approached. "How's the Cadillac running?" she asked me with a smile. "Must be nice to afford a car like that." She nodded a greeting to Jennifer.

"I've taken it back."

"And getting a Jaguar? Oh my, we girls certainly chose the wrong profession."

Then she became businesslike: "Your Mr. Gamplin is doing well. Vital signs normal. Wants to eat. Here's his chart. Dr. Saran has been in." She turned to Jennifer. "Would you mind waiting in the lounge while Dr. Betts and I see your uncle?"

The charge nurse left me at Gamplin's bedside. Since he was under the direct care of Dr. Saran for changing the dressing and generally checking his post-operative state, there wasn't much for me to do but give Gamplin my moral support and show him how to turn the television off. I assured him he wouldn't have to worry about the expense he had incurred. I can't say that the conversational exchange flowed; like most inhabitants of rural Maine, Mr. Gamplin expressed himself in laconic monosyllables or not at all.

I came out and told Jennifer things were going well and that there would be no need for her to stay. I expected her uncle to be in the hospital for about a week. She smiled and asked if she could have a ride back to Albion. I told her she could come along but that I had a few duties to perform before I left the hospital. She said she'd be happy to wait, and I told her to get a good book and I'd find her in the foyer.

I mentally assessed the morning ahead. I'd need an hour to see the strep family, but first there would be the medical clinic until noon. Then I could squeeze in another house call by taking the Benton route back to Albion, and I'd be ready for the afternoon office at two. This left about fifteen minutes in which to see the administrator about reducing or voiding Mr. Gamplin's bill.

I set a course for Miss Fisher's office.

CHAPTER

I FOUND PEARL FISHER SEATED behind her desk in surroundings delicately reflecting her personality. The gray filing cabinets and books bespoke her formality, order, and authority. Her pink telephone and vase of flowers spoke for her femininity. And the beige wallpaper, watercolor prints, light yellow curtains, and petite armchairs expressed her warmth and welcome.

I tapped on the door. Miss Fisher smiled and stood up.

"You've been busy, Doctor," she said softly and indicated for me to sit down. "And I gather you were up in the night delivering Mrs. Koncassis."

"I had an hour or two of sleep, but my shift isn't over yet," I said ruefully. "I have to face a medical clinic in a few minutes. Dr. Hill snared me in the doorway."

She laughed. "Snared you, did he?" And she almost giggled as she went behind her desk. "Well now, what can I do for you?"

I sat down and tried to collect my thoughts. Here, once more, I found myself disarmed by my inherent weakness and trapped in a financial negotiation. Whether I was buying a car, asking a patient for a fee, or, as in this instance, trying to get one reduced, I always saw both sides and mentally pleaded my adversary's case: Why should I be depriving this poor car salesman of his list price plus undercoating and whitewall tires? Wasn't it mean of me to expect a sick soul at two in the morning in the depths of the countryside to fork out five dollars for a house call? And why should the hospital give Mr. Gamplin free board and lodgings and operating room time?

Such arguments infiltrated my mind like the coarse mutterings of a mediaeval tempter. My mind went round and round and never reached the point of presenting my case. It was Miss Fisher who nailed me down by asking flatly whether I was trying to get her to void Mr. Gamplin's bill.

I nodded vigorously.

"We'll have to see," she said. "But I can appreciate what you're saying."

"You can?"

She could. She was used to similar requests, although it was unusual for a patient's physician to make them. She would try to help, and she thought the state might come to Mr. Gamplin's rescue. If, after that, there was an outstanding balance, she had ways to deal with it.

I was relieved, and after thanking her for her generous advice, I asked her if she didn't think Dr. Saran and Dr. Moore would forgo their fees. The moment I asked I instinctively regretted it. The question just slipped out. Miss Fisher was one of those sympathetic people to whom one seemed drawn to unload one's soul, to ask advice and seek comfort.

For the next five minutes she addressed me as a mother superior might in counseling a troubled novice. She hinted that I had a lot to learn about the real world. She thought I would find it difficult and hazardous to broach such a delicate matter as fees to any doctor. Doctors, and here she smiled reminiscently, were extraordinarily sensitive about money matters. It was their private sanctum wherein the fees and schedules resided. Financial transactions were strictly private between a patient and physician. She had never, never, herself approached a doctor about his charges.

She paused, and for a moment a faraway look came into her eyes, as if she were reliving some specific poignant moment, and with a wry smile she confessed that there had been one occasion when she had been more than tempted to intervene.

As she saw me to the door, her last words were of caution: I'd be treading on thin ice, and I'd better be careful if I did venture onto it.

I left her office and headed for the medical clinic. On the way I decided that perhaps it would be wiser to table the question of the doctor's fees until I'd had another think.

That day, since I was so bent on spreading the gospel of charity, it seemed ironic that at the free medical clinic I should see two of my own patients from Albion.

I think they were as surprised to see me as I was disappointed to meet them. And I was itching to ask each why he had troubled to come all the way into Waterville when I was available in his own town. Didn't either of them trust my medical skills? Did they think that a doctor endorsed by Thayer Hospital to work in its clinic was a better bet than the new doctor on the block? Or was it a question of money—my fee for an office visit versus the cost of a twenty-six-mile car journey?

I was filled with indignation and hurt pride, but ethics and dignity prevented me from broaching the subject. Instead, I indulged my anger by taking an inordinate amount of time with them. If they wanted the royal treatment, they were going to get it. I was excessively polite and thoughtful, asking superfluous questions and listening intently to their rambling answers, which, if obvious, I asked to be repeated. My physical examination was meticulous. One man had trouble with his knee joint, the other abdominal discomfort, but I examined the ears, eyes, nose, throat, and the nervous system of both of them. They wanted the best service, and they were damn well getting it. At the end I suggested each return for a follow-up visit in two weeks, casually adding that they could, of course, see me in my office in Albion and there would be no charge.

Some months later an experienced, mellowed family doctor took me aside and told me it took five years to learn a bedside manner. And it took twice that for one's skin to grow thick enough. If it didn't, a heart attack was inevitable before one was fifty.

At present, my skin was so thin that I was as sensitive as a schoolgirl. I couldn't take being brushed off, criticized, or ignored, and I had a difficult time asking a favor. But at least I recognized myself as an angry young man when I left that medical clinic and went to find Jennifer.

Fortunately, she was good company in the car, chirping away like a bird about her college and ambitions. By the time I made the stop for the strep family I had cooled off. So had the family—all temperatures were normal.

The house call turned into a pleasant visit, with good humor all around and the children frolicking like a bunch of monkeys. I was offered a cup of coffee, as was my "daughter in the car."

The next few days passed routinely, and when I next dropped in to see Mr. Gamplin at the hospital, he was recovering well. I also had time to see Dr. Saran.

Perhaps I picked the wrong moment, or approach, or both. He seemed anxious to get away, especially after I started to comment on the decline of the farm in rural Maine. When finally I got around to asking him if he could forgo his fee, I was met with a hard stare and told that Mr. Gamplin was not the first patient in distressed circumstances that he had operated on. He added that he might appear uncaring, but it had occurred to him that Mr. Gamplin seldom dined at the Ritz. And for my information and even enlightenment, I should know that he always sent a bill for the standard fee. This allowed the patient to know that the work performed on him was worthwhile and had value. To receive such a bill did not undermine the patient's self-respect by thrusting charity down his throat. If, after receiving the bill, the patient asked for a reduction because of poverty, I could count on the fact that Dr. Saran would know whether to respond. He would like me to know that he was not a grasping individual, and being a native born in Maine, was not unaware of the financial embarrassments in the rural areas. And now, if I would excuse him, he was due to operate on another indigent patient.

After that I decided not to tackle Dr. Moore. Instead, he tackled me in the coffee shop. I felt a hand on my shoulder as he slid onto the stool beside me.

So, I was taking the hat around for Mr. Gamplin? Very commendable of me. Pity a few more referring physicians didn't go to bat for their patients. He'd just had a chat with Dr. Saran, who was going to waive his fee, and had urged him to do the same. As a result, Dr. Moore had told his office girl not to send a bill.

On the other hand, he didn't see why I shouldn't be paid. After all, I'd gone out into the boonies at an ungodly hour and deserved something for it. Besides, word spread quickly in the countryside, and before I knew it, if I set such a precedent, I'd be filing for bankruptcy. He paid for my coffee and English muffin and slipped off.

I suppose I learned something from all this, but I wasn't sure what. On Gamplin's last hospital day he had a heart attack. An internist, a cardiologist, and a pulmonary specialist were called in. Mr. Gamplin was transferred to an intensive care area for a week and remained in the hospital for a further twenty-one days.

Over that period, whenever I met Miss Fisher in the corridor, her fixed smile became gradually more glacial. But I made no more attempts to influence her or any doctor about the mounting bill.

It was the internist who suggested that Gamplin could go home

"He should stay, but I expect you could look in on him each day, couldn't you?" he said.

"I could. He only lives twelve miles down the road."

"I'm really discharging him on economic grounds. Miss Fisher said his bill was reaching the sky."

"Really! I expect she's getting worried."

"Yes. She hinted that the doctor's bills were getting up there, too. I told her I'd cut mine back."

The next day Gamplin was ready to leave the hospital. Jennifer's aunt had taken over his house, and the two women had made it clean and tidy. The effect was pleasing to everyone except the old boy himself, who "couldn't find a dang thing."

On my second visit, the aunt showed me a pile of bills on the kitchen table amounting to several thousand dollars. She pointed out that there wasn't one from me, but that I might as well send one, just for the record.

By the last of summer, Mr. Gamplin was on his feet and back to tending his bees. One day he drove over to Albion and parked his dilapidated truck in our yard. After looking him over in the office, I told him it was the last time he need see me.

"Guess so," he said. He stood up and reached into his back pocket for his wallet. "What do I owe you, Doc?"

I looked at him. I wasn't going to shove charity down his throat. A night call, transportation, assistance at the operating room, fifteen hospital visits, ten or more house calls, and now an office visit—

"Five dollars."

He methodically peeled off five ones and handed them to me. I thanked him.

"Just a minute, Doc. Where's the missus? Can she come to the truck?"

He went outside and I fetched Mary. We walked across the gravel drive to where Gamplin waited for us at the back of his pickup. He reached up and took a gallon jar in his arms and passed it to Mary.

"Honey, Mrs. Betts. One for you, and here's another for your husband. It's good honey; did it myself. Thanks for everything. Sorry for your trouble."

I never saw him again.

CHAPTER

B Y NOW IT WAS LATE FALL. The leaves had fallen and the clocks had been set back. I was in China, doing my last visit of the day, when I received a call from Mary. It was unusual for her to telephone me unless there was an emergency, but when we spoke she only said that there were one or two patients at the office.

"What's the problem then?"

"There's a patient—a woman sitting in her truck—and she can't get out. She's been here about half an hour and it's cold. Can you hurry?"

I had already come to rely implicitly on Mary's judgment in the practice. She had an instinct for what was necessary. I would never have gotten through all the scrapes and adventures of Eagle Lake and Albion without her help. She'd stand by with scissors and forceps when I was stitching up a gash, chaperon for a pregnancy, clean up the office, sterilize syringes, and keep the books.

There was one evening when a man came in clutching his hand, which was wrapped in a bloodstained towel. He'd brought an ax down on the back of it, and when I cleared away the blood I could see the severed tendons in their sheaths. They were still precisely in position, and I knew that if he moved his fingers or wrist, the tendons would retract up their sheaths and make the surgeon's task much more difficult; so I decided to tack them together with catgut.

I washed out the wound with a sterile solution and local anesthetic. Then I needed Mary's help. She stood beside me and handed me instruments and sutures as I brought each tendon together and sprinkled antibiotic powder into the wound before closing the skin. Mary found a short piece of wood I could use to splint the forearm and wrist. Any orthopedic surgeon reading this today would wince, as I do now. (Nowadays this situation would have a medical malpractice lawyer licking his anticipatory chops. Thank heavens in those years that that breed hadn't yet hatched, or mutated.)

But the impressive thing for me was Mary's stoic aid. That gash from the ax was a nasty sight, and most helpers would have passed out. I never dreamed, when first we met, that this would be one of her roles in my life.

I remembered Sister Euloge once asking me whether Mary was a nurse, and I had replied that she was an x-ray technician.

"Then how did you meet, Doctor?"

I told her the story of how one day, as a medical student, I had been examining a patient on a ward when I looked up to see the most beautiful, slim, blonde girl pushing a portable x-ray machine toward the door. I rushed to open it for her. All I received was a smile and a quiet thank-you, but I was hooked. So were what I estimated to be two hundred fellow students and half the junior staff. Who was the strawberry blonde?

After extensive research I found she worked in the depths of the x-ray department. Whenever I ventured into that sanctum, however, I found her either busy taking pictures of patients on their backs under some massive camera (and chaperoned by a middle-aged gorgon in a rubber apron), or closeted in some back room with a gaggle of radiology students. Either way, it would have been easier to date her by scaling a tower in some mediaeval castle.

My work suffered as I languished. By waiting in Whitechapel Road station, I learned that she took the London Underground northern line and changed trains at Moorgate station. She seemed to be either unaware of my existence or indifferent to it.

Then fate intervened. Hospital tradition had it that the final-year students put on the Christmas show. This was a big annual affair staged in the vast library, which was converted into a theater for the purpose. A group of students from Oxford were asked to write one part, and my friend Alan Young and I composed the other. The Oxford "playwrights" had the advantage of being led by David Oppenheimer, who had taken an honors degree not only in music, but in Greek and Latin before deciding to study medicine. He and a fellow student, John Blandy, wrote a short pantomime; Alan and I settled for a sophisticated musical comedy.

We then planned auditions. With delighted anticipation we realized that we needed two choruses of women and some female leads. We moved a piano into the bursar's office and advertised throughout the hospital for any nurse or technician to come for a tryout.

David sat at the piano and kept a yellow pad ready for assessing the auditioners. He was determined to keep the classification in Greek, giving alpha, beta, and gamma ratings for singing ability, charm, legs, and so on. It was a miracle of male chauvinism.

The turnout was terrific. Student nurses, ones we had been dying to address, suddenly appeared. After lots of charming explanations, they were asked to sing briefly and read a couple of lines. Then the door would be closed and David, after consultation, would pronounce:

"Gamma for legs; beta for charm. Next."

One of the next was my strawberry blonde.

She couldn't sing, and we could barely hear her voice when she read.

"Alpha for everything," I declared.

And it has been alpha ever since. I believe I proposed in Moorgate Station. Mary was dressed as a Girl Guide. In reply I got whatever is the Greek equivalent for "maybe."

It turned out that, like me, Mary was a Londoner and had experienced the Blitz. From this encounter with nightly bombing she had learned that a cup of tea could cope adequately with most emergencies. We had tea for breakfast on our honeymoon.

In Eagle Lake she had been capable of everything from chucking logs from the snow-drenched shed to the back door at four in the morning, to taking every type of telephone call and still attending to Sara and Ann, whom she bribed into silence with lollipops.

Mary said her most memorable telephone message of our northern Maine days had been from a lady in Plaisted (five miles north of Eagle Lake) who had said she would be having a baby during the following week. Mary asked if she wanted me to see her. No. Just wanted to make sure the doctor was around. Probably wouldn't need him—and she didn't.

Now, in Albion on a cold autumn night, Mary was anxiously waiting for me to return and deal with the evening office calls. It was just after seven o'clock and dark. As soon as I arrived she came over with a cup of steaming tea in her hand.

"Darling, before you go into the office you must see to this lady in the truck."

I walked over.

"She's been sitting there waiting for more than half an hour. She won't come in. I put a blanket over her and was about to give her this tea."

I could see a gray-haired, middle-aged woman in the driver's seat. She didn't look at me as I approached, and when I opened the door I could understand why: she was stone dead. Her bare arms were like ice, and her eyes were fixed, staring blindly at the windshield. I looked down. On the floor between her feet were a set of teeth.

Mary was behind me, but I made sure she couldn't see.

"Here's the tea," she said.

I turned and took it from her. "I'll give it to her. You'd better get back to the house. Tell the patients I'll be there in a minute."

As soon as Mary turned away I surreptitiously poured the tea onto the driveway.

"What did you do that for?!" Mary had seen. She came slowly to stand alongside, and caught sight of the teeth.

"How long has she been like that?"

"Half an hour, probably."

"But I spoke to her . . ."

"Did she reply?"

"No, but they often don't. I put a blanket over her shoulders."

I closed the truck door, and with my arm around Mary, walked her back to the house. It took a long time for her to recover. But when I said, "Always alpha for charm," she managed a smile.

"And Phi Beta Kappa for being you," I added.

She gave me another smile. "I'll call the undertakers. Your first patient is old Mrs. Foss."

"Oh, dear."

"Mickey Marden left us some steak."

"Wonderful."

"And I'll make you some fresh tea."

CHAPTER
30

RACIAL SEGREGATION WAS UNIVERSAL when I arrived in America, and on the medical front an iron curtain separated the allopathic physicians (M.D.) from the osteopathic (D.O.). Neither faction recognized the abilities or the existence of the other. In northern New England, the medical diocese of Boston, hospitals did not have M.D.s and D.O.s. on the same staff.

These racial and professional doctrines had been drummed into me at Trenton State Hospital, and I found that the M.D./D.O. standoff was also firmly established in Waterville, Maine. Each cult professed better training than the other; each had its own hospital.

In Unity there was a popular osteopathic physician, Dr. Hanscome. He lived in a white house opposite the drugstore. Rarely, when he was out of town, I would see one of his regulars in my office. I never converted one, though; they always went back to him.

I used to wonder why patients stayed with him when I, an M.D., was so close by. Surely people would know how inferior the osteopathic training was? How could anyone believe that every disease was caused by a misplaced piece of the backbone? These indignant questions flooded my mind, especially if my waiting room was deserted when I had expected it to be packed.

One day came an episode of triumph when Mrs. Sharon Brown entered my office. She was from a local family with a strong allegiance to Dr. Hanscome. She was in her twenties and had neat, dark features. Her brown eyes and firm mouth suggested a frank and determined attitude.

Sharon Brown was six months pregnant and wanted me to deliver her first baby. She confessed she had already been examined by another doctor.

"Another doctor?"

"Yes, Dr. Hanscome."

"I see," I murmured. "But you wanted to change because . . ."

She flushed and looked down. "We . . . we couldn't get along."

"Quite so," I said, at my smoothest.

After a few pleasantries I asked her the usual questions about her pregnancy and family history. She had some complaints: a little nausea during the first two months and now some swelling of her ankles.

So far so good. I asked her to wait and went to get Mary to prepare her for an examination. I stood on the porch feeling pleased.

When I returned, the patient was lying on the examining table. I said a few words to help her relax and wrapped the blood pressure cuff around her arm. Two readings showed her blood pressure was abnormally high, even allowing for first-visit nerves.

I listened to her heart and lungs. Mary readjusted the blanket.

I said, "I deliver my patients at Thayer Hospital. Do you mind?"

While she was telling me she had no preference, I gently pressed her ankles. The deep imprint of my fingers indicated an excessive retention of fluid.

Her abdomen was bigger than it should have been for a sixth-month baby. I asked her to check her dates. She was sure of them.

"You don't think I'm having twins, Doctor?"

"Would you like that?" I asked

She shook her head and smiled. "Twins don't run in my family."

I smiled back, but I was worried. I could feel nothing firm in her abdomen. Where I should have been encountering the bony outline of the fetus's head, shoulders, legs, or arms, my hands met nothing but a mass of soft dough.

I tried to control my anxiety as I continued the examination, but at last I stood back. I had a suspicion of what I was encountering, but I needed time to think. To gain that time, I listened with my stethoscope in four or five areas. Dead silence. No heartbeat.

"Is it one or two, Doctor?"

"I can't really tell. Have you felt any movements?"

"Oh, yes. Especially at night."

I forced a smile. "That's when babies are most active," I said.

I told her to get dressed and asked if she had brought a specimen of urine. It was important to see whether she was losing protein. Mary took over, and I left the room.

From the bookcase in the back room I took down a textbook on obstetrics. I needed to refresh my mind on a condition known as a hydatidiform mole. I soon had the page, and what I read there reinforced my suspicions.

A hydatidiform mole is a tumor of the placenta. It is a rare abnormality where the baby is never formed beyond a few cells, but the afterbirth grows into a huge mass of little balloons, or vesicles, made from the membranes.

There were two dangers for the patient. First the "tumor" could spread to the lungs and grow there. Secondly, it raised the blood pressure and affected the kidneys, with serious and even fatal consequences. The cure was surgery to remove the tumor. Possibly the womb would have to be sacrificed; if a portion of the tumor had penetrated the muscle wall it could grow again or cause a rupture.

I returned to the office, where my patient was now seated beside the desk.

"Mrs. Brown, are you certain you've felt movements?"

She nodded.

"But I don't see how that's possible."

Her eyes met mine. "Why? Isn't it usual at this time?"

"Yes, it is." I hesitated. "But I'm worried."

"Worried?"

"Yes. I hate to tell you, but I don't believe you're really pregnant with a child."

She stared at me with a white face: "That's stupid! Don't be silly. Not pregnant! What do you think *this* is?" She put her hands to the sides of her body. "Just ask anyone. Ask my mother. Ask my husband."

As sympathetically as I knew how, I tried to explain to her what I thought had happened. She was deaf to anything I had to say.

"Is your husband or mother with you?" I asked.

"My husband. Out in the truck."

"May I fetch him in?"

"You can. He won't believe you any more than I do."

From the window I could see there was only one truck in the parking area, a new red pickup. I walked out to the man seated at the wheel. His window was down and his elbow rested on the frame. He wore a red-checked lumberman's shirt with the sleeves rolled up. His head was shaved like a marine's. From his build and hostile gaze, he might have been one.

I introduced myself, and he gave me a curt nod.

"Mr. Brown, I've just seen your wife. I'm afraid there may be a serious problem."

He ran his tongue round his cheek. "Problem? What do you mean? Kid's wrong way up?"

I began to explain the problem to him. But it was difficult to make contact. I was at a disadvantage with him seated above me, abrasive and hostile. He continued to look at me with cold blue eyes, determined not to move. I told him my conclusion.

"Don't talk crap."

We stared at each other. "It isn't crap, Mr. Brown. Your wife may have a dangerous condition."

He turned away.

"Mr. Brown."

He looked me in the eyes. "May have? So you don't know, do you?"

"No, but I'm almost sure, and I can prove it to you. Let your wife be x-rayed at the hospital. If I'm right, it won't show the bones of the child. Also I'll arrange for a specialist to see her at the same time, so that you can have an independent opinion."

He gave a short laugh. "He'll say the same, won't he? You doctors always hang together."

"That's not fair. What have I to gain?"

"Don't make me laugh."

But he opened the truck door and made for the house. We entered the office. Sharon Brown had remained in her chair. I went and sat at my desk. Mr. Brown shut the door and leaned his back against it. Neither husband nor wife spoke, but they looked at me, united in their common opposition.

"I've told your husband, Mrs. Brown."

She turned toward him. "What do you think, George?"

"Crap. Same's I told you at Hanscome's."

I looked at him. "And what did Dr. Hanscome say? Did he advise an x-ray?"

"Maybe."

Another long silence. I went over the position again. I found myself pleading with them to have the proof from an X ray and the opinion of a specialist.

They looked at each other. I sensed they were weakening. I said it was too late in the day to go to Waterville. I would meet them there first thing in the morning. I'd book the x-ray and speak to a specialist. I left them to talk it over.

The brief reprieve let me vent my exasperation. I was mad with myself for getting personally involved in the problem. A good doctor should be able to view a patient's trouble with detachment. In a calmer frame of mind I returned to the office.

As if they were doing me a favor, the Browns said they might be at the hospital at 8:00 A.M. the following morning.

They left, and I gave Dr. Southern a call to ask him to see Mrs. Brown. Dr. Edward Southern was a certified gynecologist and another emigrant from Britain.

"You say a hydatidiform mole, old boy?" he said with an impeccable Oxford drawl. "By Jove, I haven't seen one of them since I was in the navy."

"When you were on submarine patrol, I assume?"

"Near miss, old boy. Actually, Aden. A charming Wren who'd been frolicking in the surf on Christmas Day."

"Of course."

"Cross my heart. My first and last hysterectomy on the equator. See you and your Mrs. Brown in the morning, eight o'clock in the Thayer foyer."

I wasn't at all sure he would. At eight we both were waiting. I explained to Dr. Southern that my patient and her husband were not like the general run of London society he had been used to.

"Don't fuss, old boy. I did my first American residency in Harlem."

Ten minutes later the Browns arrived. Mr. Brown was still belligerent and his wife quiet and reserved. I introduced Dr. Southern and told them he was very experienced in complicated pregnancies.

"You mean complicated crap."

Teddy Southern gave a guffaw of laughter. "Perhaps you're right, Mr. Brown. *Vox populi*, don't you know."

I shuddered, but oddly enough this bizarre, ultra-British manner seemed to thaw George Brown. Before long Dr. Southern was examining his wife in an alcove in the clinic.

"I'm afraid Dr. Betts has got it right," Dr. Southern said when he was finished. Mrs. Brown began to weep.

"I'm terribly sorry, Mrs. Brown. Frightful bad luck. But you must believe us," Dr. Southern continued. He took her hand. "Look, my dear, we'll take an x-ray. That will convince you that we've made the correct diagnosis. Then we can have a good long talk. I know it's terribly upsetting both for you and Mr. Brown."

By now two nurses had joined us and added their weight trying to persuade the Browns to take our advice. Ultimately it was Miss Fisher who managed to tip the scale. She had the uncanny knack of appearing on the scene at exactly the right moment.

Half an hour later the radiologist, Dr. Southern, and I stood before a viewing box. On the film, where the bones of a six-month fetus should have been, was a cloudy white mass.

"I also took a chest film," said the radiologist. "It's clear. No tumor." And he put the films on the box.

"With that picture, the history and physical examination, and the ton of protein in her urine, she's got a hydatid," said Dr. Southern. "The sooner we operate the better. Let's go and talk to them."

The Browns were seated in the outpatient waiting room. Dr. Southern elected to do the talking. He told them that we were now certain of our diagnosis and that it would be dangerous to postpone an operation.

"What operation?" asked Brown.

Dr. Southern explained that he would have to evacuate the tumor. He would try to save everything else.

"And what about the baby?"

"Mr. Brown, I've told you. There is no child."

"That's not true. Look at her. Look at her belly."

Dr. Southern took out the X rays and held them up to the light. He demonstrated the anatomy of the pelvis and the absence of any baby. The Browns were not convinced, even after Dr. Southern had obtained another X ray from a patient where the fetus could be seen. I added my voice to the argument.

It was a standoff. The Browns sat mute on a settee and Dr. Southern and I waited in silence before them.

Brown stood up. "C'mon Shar. Let's quit." He avoided our eyes and waited while his wife struggled to her feet.

They walked out.

"Oh, what fools we mortals be," murmured Dr. Southern. He shrugged his shoulders. "Let me know what happens."

I heard no more for a week. Then the telephone rang and I found I was talking to Dr. Hanscome. Mr. and Mrs. Brown were in his office. They had told him about going to Thayer Hospital. Would it be possible for him to see the X rays?

I told him that if Mr. Brown went to the hospital, I would arrange for the x-ray department to let him have them.

Three days later Mr. and Mrs. Brown entered my office. Mr. Brown placed an envelope on my desk.

"What can I do for you?" I asked.

"She's going into the hospital," said Mr. Brown.

"The Osteopathic?"

"No, Thayer. We want Dr. Southern."

I turned to Mrs. Brown and she nodded. Did she believe the diagnosis? From her silence I presumed she did. I said I was glad they had reached that conclusion, for I had been very worried. What had made them change their minds?

"Hanscome," said Mr. Brown. "We went to see him first. He'd said the same as you, but we thought he was up the creek and came to you. You was no different. Then this Dr. Southern fella said the same. He sounds like a queer, but she liked 'im. Believed 'im, in fact. Can't say I did. So we went back to Hanscome, and he reckons we'd better do as Dr. Southern says."

"So you have faith in Dr. Hanscome?"

"Always have and always will."

I telephoned Dr. Southern and made the hospital arrangements before they left the office. After I had seen the last patient for that day, I put through a call to Dr. Hanscome. I told him I had just seen Mrs. Brown, and she was going into hospital.

"She has great confidence in your opinion," I said.

He thanked me. He was pleased that I had agreed with his diagnosis of hydatidiform mole. It was a rare condition, and he had only seen two other cases, one when he was training.

"You mean you told the Browns there was no fetus?"

"Yes," Hanscome said. "They were reluctant to believe me, so I suggested they go to you for a second opinion."

"To me!"

"I think it's good to exchange ideas now and then. Perhaps we could meet sometime when you're free."

Mrs. Brown's operation was a success. She was happy to learn that she could have more children. She planned to use Dr. Hanscome as her obstetrician.

CHAPTER

31

CHRISTMAS WAS JUST AROUND the corner when we had our first blizzard. The snow was about six inches deep on the sidewalks and the roads had a dusting, but Mary and I had spent our apprenticeship on the highways of Eagle Lake, so getting around Albion was child's play. Now as I looked at the houses when I journeyed into Waterville I saw them sparkling with colored lights. The landscape on a crystal clear night looked like a fairyland. We began to receive cards from patients and party invitations from the hospital and staff. House calls were rounded off with cups of eggnog, and Keay's store was festooned with gifts.

The precise date of Christmas Day has been disputed over the centuries, but its association with happy, miraculous events remains strong. The spirit of Dickens's A *Christmas Carol* seems ever-present. By a remarkable coincidence, I was involved in a similar type of story in my Albion practice—my own Christmas miracle. It happened five days before our first Christmas in the community.

There were always some households in my practice area where I had to make visits at regular intervals, especially now that cold weather had set in. The Cornforth residence was one.

From the day I had opened my office door, Mr. Cornforth would walk up the hill to my office once or twice a week to ask me to see his wife because she was again suffering severe pain. Mrs. Cornforth was bedridden and had to be helped in everything she did. Both she and her husband were about seventy years old, and it was touching to see how devotedly he looked after her.

Mrs. Cornforth's chief problems were a paralyzed right leg and a weak left arm. She had to have a wheelchair at the bedside, and Mr. Cornforth was forced to take her to the toilet as if she were a child. He would cook all the meals, and she preferred to be fed in her bed. Sometimes she was in pain, and when it was severe I would be summoned to give her relief.

Whenever I saw her I had difficulty in finding the cause of any of her complaints. Her pains would change from place to place, and when I examined her she would say that my touching her was agonizing. As I palpated this or that part on her body she would stiffen to bear the trauma like a stoic martyr.

It was after the second or third visit that I suspected that Mrs. Cornforth was an hysteric. When I examined both her legs they appeared identical; there was no muscle wasting. By asking the same question in different forms about her sense of feeling in the bad limb, I would often obtain conflicting responses. More telling was the fact that her reflexes—knee and ankle jerks and the way her toes responded to stimulation—showed no evidence of a nerve lesion. Similar results came when I examined her arm.

Mr. Cornforth had told me that his wife had been a cripple for more than thirty years. He had never been able to leave her for more than a day. She had been seen by many specialists, and had visited the finest clinics in Boston and New York. No one had been able to find out what was wrong with her. He had spent a fortune on her care, and with dwindling funds they had retired to a simple home in Albion.

Due to terrible abdominal pain she had been in the hospital for a week just before I had come to town. The surgeons had refused to operate, though both Mr. Cornforth and his wife had begged them to make an exploration. I had looked up her hospital record—a thick folder of notes crammed with reports from the radiology and laboratory departments and letters from consultants. Everything was normal, and the conclusions of the many physicians had been consistent: Mrs. Cornforth was an hysteric and should have psychiatric help.

I had discussed these findings with her husband. He refused to believe that there was nothing physically wrong with his wife. It was we doctors who were failing to discover the cause.

I didn't press him, because I knew it would be fruitless. I was also particularly cautious in dealing with her, for I remembered an extraordinary lesson I had once received about the pitfalls of giving a patient the diagnosis of hysteria.

It was during a teaching round in my last days as a medical student. I was one of six students awaiting the arrival of Dr. James Hamden, a junior physician on the teaching staff at the London Hospital. He was a rising star in the medical firmament and was thought to be the most exciting and dynamic teacher on the staff. As students, we were lucky to have him for the three months of our medical rotation.

Dr. Hamden must have been in his mid-forties and had enormous energy. He sported a luxurious handlebar mustache, and his dark brown eyes often would light up with laughter at some point during his round as he recalled some amusing anecdote. He could expound on any medical condition with infectious enthusiasm.

On this particular day he came bounding up the stairs to Rothschild Ward while his intern, loaded down with a raft of x-ray folders, plodded along a flight behind.

"Good afternoon, gentlemen—and ladies." Dr. Hamden grinned. *"I always forget you two, sorry."* He nodded toward Margo and Hilary, who together with Jack, Jim, George, and me made up his group of students.

"Now, before we go in the ward I want to tell you that you are going to see the most fantastic case of your lives. Fantastic! I myself have never seen anything like it, and I'll guarantee you never will in all the years ahead of you.

"He's a forty-seven-year-old man, a printer. Married. Happy home life. Two children. Suddenly he starts having bouts of weeping. His wife asks him what troubles him, and he complains of every bizarre symptom under the sun: indigestion, pain in his right foot, pain in his shoulder, pain everywhere, headaches all the time. Says he can't breathe. Then he itches. On and on he goes.

"He's been like this for months and is driving his wife mad. He's seen dozens of doctors and no one can find anything wrong with him, so they sent him to me in my chambers in Harley Street for an opinion. I've brought him in for investigation and observation, and he's going to be under your care, Betts, so take a good history. He only arrived this afternoon, but we'll have a look at him right away, because he's such an excellent lesson for you. Follow me."

He swept into the ward and greeted Sister: "Where have you put Mr. Elttingham?"

She led him to the first bed, and we gathered around. The patient was curled up, clutching his pillow.

Dr. Hamden bent over and spoke to the patient quietly. I heard him explain that we were students and ask if he minded our being told about his case.

"You're not in too much pain?"

Mr. Elttingham tried to shake his head.

Hamden turned to us. "Fantastic case. Come over here."

We all followed him across to the far window and out of earshot of the patient.

"Now, I'm going to ask him to get out of bed and walk the four or five yards to the x-ray viewing box and back. Watch his gait. Watch it. You really don't need a history and physical in this case, because the gait is absolutely diagnostic. And if you don't get the diagnosis right first time, none of you deserve to hang out a shingle. None of you."

He went back to the bed. "Sister, we'd like Mr. Elttingham to get up and walk over there and back. Tell him to take his time."

While Sister helped the patient out of bed, Dr. Hamden joined us. We stood like a group of conspirators. "Just watch this," he said in a loud, theatrical whisper.

Mr. Elttingham took a long time to sit up on the edge of his bed. Sister stood by to help him, but Dr. Hamden motioned her away.

Then in a clumsy, staggering walk Elttingham lurched across the ward. One leg dragged behind the other, an arm clawed the air and his head shook with a coarse tremor as he reeled toward the x-ray box. He didn't make a sound as he turned and repeated the same gyrations going toward his bed. Sister was there to help him.

Dr. Hamden went over. "You all right, Mr. Elttingham? Good. Thank you."

Twisting his mustache, his eyes glinting with excitement, Hamden returned to us. Still in a loud stage whisper he asked: "Well, what do you think, eh? That gait. Fabulous. Absolutely fantastic. That gait tells you everything. What do you think, Betts?"

"I was thinking of some advanced neurological disorder like—"

"Nonsense. There is nothing that will produce a picture like that. What do you say, Mr. Rogers?"

"Syphilis, sir?"

"Not even on the cards. Anyone got an idea?"

We all hazarded a guess at the diagnosis. Of course, none of us had had the advantage of taking a history or examining the patient, and Dr. Hamden knew it and made an allowance. He was anxious to press on with the teaching aspects.

"It's the gait. You don't need to see anything more. Ladies and gentlemen, this is hysteria. Hysteria—nothing more, nothing less."

He paused to let it sink in.

"You are seeing the most classic case of hysteria you will ever encounter in your life."

And for five minutes he went on to give a brilliant dissertation on the salient features of hysteria, invoking Freud, Charcot, Mesmer, Henry Head, and a host of other authorities. We all looked at each other, impressed with the vigorous and amazing demonstration.

Meanwhile there was a diversion at the x-ray viewing box, where Hamden's intern was shuffling through some films. After a moment he hurried over to Dr. Hamden and interrupted his flow of teaching.

"Yes, yes. What is it?" Hamden almost shook him off.

"I think you had better see the pictures for yourself, sir."

We all clustered in front of the fluorescent screen, which glowed brilliantly in the dim light of the ward. The intern put up an X ray of Mr. Elttingham's pelvis.

Even we, not experienced in viewing such pictures, could see the white splotches and the myriad of little white dots breaking up the bones. The man was riddled with cancer.

Hamden stared at the films in silence. Finally he asked, "And the chest?" The intern put up another film. A mass the size of a grapefruit obliterated the lower part of one lung.

Dead silence prevailed as further films went up on the screen. There was hardly a bone that was not partially replaced by spreading tumor.

I have always remembered Dr. Hamden's next words: "I told you this would be the biggest lesson you'd ever learn. It is for me.

Beware of jumping to conclusions and labeling anyone an hysteric or a neurotic. Rule out everything else first."

So I was being cautious with labeling Mrs. Cornforth. Then, five days before Christmas, my miracle took place. Mr. Cornforth, as he walked to the entrance of Keay's store, slipped on the ice and broke his leg. I was across the road in my office when they came to fetch me. When I examined Mr. Cornforth he exhibited the classic signs of a broken head of the femoral bone.

In a matter of minutes we had him splinted, relieved of pain and the possibility of shock, and on the way to Thayer Hospital in a station wagon. I followed, and within the hour we had Mr. Cornforth in the x-ray department. Later that morning an orthopedic surgeon "fixed" his hip while I had my usual role as assistant.

When I arrived home I made a quick trip to see how Mrs. Cornforth was getting along. I was let in by one of the neighbors, Mrs. Glowearth, and found Mrs. Cornforth sitting in a chair. The room was warm and had been decorated for Christmas. A small tree twinkled with lights in one corner. It hadn't been there two days previously. But Mrs. Cornforth had not been able to sit in a chair two days ago either.

"Just thought I'd look in and tell you that Charlie is doing fine," I said. "We might be able to get him home for Christmas. But we'll have to make some changes here. He'll have trouble getting around for a while."

"That's all right, Doctor, "said Mrs. Glowearth. She was a heavily-built woman in her mid-forties with short hair and glasses. She and her husband lived in the house on the other side of the road. "We can be in and out to give them a hand. Not that they'll need much help."

I gave her a puzzled look.

Mrs. Glowearth smiled. "Just watch." And she turned to Mrs. Cornforth. "Go on, Edith. Show the doctor."

Well, it might not have been as dramatic as Lazarus rising from the tomb or loaves and fishes appearing on the table, but Mrs. Cornforth getting out of her chair and crossing to the sink was good enough for me.

"I was as shaken as you, Doc," continued Mrs. Glowearth. "I've known Edith more than ten years, and I've never seen her out of bed without help. Look at her now. When I came over first thing, she was in bed, same as usual. I told her about poor Charlie and said I'd be back to help with the chores. It wasn't an hour later, I let myself in and there she's up at that table. You could have knocked me down with a feather."

I must say, it took me a minute or two to adjust.

"Mrs. Cornforth, let me see you walk across the room."

She gave me a smile and went from the sink to the table and then back to her chair.

"What about the pain?"

"What pain?"

The day after Charlie Cornforth came home, I made another visit. It was almost comical. There he was, propped up in bed, and Edith was serving him his lunch. And it was as if she had undergone a personality change; she was almost chatty, the very reverse of the morose, pain-ridden woman I had known before.

There was an extraordinary and ironic sequel. I hope it wasn't scripted in heaven. Six weeks later Mrs. Cornforth went to Keay's store to replenish her cupboard. It was a bitter January day with a mixture of ice and snow on the ground.

She fell down and broke her leg about two yards from where her husband had done the same thing.

CHAPTER

32

A S WE CAME INTO MERRY MAY in Albion, with all its false hopes of spring and darling buds, Mary and I felt we were only just keeping our heads above water. In spite of the town's assurance of a five-thousand-dollar guaranteed income, when the cash flow went down to a trickle, we both in the wee hours envisioned the specter of ruin and bankruptcy.

Actually, if we had known that what was on the books was going to realize less than half its value, we'd have been even more panic-stricken. Mary kept the ledger and made her entries at the kitchen table. She had not yet seen the emerging pattern of several patients running a tab.

What really pushed the panic button were the days when I would return from the hospital to find the waiting room empty. I was sure that all the sick were seeking help elsewhere. I was convinced that the osteopath in Unity was draining off my practice, that people were sneaking into Waterville to see specialists, that specialists were sneaking into Albion. But there was nothing I could do about it except gloomily visualize a return to Trenton and look at the vacancies advertised in *The British Medical Journal* for assistants in Malaya or the Fiji Islands.

Mary would try to shake me out of my acute, bleak, paranoid depression by organizing outings with the children. Sometimes it was to Unity Lake or Lovejoy Pond. Occasionally we steered a course for Belfast, on the coast. In those days a journey down Route 137 to Belfast was certainly a diversion and would satisfy most souls needing a shake. Next to the Monte Carlo Rally, the road was probably as good a test as any for the durability of a vehicle.

Nor was Belfast, especially in early spring, the reward Monte

Carlo would have been. It was then a gray, seedy town that had seen better days at the turn of the century, when seafaring clipper captains and owners had viewed the horizon from lofty homes that were now falling apart. The shore could only be found by crossing the river to Searsport and plunging through undergrowth to the ever-receding sea.

But the practice's activity was as capricious as Maine weather. It could change in a twinkling of an eye, and we could become as busy as a pair of one-armed paperhangers. I say we because somehow, in spite of the demands of the children, Mary became the office manager and general factotum.

There were times when the waiting room was packed. Our record activity, our climax, came one spring evening when I was returning from a house call somewhere miles south of Freedom. I had visited a young pregnant girl who was bleeding severely.

In those days I carried Dextran intravenous fluid and a kit for such emergencies, for there was no ambulance service. So, with her mother giving a helping hand, we laid the girl down in the back of the Pontiac and headed for the hospital. Since this involved passing through Albion, I pulled into the driveway between several parked cars and a truck and sought Mary for a briefing.

She met me at the back gate to say that one of the undertakers was bringing in a man from Benton who had had a heart attack and was "pretty bad."

I went into the office. Here I found a patient beside my desk. She explained that hers was the last seat in the house. I stuck my head round the door and confirmed her statement when I saw that the waiting room was full and an overflow had seated themselves on the stairs all the way up to the landing.

"It reminds me of a Christmas game—you know, musical stairs," said the lady at my elbow when I returned to my desk.

A couple of vigorous turns of the telephone handle brought Mrs. Bessey on. She connected me with the hospital, and I warned the receiving nurse to expect my hemorrhaging patient and probably a cardiac case.

Mary came in and beckoned me into the annex. One of my heart patients had taken acutely ill. The exchange went something like this:

"Where's he? China Lake?"

"No. Upstairs,"

"Where?"

"On our bed."

"Good Lord!"

"He's having a hard time breathing."

"Our bed? I don't mind that, but you mean you got him up the stairs in his state? Why not use the old couch on the porch?"

"The man with the heart attack is on it."

"No he isn't; he's coming in Brown and Norton's hearse from Benton."

"This is another one."

"Which other one?"

I went through to the porch. Indeed there was a man on the couch. One glance and touch were enough. His hands were stiff and cold, his eyes sightless, and there was no heartbeat.

As I placed a blanket over him, I noticed a black Cadillac hearse pulling in beside the church. I looked up at Mary.

"Where are the relatives of this one?"

"Just his wife, Mrs. Cheerly. She went home for some clothes."

"Head her off, or call her, and tell her I need to speak with her. Don't give her the news."

I went out to meet the undertakers to tell them that they might have a body to deal with. In reply they said a patient of mine from Benton was lying in the back of their hearse at this moment. Seemed he'd had a heart attack.

It was the first time I had examined a patient in a hearse, and I found it cramped. (The only other time I had ministered to the sick for a long time in a half-bent position had been while delivering a baby in a thatched cottage near Stonehenge. It was curious how my mind dwelt on such irrelevancies in difficult situations.) I also thought that having a hearse in the parking lot during my rush hour was not propitious. The only good point, I suppose, was that it showed me that I could achieve emotional detachment in trying circumstances.

Even in my doubled-up position, I immediately recognized the patient as a man I had been treating, and at once confirmed the diagnosis of a heart attack. I crawled out and found my bag in my car, taking the opportunity to reassure the girl and her mother that they'd be on their way to hospital in a couple of minutes.

Then, with the bag on the hood of the car, I drew up a dose of morphine and went back to the hearse. For convenience the undertakers had partly slid the patient out on a stretcher, and I was able to inject him in a vein.

Within seconds he felt better.

"You should take him to Thayer right away," I said. "Then come back and pick up the man on the porch. If his wife wants another funeral home, I'll leave a message for you at the hospital front desk."

I found Mary in the kitchen and we brought each other up to date. Our prime need was for someone to take my car with the pregnant girl into Waterville. Mary said she'd arrange it and deal with the girl and mother.

Next I clambered up the stairs, scattering words of apology to the patients who squeezed aside to let me by, and I entered our bedroom.

Lying against a pile of pillows was a middle-aged man, blue about the lips and breathing so heavily he could barely speak. His wife was seated on the edge of the bed.

She rose to her feet, twisting her hands with embarrassment: "I'm ever so sorry for me and Harry to be in your—"

I gave her a broad smile and reminded her that I had invaded their bedroom at least three times on house calls.

"This bed," I said, to put her at her ease, "was donated by Mr. and Mrs. Honkton, of Vassalboro. Curtains by Robinson's Store; chairs from the barn." She gave a faint smile and took herself to a chair.

But it was fortunate that I had seen her husband in his home and knew his hospital record and treatment. He had rheumatic heart disease and had been in borderline heart failure for the last year. From the way he looked now, he was over that border and heading for next and last.

With all these acute cases at once, I thanked my stars that I had been the cardiac intern at the London Hospital and an emergency room officer. I had seen and handled numerous heart attacks, cases of heart failure, and bleeding.

I went down to the office (more apologies) and found a fresh sterile syringe (Mary always boiled three or four up in a certain saucepan as we went along). Again I took up a dose of morphine and returned upstairs. I checked the patient's chest and heart, gave him an injection, and told his wife I'd be back in ten minutes.

Back to the kitchen, where Mary said young Clyde Higgins would drive my car to the hospital. He was waiting for me in the driveway. The wife of the man on the porch was in my office.

"What about the bright lady who was seated at my desk?"

"She said she'd find a place on the bottom stair."

I managed in the next few minutes to talk to Higgins and send him on his way. I re-examined the man in my bedroom and found him improved. I told his wife that we'd get him home when the office work was done. Next I talked to the dead man's wife in my office, and persuaded her to accept Brown and Norton's ministrations.

It was approaching nine o'clock before I finally put my head in the waiting room to say that I'd start seeing people. It was interesting that during all this time, as far as I could tell, no one had left.

But I was not reckoning with fate. I had just sat down at my desk when I heard the crash. A car coming up over the hill from Unity had hit another vehicle turning out of the Palermo Road, just opposite Marden's gas pumps. Moments later they came to fetch me. Four people were involved, and one was dead.

Nothing like this simultaneous deluge of accident and sickness ever happened again. That all this should have taken place in a single night still seems extraordinary.

Nevertheless, on the tenth day of the following month we were still short of cash, although Mary said the amount on the books looked promising.

CHAPTER

33

I N SUMMERTIME THE lakes region of central Maine was filled
with the sound of children and teenagers at camp. They came from
every state, some from affluent families, each child equipped ap-
propriately to receive instruction in tennis, horseback riding, and
lacrosse. Some camps were run by religious organizations, which interspersed Bible study and dogma with swimming, volleyball, and
sing-along. Scout camps roughed it with overnight canoe trips, life-
saving, fire-making, and knot-tying. The music camps allotted space
behind remote trees for individual practice, and a hall for concerts
and performances before teary-eyed mothers and anxious fathers.

Many camps had names that were loosely based on Indian words,
such as Metoka, Tangeli, Manaskas. Others went New England formal: Camp Somerset, East Pond Camp, and Camp Lown.

When I set up practice in Albion in the mid-1950s, every camp
was packed and thriving in the summer. Buses, cars—even trains—
were disgorging hordes of little people in search of sunshine and freedom, fresh air and companionship. The local general practitioners
were stretched to the limit because each camp had to have a doctor
on call, and demand exceeded supply. It wasn't long before I was asked
to look after two large camps in the Belgrade Lakes region. This commitment meant a daily journey for me of about twenty miles from
Albion, and an occasional special trip when there was an emergency,
but the retaining fees made it worthwhile.

Both camps had resident nurses who knew the ropes and kept
me out of trouble. Sick call was held in one camp at 9 A.M., and about
an hour later in the other. My only experience of this type of thing had
been on the receiving end, during my first days in the R.A.F. in Africa.

There you only joined the line if you were feeling terminally ill and it was a toss-up between facing an ex–Boer War sergeant or St. Peter.

In contrast, the line at my first summer camp, an outfit sponsored by a wealthy sect in New York, was remarkably boisterous and excessively long. It began at the nurse's station and wound around a tree or two before disappearing behind the dining lodge on the edge of the lake. The campers were mostly teenagers with a language of their own, based on a New York dialect.

Fortunately the camp nurse was a tough middle-aged woman who had achieved tenure by the skin of her remaining teeth. At the end of the season I knew it was to her I owed my sanity and job security. Her name was Nurse Grizbon, and she was referred to by the inmates, out of earshot, as "Old Grizzly."

Nurse Grizbon held the reins and guided me through my first day with a firm hand. Without her I would still have been seeing campers by the light of the evening star. I had not realized that I would have to meet the entire camp population in single file on opening day. It was boiling hot, and no one could go swimming until his medical form was reviewed. One look at the line sent me into a panic. There were patients waiting to see me at the hospital, and I had house calls and afternoon office hours in Albion.

Each camper presented a long questionnaire detailing his or her medical history, immune shots, and allergies. Each document also included an elaboration on his medical condition and his parent's preferences for treatment.

It was slow going. New York seemed to have an unusually high incidence of ragweed, pollens, assorted dusts, insects, vermin, and sulfur emissions. Practically every child came equipped with vaccines to combat the onslaught, and they had to be injected at frequent and precise intervals. Logging the innumerable bottles and deciphering prescriptions took forever. Each child was anxious that I should understand the specific instructions given by his New York doctor.

Acne, in both sexes, was rampant at an age when facial appearance was vital. Girls arrived with pint bottles of antibiotic lotion to fight this adolescent blight. With one young blonde I felt impelled to give a homily on the abuse of antibiotics, but before I could get into my stride, Nurse Grizbon managed to divert me.

By the time the end of the line dragged into sight I was exhausted. The thought of facing the next camp was appalling. Nevertheless, although two hours late, I reported there. This one was a scout camp. The medical form was five lines long, and campers sailed by like a flight of birds. They were all girls about ten years old and not allergic to anything. Acne, insomnia, crying fits, and similar problems were not on their menu. An hour later, everyone was splashing and shrieking in the lake and I was on my way back to the hospital.

From then on the job became a pleasure. Medical complaints in both camps, with one exception, were trivial, and I was often able to linger at the lakeside and enjoy the marvelous surroundings. Maine in every season is glorious, but summer at the lakes, with the flawless blue sky, the sun dancing on the water against a background of green hills, is unsurpassable. To sit at the foot of a tree and watch the children laughing and playing was a splendid entertainment. Sometimes I would get a night call, and in the sharp chill of evening I would walk between the silent pines and look up in wonder at the myriad of stars twinkling with brilliant clarity.

The New York camp did provide some excitement. Thirteen-year-old Jeremy Cohen complained of feeling sick at dinner time. As soon as he reached the sick bay he had a pain in his abdomen and vomited. Nurse Grizbon tracked me down at Thayer Hospital. I went to the camp, and we both agreed that the probable diagnosis was acute appendicitis. I said he should be taken to the hospital to see a surgeon.

Dr. Saran was on vacation, but there was a new surgeon in town. Dr. Richard Hornberger had recently set up practice in Waterville, having just returned from serving as a surgeon in Korea. His major field was thoracic surgery, and he had trained in New York. Horn-

berger was a giant of a man from coastal Maine, and combined the
laconic brevity and pithy humor of his home state with the sophisti-
cation of Manhattan. We got on well from the first, and I had sent him
a few patients.

Eventually we would even share an office when I needed a base
in Waterville. And when I did, the arrangement worked well. While I
saw an occasional patient, Hornberger spent most of his time drinking
tepid coffee and writing short stories about Korea, His book eventually went into print as *M.A.S.H.*

It was about 7:00 P.M. when we assembled at the hospital to
admit Jeremy. As usual Miss Fisher had materialized and smoothed
the arrangements for admission. Dr. Hornberger, in an unexpectedly
shy but gentle manner, questioned and examined our patient. The
laboratory confirmed the diagnosis. Dr. Hornberger said he ought
to operate right away.

"There's the matter of getting parental permission," I said.

Nurse Grizbon had brought in Jeremy's file from the camp. His
parental permission form allowed us to give medicines, but for any
surgery we had to call a Manhattan number. She gave the file to Hornberger.

"He lives in the right neighborhood. Maybe I'd better make the
call." He turned to me. "I speak the language," he explained.

He sat at the nurse's desk and dialed long distance. I heard it ring-
ing and after a moment or two I could hear a well-disciplined voice.

"Who?" asked Hornberger. I heard another rhythmically slow
reply.

"Ambassador! Jesus!"

A pause. A faster garbled sound.

"In Mexico? Where? You don't quite know?"

Longer pause. "Consulate! Do you have the number?" Pause.
"But how—? Oh, for God's sake. O.K., O.K. Thank—thank you.
Thank you so much."

He replaced the telephone and stood up. I waited while he lit a cigarette. Then he said, "His father is ambassador to Luxembourg, Lithuania, Ruritania, or something. He and his wife are cruising around Mexico. The flunky doesn't know where."

"So what do we do now?"

"Try the American consulate in Mexico City, I guess."

It took about three hours to trace Jeremy's parents. Heaven knows what the telephone bill was, but ultimately a red-faced, exasperated Dr. Hornberger spoke to Jeremy's father.

Ambassador Cohen had grave reservations about the ability of an unknown surgeon in Maine, and about it being safe to remove his son's appendix in that domain.

Dr. Hornberger's language began to resemble parts of his forthcoming book. It ranged between icy comments and red-hot expletives.

"We don't operate with wooden forks and spoons up here," was one of his lighter replies.

"Maine was incorporated in 1820," was another.

"Sure, and I could remove his lung if it was called for."

"Call Columbia and ask if they remember Hawk-eye."

"Hawk-eye. H, A, W, K—Oh, for Christ's sake! Call your own Foggy Bottom, if you know how."

Even so, the ambassador, no doubt well-versed in tense negotiation, persisted in exploring Dr. Hornberger's qualifications and the background of Thayer Hospital. Surgeons who had trained Hornberger were called to verify his capabilities. The army came back with a report on his spell in a Korean surgical unit.

Finally, around midnight, we got the go-ahead. Hornberger by then was seething with frustration. He was torn between his moral duty as a doctor to attend an emergency and his frustration at being forced to reason with a stubborn father who had legal rights and a heavy load of ignorance.

The operation took place in total silence. Just the sound of suction and the clink of instruments. Hornberger didn't even comment on my talent as an assistant. Everything went well. An inflamed appendix was removed, and Jeremy was returned to the ward in stable condition.

Miss Fisher offered to give the good news to the ambassador, and neither Hornberger nor I objected.

A week later I met Dr. Hornberger in the hall. He was in a genial mood and gave me a welcoming grin.

"I sent that Mexican grunt a fat bill and put one in for you. Bastard."

"He wasn't a Mexican. He was just visiting."

"Well, screw him anyway." He paused to light a cigarette. (He was the second thoracic surgeon I had met who got through two to three packs a day.) "Say, I've got a job right in your line. You free next Sunday afternoon?"

I nodded.

"Camp Bombazine. They've got five hundred Boy Scouts coming in. They have to be checked before they're allowed to swim. Got a stethoscope?"

"Yes."

"O.K. I'll see if I can snag one. Meet me there at three o'clock. I've got a tee time at five. We ought to get an operation or two by looking after them for a season."

But I'm glad to report we didn't.

A year or two later Hornberger's wife called me. "Dick's sold his book, and they're going to make a movie."

All I can say is that any resemblance between Hawk-eye and Dr. Hornberger is very close.

CHAPTER
34

THE ONLY OTHER SOURCE OF medical advice in the immediate area was the osteopathic physician, Dr. Hanscome. However, in spite of his friendly invitation after the Sharon Brown affair, I had never consulted with him. Hanscome had a big following. It would have been easier to land a salmon out of Unity Pond than snare one of his patients. The only time I netted one was when he went away on vacation. It was only a temporary arrangement; as soon as Hanscome returned, the patient rejoined the ranks as though he'd been AWOL.

I found it difficult to understand why the public had this preference. Osteopathic therapy was based on attributing all ailments to bone displacement, especially of the back. How could any sane individual accept that? But osteopathic physicians were licensed to use medicines and could supplement their bone manipulations with antibiotics and pain pills. Sometimes I wondered, ironically, whether a patient with a strep throat received a preliminary neck twist before a jab of penicillin.

For some M.D.s, all osteopathic physicians were beyond the pale. To mention anything favorable about them within earshot of Dr. Frederick Hill was the equivalent of putting a firecracker in his shorts.

On the other hand, if osteopaths were "inferior," as the M.D. world asserted, why didn't they get into more trouble with difficult obstetrics, blood transfusions, and so on? It seemed they must be doing most things right or they would be sued out of existence. And their patients swore by them, loyal as the legions of Rome.

Dr. Hanscome and I seldom came into direct contact. If we passed each other in our cars or on the street, we'd wave and give a short greeting. But there our social and professional interaction ceased. Then, one evening, I came to understand part of the D.O. secret, the basis on which they were so revered by their patients.

One of the selectmen asked me to visit a young woman nearby who was mentally ill and might need commitment to a mental hospital. She'd been making threats and had odd and dangerous ideas about the use of fire. The sheriff had been called in twice. Two doctors were needed by law to certify that a patient should be committed to an institution. I was to be one of them.

"It's Dawn Spooner. She married young Jim, works at the mill in Thorndike," said the selectman. "They're living with his mum and dad, just after you cross the railroad tracks. Rucksome's—third house on the left. Doc Hanscome said he'd be there 'bout six."

"I've got office hours at seven."

"Maybe you'd better go now. I'll tell Doc Hanscome."

"You mean you want *me* to consult with an osteopathic physician?"

"Sure. What's wrong with that? You both treat the sick, don't you? It don't say nothing on this committal form about what kind of doctor you have to be."

By now I had at least learned not to argue with the public, and certainly not with their elected representatives. I'd already had a run-in with the local state trooper for doing eighty miles per hour at two in the morning. I didn't argue then, and it was only when he discovered that I was on my way to see his pregnant wife that he put away his ticket pad and led the way.

"O.K., I'll be there," I told the selectman.

On the way I tried to recall the correct approach to the mentally sick. I hadn't met many obvious ones except a plumber's wife who, although she thought she was connected to the electric light and was a squaw, was pretty docile—unless you switched on the light. Her husband used to remove the fuse before I made a house call.

Of course, I had done some basic psychiatric training at Trenton State Hospital, and learned to do a mental status appraisal—a systematic questioning to see whether a mental patient was oriented in time and place, intellectually sound, had an intact memory, and so on. Dr. Sharp hadn't been too impressed with my ability, but I didn't know what else to do in this case.

As I looked for the house, I speculated somewhat sardonically about what Dr. Hanscome's approach would be. Did bone manipulation come into the treatment of delusions and hallucinations? A Ford parked in the driveway with a plate displaying the letters "D.O." showed he'd already arrived.

The door was opened by an agitated middle-aged woman in bedroom slippers. "You Dr. Betts? I'm Mrs. Rucksome. The *doctor's* here already."

She left me at the door and clambered up the stairs. From above I could hear someone crying, and there were shouts of "No, Cheryl, you're not to."

I closed the door, took off my overshoes, and with bag in hand made my way up to the landing. Here a big man in his shirt sleeves, looking like a variation on Rodin's *The Thinker,* leaned on the banister and gazed at me gloomily.

"Dr. Betts," I said.

He inclined his head. "She's in there."

The bedroom was crowded. The centerpiece was a bed, and on top lay a young woman in a nightdress and dressing gown. Her blonde hair was disheveled, and her face was blotchy and freckled and bore remnants of eye makeup that had been distorted by tears. She kept staring out the window and clenching her hands.

Everyone turned toward me as I entered the room: three women and two men. All except one were dressed in rural Maine attire of multicolored wool. The exception, Dr. Hanscome, was in a tailored dark suit, white shirt, and tie. He was about fifty-five, medium build, and his silver hair was smoothly brushed back.

He came forward with the assurance of a *maître d'hôtel,* hand outstretched. "Glad to see you, Doctor. This is Cheryl, and here is her husband." He gestured round the group, making the introductions with quiet charm.

"Cheryl has been a little upset—so much that she can't stop crying, can you dear?" he said.

He moved toward the bed and removed a laundered handkerchief from the top pocket of his jacket. The girl took it from him and blew her nose.

"Perhaps you'd like to talk to her first, Doctor," said Hanscome, stepping back.

I nodded, but approached the patient's husband. He was a thin, sulky looking man in his twenties. He was partly sitting on a dressing table, cleaning his nails with a penknife.

"How long has she been this way?" I asked him.

He looked at me as if he didn't comprehend the language. "Gee, I dunno. Guess about a month—eh, Ma?"

"More like six weeks," an overweight woman in trousers said emphatically.

"Seven," echoed another.

"Too damn long," came a voice from the landing.

I went to the bedside. There was no chair, so I sat on the edge of the bed. The patient looked at me for an instant, then turned her head away toward the window.

"How are you feeling, Cheryl?" I asked.

She didn't answer, and while I waited, Dr. Hanscome crept forward and retrieved a hot-water bottle from the edge of the bed. He tiptoed toward the bathroom bearing it aloft in explanation of his motive. He moved cautiously, as if trying to avoid interrupting a prayer meeting. "I'll just refill this. Make her feel better," he whispered as he passed one of the women.

"Let me help you, Doctor," she said, following him.

"Cheryl, do you know who I am?" I asked. This was question one on the Trenton admission form.

No reply.

I repeated it. Then: "Do you know where you are?"

"She knows that all right," said the heavy woman. "In our house, that's where she is."

Dr. Hanscome crept back with the hot-water bottle and placed it gently at Cheryl's side.

"What day is it?" I asked, undeterred. I waited, and Cheryl began to weep. She wiped her eyes. Dr. Hanscome took back his handkerchief and gave her a replacement. He smoothed her pillows.

"Dr. Betts wants you to tell him what day it is, Cheryl," he said. "Is it Sunday?"

Cheryl unleashed a volley of obscenities. She knew it wasn't Sunday.

"How do you know?" I asked. I watched and saw her looking intently at the upper corner of the room. Her lips were moving. She was hallucinating.

By now I realized that the Trenton questionnaire didn't work in the real world. There was no point in asking her to name the last five presidents, subtract nine from a hundred, or tell me who George Washington was. Of all the people gathered in that room, it seemed as if only Dr. Hanscome would have scored in any category.

I turned to the large lady. "Are you her mother?"

"No."

"Her mother's up in Bangor Mental," volunteered Cheryl's husband.

I stood up and went over to Dr. Hanscome. "Have you talked to her?"

"Oh, yes. Cheryl and I are old friends—aren't we, dear?"

"Has she been making any threats?"

Hanscome shrugged and turned with a smile to the mother-in-law. "Threats, Mrs. Rucksome?"

"Not since yesterday."

"Oh? What were they?"

"I'd rather not say. They wasn't very nice."

"Had she said anything like it before?"

"She certainly has. Ever since she stepped foot in my house."

"And did you do anything about it? Seek help?"

"Only from Doctor Hanscome and the fire marshal."

I looked around at a series of belligerent faces and asked Dr. Hanscome to step into the bathroom with me for a few private words. He made a gesture for me to enter first.

"We'll be with you in a moment, Cheryl," he said.

I sat down on the toilet seat and Hanscome leaned against the bathtub. "What's this about threats and fire?" I asked.

Hanscome explained that the patient had been like this for years. She set fire to the back of Elmer's barn when she was ten. Since then she'd had to be watched. The school had been worried, but the family had cooperated and had been pretty successful about keeping her in control. With her marriage to Jim she'd become harder to manage. When she'd burned up his mattress three weeks ago, Jim had said he'd been lucky to get out alive. Now she'd got a thing about knives.

I asked Dr. Hanscome if he had any idea why she was doing this. He said he'd tried to talk to her and had gathered that she thought she was under some orders from a gang in Augusta.

"That's a delusion," I said.

"Perhaps so. We ought to check."

"Also she's hallucinating," I said. "She was listening to voices when I was questioning her."

"That's nothing new. She thinks she can hear Satan. I put her on phenobarbital, a half-grain three times a day. Quieted her down some."

I stood up. "Well, there isn't much doubt that she's a paranoid schizophrenic and potentially dangerous. She has delusions, is hallucinating, and is withdrawn. I think we should sign the commitment papers."

Dr. Hanscome demurred. He didn't think we should be too hasty.

The family had feelings of guilt already about the mother being in Bangor Mental Health Institute. It might be wiser to wait a while.

I disagreed and was annoyed at being contradicted. "Let's talk to the family."

We returned to the bedroom, and Dr. Hanscome announced that I had something to say. I was not quite prepared to take the lead. After all, they were all his patients, and he'd known them for several years. He should have spoken first, but now I was in an awkward position.

I addressed the mother-in-law, speaking quietly so that Cheryl might not hear. I explained that I thought the patient was mentally sick and needed treatment. I also thought she might do something violent and harm someone in the house. I was therefore going to sign the commitment form.

"Have you ever been in one of them places, Dr. Betts?"

"As a matter of fact I have. I worked in one."

"Then you know it's the cruelest thing you can do, sending Jim's wife up there."

"What will people say?" chimed in another.

"Disgrace."

"I told you this would happen if you had Dr. Betts," came the voice from the landing.

Dr. Hanscome sat on the bed and took Cheryl's hand. "Would you like to go to the hospital, or would you rather stay here in your home with your family and friends?" He spoke soothingly.

Cheryl only sobbed.

I sensed the hostility. "Have you got the papers?" I asked Dr. Hanscome. He gave them to me. They were similar to the many I had seen at Trenton. I filled in the relevant information and signed it.

"I don't think I can do any more for you."

"Dr. Hanscome is our regular doctor, thank you."

I picked up my bag and left the room. The man leaning on the banister hadn't changed position, and I had to squeeze by to get down the stairs. I got into my car and headed back to my office in a bad temper.

The following day the selectman came to my door. He had the commitment papers in his hands and wanted to confirm my signature with his own. I saw that Dr. Hanscome had also signed them and expressed my surprise.

"He called me this morning," said the selectman. "He said he'd talked for an hour with the family and they'd finally agreed that it would be best for Cheryl to get expert treatment."

"Good."

"Nice fellow, Hanscome. Thoughtful and kind."

"Yes."

I went back into my office with the new realization that the osteopathic physician had the M.D. beaten by a knockout in the first round, hook, line, and sinker, and ten strokes on the eighteenth when it came to PR and bedside manner. They get specific instruction in the art of handling the patient's personality, and many M.D.s could benefit from a similar course.

CHAPTER

35

MY MOTHER MISSED the grandchildren, and after several letters and some exorbitantly expensive transatlantic telephone calls, she was determined to come and see us. In August she boarded the SS *Ile de France,* bound for New York. There she was met by an agent of my father's company, and after a night in a hotel, she was put on a train for Waterville.

My mother's knowledge of America was limited and had been

acquired mostly from Hollywood movies, of which she was a great fan. For the past three decades, Hollywood productions had reached their giddiest heights. Slick, sophisticated films like *The Thin Man, Top Hat, Broadway Melody*, and *Gone with the Wind* had been part of an endless stream of exports to the London cinema belt.

In Hollywood's America, skies were forever a brilliant cerulean blue, the citizens always prosperous, alert, and witty. Cities soared with lofty skyscrapers, inhabited by suited men in trilby hats who held open massive glass doors for elegant women and waited for the elevator to the sixty-fourth floor. The suburbs contained nothing but energetic, handsome men with crew cuts who tended manicured lawns in front of brick ranch houses while their wives stepped out of vast station wagons and released exuberant children.

This was in contrast to London, which was still a gray, austere city of postwar years, with a climate dominated by fog and rain.

Mary and I and the children waited for my mother at Waterville's rail depot. I had parked our car close to the curb at a convenient corner of the vast parking lot. (Urban planners had overestimated the level of traffic on the railroad line, and there were about two acres of tarmac.) We watched as the train, comprising one coach containing, as it turned out, only my mother, was pulled toward us by a massive steam locomotive. It shuddered to a standstill.

We walked toward it, shielding Sara from the puffing green monster, and I saw my mother, looking like Mrs. Roosevelt alighting at a whistle stop, being helped down from the coach. Mother was in her early fifties and had handsome features and dark hair with a touch of gray. She was dressed in a tailored suit and wore high heels and a wide, floppy hat suitable for a modest English social occasion such as Henley or Wimbledon.

It was midsummer, hot, and the skies were very blue, but Waterville revealed a marked absence of skyscrapers, executives in Brooks Brothers suits, ranch houses, and all the rest of the Hollywood scenario.

I don't think my mother noticed these deficiencies. She made a beeline for Sara and lifted her into her arms, then, beaming with tears, turned to Mary to embrace and admire Ann. Meanwhile, I was collecting the luggage and hauling it to the car.

At the curbside I saw that I had been trapped. A second car—there were no others in sight—was parked one foot behind me and the owner, the local taxi driver, had departed.

"That's not a very nice thing to do," remarked my mother.

"No," I agreed.

"After all, there does seem to be a considerable amount of space available."

"Indeed there is. But the taxi sign is here."

"They wouldn't do that even in London." She got into the car.

In Cairo, where this type of incident had been common, I had learned an infallible method of tackling the problem, but, not having a fortified jeep in this instance, I decided to forsake the "back up and bash" technique. Instead, I started to shunt the car back and forth, with a twist of the wheel at the end of each foot-long run.

"What a beastly thing to do," said my mother from the back seat.

I continued the work and was getting very warm.

"So thoughtless," she went on. "Do people often do things like this, over here in this country?"

"We had taken the cab's space," Mary murmured.

"His space? I was given to understand that this was the land of the free." My mother liked to accompany her ironic comments with a quizzical raising of her eyebrows and a shrug of her shoulders.

We freed ourselves after about the thirtieth maneuver, and I decided to skip any sightseeing and head for Albion.

I chose the road via China because Sara loved that ride, a stretch of highway that had a succession of sudden rises and falls that she said did funny things to her stomach. At any speed over thirty miles per hour, passengers rose up and down in the air. It was just like a bumpy ride in an aircraft. Sara used to be convulsed with infectious giggles as we sailed over the humps.

"Don't they ever mend roads like this over here?" asked my mother after a couple of miles.

"Maine's a big state. Lots of roads. This one hasn't made the list."

"In Germany, where your father and I have just been on holiday, they're building autobahns everywhere. Absolutely marvelous. We ought to have them in England, but of course there simply isn't the money." She gave a shrug. "Although I believe we did win the war."

"We're getting a turnpike from Kittery."

"But it won't go to your Albion, surely?"

We reached China Lake, and at Bailey's Store I turned toward Albion. I gestured toward the shimmering water. A motor boat was towing a skier. "Pretty sight for a summer day," I said.

"Yes. Quite nice. But did we ever take you to the Lake District? The green rolling hills, the distant mountains—"

"No, you didn't."

"Oh! Well then."

She watched the farmland go by until Robinson's store hove into sight, and then Keay's. I pulled into our parking lot and came alongside a pickup. As I opened the car door to help my mother out, an elderly farmer emerged from the truck.

"You open for business, Doc?"

"Sure. Be with you in a minute. This is my mother, Mrs. Betts."

He stood his ground: "Pleased to meet you, ma'am. Joe Higgins. Great day." He took a deep breath. "Sure glad you let your son come to stay with us."

My mother inclined her head like the Queen Mother receiving a small bouquet. I took her arm and we walked toward the front door, followed respectfully at ten paces by Higgins. Mary and the children had taken the kitchen route.

As I ushered mother down the hall into the living room, I explained that I had better see Mr. Higgins and would leave Mary to show her to her room.

By the following morning Sara had been won over by her grand-mother and Ann had stopped her objections to being held. We had sat up for a long time catching up with the news from "home," and my mother had been given an early-morning tour of the house, the garden, and the barn. Her reactions were a little restrained, and Mary had fallen back on the defensive. When I suggested I take my mother on the round of house calls, she gave a tight smile and agreed.

"Then afterward you could take her on to the hospital," Mary said.

"No, I think we'll come back for lunch."

"Oh! Right. Jolly good."

We set off in the Pontiac. The car was twice the size of my father's Hillman and several years more modern, but I waited without success for any appreciative remark. As we edged out of Albion I showed her the salient landmarks: Marden's gas pumps, the dirt road to Palermo, Higgins's new chicken house, and the turn-off for Route 137.

We were halfway to Unity when she asked: "Do you think you'll be staying long?"

"Where?"

"In this place. In this midst of nowhere. You can't mean to settle forever."

"Why not?"

"Why not? My dear boy, you didn't put in all those years of study in London to be doing this."

"I'm doing what I like. That's what matters."

She gave a snort.

By the time we entered Unity I was resolved to demonstrate that I was engaged in a rural practice as rewarding as anything available in the Old Country. Indeed, I had one patient up my sleeve who lived in a style that could compete with the minor aristocracy.

I pulled into the driveway of a brick mansion in the center of the town, the home of Mrs. Randolph Welsome. It had a walled garden with trim lawns and beds filled with flowers and shrubs. The roses were in bloom and made a beautiful display. Four elm trees, a huge oak, and a willow threw a dappled pattern of sunlight and shadow over the lawn and walls.

I drove down the gravel drive and parked opposite the front door. Leaving my mother in the car, I rang the bell. The door was opened by Elsie, a servant companion, who today, much to my regret, was not attired in a white cap and frilly apron.

Mrs. Welsome, a gracious white-haired lady in her sixties, was the widow of a successful publisher. She had a slight weakness of her heart and needed to be checked every month.

I found my patient in the front room in her usual armchair by the window. Newspapers and magazines covered a table in front of her. Ever since my first visit she had always offered me coffee, but this time I explained that my mother was waiting for me in the car and I could not stay.

I asked her a few questions, checked her blood pressure and pulse, and looked for any signs of heart failure. As I wrote a fresh prescription, she said, "I'd like to meet your mother, Dr. Betts."

"She'd be delighted."

Mrs. Welsome rose and accompanied me to the front door. We both stepped out on the gravel driveway. I went ahead to the car.

"Mrs. Welsome would like to say hello," I said.

"What?"

"Good afternoon, Mrs. Betts," Mrs. Welsome had come up beside me. "I hope you're enjoying our country."

"Oh! I am. I am. Immensely."

"If it wouldn't delay the doctor on his round, I'd offer you a cup of tea."

My mother beamed. "How very kind."

Mrs. Welsome continued, "Perhaps another day—next week. May I call your son?"

There was a silence in the car as we drove away.

I decided my next stop would be at Mr. Reed's pharmacy. I was anxious to see how this scene would play. I brought the car to the curbside and asked my mother to come in and see a real American drugstore.

We stepped inside, and Mr. Reed emerged through his back room curtains. He brushed the remnants of his gray hair back with his hand and readjusted his steel-rimmed spectacles.

I introduced my mother.

"Glad to meet you, ma'am. Now I've seen the whole family." He turned to me. "But when are you going to bring your lovely wife and those cute little daughters to see me? Don't they want more ice cream? Mint chip, wasn't it?"

He chuckled, and addressed my mother. "So you're checking up on your son, eh? Well let me tell you, ma'am, he's doing O.K. Mind you," he smiled, "at first we had our problems making out his la-de-dah accent, but people round these parts are getting used to him. Very pleased to meet his mum." He put out his hand with a broad smile.

"What a fascinating shop you have. I must buy some postcards."

"Sure is," agreed Reed. "Now, while you look, what can I get you? Your granddaughter likes a cone of mint chip."

We emerged with my mother bearing a sugar cone topped with a double scoop of green ice cream. For the next mile she was too busy to offer any comments.

Next I went toward Thorndike, and beyond the railway tracks I swung into the yard of a dilapidated clapboard house with peeling paint. The unweeded yard displayed two battered garbage pails, empty tins, loose sheets of an old *Morning Sentinel,* and scraps of paper and boxes. In the center sat a lopsided and battered television set and a two-tone Chevy with flat tires.

Mrs. Wiggins and her seven children were all at home. She was nearing the time when she would deliver her eighth. I had told her that it was easier for her to be checked at home when I was passing than for her to trek to my office.

Appearances belied the character of Mrs. Wiggins. She was a kind, intelligent, and educated woman, but given some knitting, she could have easily been cast as an extra for the front-row guillotine scenes in *A Tale of Two Cities*. She had no teeth, her long black hair hung down each side of her gaunt face. She had a baby in her arms and another, who needed a diaper change, clinging to her leg. The others roamed randomly at large.

In the kitchen I asked her some routine questions. But there was a problem when it came to checking her physically. On these occasions a neighbor usually came over to watch the children. Just as Mrs. Wiggins was about to dispatch one of the children to fetch someone, my mother appeared at the back door leading two children by the hand.

"I'm sorry to interrupt," she said, "but Jane and Jason insisted I bring them to you."

Mrs. Wiggins flushed. "They're so naughty," she said.

"This is my mother," I said. "And this is Mrs. Wiggins. She has a large family."

"Like the old lady in the shoe," said Mrs. Wiggins with a toothless, apologetic smile. "And another on the way."

"And that's the difficulty," I went on. "Because I have to examine Mrs. Wiggins, and—"

My mother moved forward. "Can I help?" She turned to me. "You forget, Anthony, that I was a qualified nurse in the war." She gave a shrug. "Where shall we go, Mrs. Wiggins? You children stay there for a minute."

From her handbag she distributed lollipops to several grubby outstretched hands. "I bought them at your Mr. Reed's. I'll get some more for Sara later. You don't mind, Mrs. Wiggins? Now then, where shall we go?"

After my stop at Mrs. Wiggins's we moved on to Freedom to see another cardiac patient, and I found myself telling my mother the history and background of some of my patients. She was right; I had forgotten her nursing experience. She had been a V.A.D. nurse in the First World War and had gone back to nursing during the London Blitz. She had never taken much interest in academic medicine while I was a medical student. Now, out in this country practice, she was full of questions, but when I suggested that we might visit the hospital she declined, saying she'd rather spend some time with our children.

A week went by, and my mother began to be acclimatized. We took a trip to Monmouth Theater—a gem of a building and completely new in my mother's experience—and saw the New York Savoyards playing Gilbert and Sullivan's *The Gondoliers.*

"Do you remember the first time you saw this?" she asked as we promenaded in the theater yard.

"When I was five, I suppose." I smiled at Mary.

"No, you were six, and we took you to see the D'Oyly Carte production at the Golders Green Hippodrome in London. It was Sir Henry Lytton's farewell performance as the Duke."

"And now you're seeing it in the backwoods of Maine."

She looked at me with a suppressed smile. "I must admit, it is rather remarkable."

We walked across the beautiful campus of Colby College at sunset and listened to chamber music. And we went to a dinner party given by Flora Champlin, done in a style, as my mother remarked, "fit for Noel Coward." She had learned that Flora had played sophisticated comedy on Broadway, and I overheard my mother telling her how she'd seen "Noel and Gertie" in *Private Lives* in London.

In Keay's store she bought a pair of sandals. There was nothing remarkable about the transaction except for the closing dialogue, which I heard as I stood beside her:

Mr. Keay: "Eight dollars and twenty cents change."

Mother: "Thank you."

Keay: "You're welcome."

Mother: "How nice of you to say so."

Keay: "My pleasure."

Mother: "Thank you."

Keay: "You're welcome."

Mother: "Forgive me, but why do you keep on saying that?"

Keay: "Saying what?"

Mother: "You're welcome."

Keay: "Thank you."

Mother: "There you go again. You're welcome."

Keay: "My pleasure."

Mother: "Good God!" Followed by uncontrollable laughter.

In the middle of the last week of her visit we found that the corn in the garden that Mickey Marden had made for us was ripe for picking. Mother climbed the hill in her new sandals and helped, then sat on the back steps and shucked the ears. Another day she took herself down to Robinson's store and browsed all afternoon. She returned bearing an assortment of drapery items that she said she hadn't seen since she was a child scouring Petticoat Lane market in London.

A few days later I drove her back to take tea with Mrs. Welsome. For this occasion my mother wore the splendid hat she had bought in Harrod's, high heels, and a silk dress appropriate for opening day at Ascot.

By the time I took her to New York for her return boat, I think my mother had come to understand why we were settling in America, though she departed convinced that the Old Country had more to offer in culture and tradition. "But I suppose this place has its attractions. Perhaps I'm getting old," she said with a shrug.

I knew she was heartbroken at leaving the grandchildren, though she didn't say anything. It was the same when I was seventeen and she saw me off at Waterloo Station during the war: just a hug.

We parted at the gangplank. I kissed her good-bye. "Thank you for coming," I said.

She walked two yards, turned, and smiled. "You're welcome," she said and went aboard. Unfortunately, she never came for another visit.

CHAPTER

OUR NEXT WINTER IN THE Albion practice proved to be even more trying than the conditions we had faced in Eagle Lake. There was less snow and it was warmer, but driving around the back roads and up and down the hills was worse than slithering along Route 11 to Fort Kent. The narrow back roads were often not plowed, and snow concealed underlying patches of ice. On several occasions I had to be hauled out of ditches or snow banks.

One night I visited an egg hatchery in Unity and made the mistake of going up the drive. About halfway, the rear of the car fishtailed and left me sideways across the drive. When I got out, I found it impossible to keep my feet unless I held on to the car. The driveway was a treacherous mixture of ice and snow. The house was still twenty yards above me and the road about sixty below.

I crawled into the car and sounded the horn, unconsciously giving the SOS in Morse code, a legacy from my flying days. I was rewarded after five minutes with the arrival of a small child, apparently immune to fractured limbs or concussion, schussing down on skis to tell me that her father, the owner of the several thousand adjacent hens, was organizing a rescue party.

Eventually this materialized as a length of rope, and I was hauled to the summit. From there I had a splendid view of Unity in the valley beneath a starlit sky.

After I had attended the patient, who fortunately justified the call, the father and I faced the problem of my descent. He apologized for the situation. He explained that while he was in his hatchery, his children, without permission, had groomed the drive as an intermediate ski slope. He said he'd been a fool not to have warned me.

I agreed.

As it was, until he could sand the slope, he was equally stranded. Both his Cadillac and the Buick were in the garage. He supposed I wouldn't care to ski down. I told him he supposed right.

He made a series of calls to friends who might want to try and tow my car out, but there were no takers. He ruled out the fire station. He offered to lower me on the rope but feared for my long, freezing walk into town. Other suggestions were similarly ill-conceived or halfhearted, including trying to coax the town taxi to come out, which he said would be harder than enticing a stoat from its lair. Other than that, I was welcome to spend the night. There was plenty of food and, since I wasn't going to see any more patients, beer.

I gave Mary a call and settled for the beer. After some breezy conversation my host said he had heard I was fond of music and played the piano. He was keen himself and had a saxophone. Why didn't we try a number or two? Otherwise there wasn't much left for amusement except to grade eggs.

I went for the eggs.

A brief explanation: during the war I had obtained a clarinet in Cairo while on my way to a squadron in Aden. There I intended to master Benny Goodman's instrument in the desert's long night hours. After my first practice, I went into the mess to ease my parched lips.

At the bar a senior officer bought me a drink. After a few pensive draughts, he inquired if I wasn't the fellow who had been playing the clarinet in the rooms below him. I confessed that indeed I was the musician, but just a beginner. His eyes lit up as if he'd located his target and was going in for the kill.

He ordered another round, and as he placed his empty glass on the counter, he mentioned that he had some bagpipes. He hadn't been playing them as yet in order to spare his neighboring officers. He now had a proposition. During his remaining eight-month tour, if I would refrain from the clarinet, he would dispense with the pipes. Fair enough?

My dislike for the saxophone ran neck and neck with my repugnance toward bagpipes. The more distant the pipes swirled in the far, misty Highlands, the happier I was. So, in Unity, I settled on sorting eggs, and this I did into small, medium, and large for the next two hours. I was rewarded with a box or two of the best, and the following morning, when I made the descent, the eggs and I completed the journey intact.

Eighteen holes of golf followed by playing chamber music until midnight had been my father's recipe for the blissful life. That he played his viola slightly sharp and his putting was a lottery didn't trouble him. His philosophy was that if a thing was worth doing, it was worth doing badly.

In the fall of 1956, with the approach of another year, I had a similar attitude in mind. And as the last scarlet maple leaf was swept from the lawn, I felt I had to get some balance into my way of living.

For the last two years I had found myself working every hour of the day and most of the night. The only time I had to myself were the hours spent on the road. Mary was getting a raw deal, and I saw almost nothing of the children.

Rural practice had been a rewarding but exhausting business. I often wondered if it had always been that way. Had the automobile now changed the rural doctor's way of life? I suppose in bygone days, a house call meant either a walk or a journey with a horse and buggy. Each must have taken time, and the pace of practice probably wasn't as frenetic.

Now the automobile allowed me to race from house to house, a dozen miles in this direction, fifteen miles in that. Then a frantic rush to the hospital in Waterville for a delivery, then back to the office. And with obstetrics I was always on tenterhooks, trying to time the delivery.

I felt I must discipline myself, take an hour or more each day for myself and the family, and involve myself in something other than medicine.

Apart from the meager income, everything was going well. The people seemed to have accepted me, and there had been many acts of kindness. One of the most remarkable was when, unheralded, Mickey Marden and the search committee brought an upright piano through the front door in the middle of office hours and deposited it in the back room. It was a gift. Word had got out that Mary and I loved to play duets and missed our music.

And the hospital staff had been kindness itself. Their leg-pulling about my British habits and accent was good gentle humor. I felt very much at home.

The problem was to find some spare time and a little more income.

We still had quite a way to go in understanding America and Americans. Without the benefit of going through a school and college in the States, it was difficult to appreciate many of the customs and manners: cheerleaders; basketball (called "netball" and restricted to the fair sex on the other side of the Atlantic); radio commentators; two-toned, high-finned cars; tea bags; and native idioms such as "you're welcome," and the imperative "why," were only a few of the inexplicable mores and fads of the native-born.

But for the time being we thought we had found our niche. It was a matter of standing back and getting everything into perspective. So we decided we ought to get away for a couple of days, our first vacation in months. Mary, as if released from bondage, soon found a baby-sitter willing to stay overnight. And so, with the children settled, we made a weekend trip to Boston to see a play and hear the Boston Symphony. The mini-vacation was just what we needed, and we came back feeling renewed.

However, even before Mary had taken our sitter home, Mrs. Bessey was on the telephone to say that about a dozen people had been looking for me, and most of them were "jumping mad." Before I had replaced the telephone one such disgruntled patient appeared at the door.

"You was gone when I needed you, Doc. Suffered with this knee all night. Then you wasn't here Sunday."

"Sorry. You see—"

"When you came to Albion, you promised you'd be around, not independent, going off like that."

Others were even more vocal. I apologized and tried to smooth things out. At the gas pumps I vented my feelings to Mickey. I explained that I had put a notice on the door that we had gone for a couple of days and that they could call Dr. Beckerman in Waterville for an emergency.

"What else did you put on your note, Doc?"

"That we had gone to Boston to the theater."

He laughed. "Of course they're mad with you. Now, if you'd written that you'd gone hunting, you wouldn't have heard a word."

"The arts don't count for anything?"

"Lor' no! Not in these parts. Only make them madder. Just you put 'gone hunting' next time, and you won't hear a murmur."

"That only covers November."

"'Gone fishing' will do for the rest of the year."

He was right. "Gone fishing" covered a performance of *The Messiah* in Portland, the Beethoven cycle of quartets, and two trips to the Boston Museum of Fine Arts. We never had a peep out of any of our regulars, and only an occasional inquiry about our catch.

Setting aside an hour for myself on a regular basis took a more determined effort. Stimulated by remembering the joy my father derived from playing the viola, I decided I would learn the cello.

I had seen a pre-owned instrument propped up in Al Corey's music store in Waterville. I bought it for twenty-five dollars. It had a nice new "Stradivarius" label gleaming through the *f*hole. Al Corey (who played the saxophone in his dance band) said it had a good tone for something made of plywood.

As I carried the instrument out of the shop, I vowed I would learn how to play it and practice for half an hour a day. Only an emergency or a delivery would interfere with that sacrosanct half hour. Al Corey followed me to the car, telling me I had a bargain, and suggested I take lessons from a Miss Marcoux, who lived above a variety store in Winslow.

So began my journey toward quartets until midnight. (Mary, in self-defense, took up the violin.) My golf swing came several years later, although in the meantime I tried an occasional round on the Unity course and lofted multiple drives into the lake.

It was a theater outing that led to the most unusual "house call" I ever made.

Dr. Andrew Halliday and his wife came to stay with us for a few days toward the end of summer. He was considering emigrating from England and wanted to see what things were like. I took him around the practice and hospital, and Mary showed his wife the domestic aspects of life in America.

For entertainment we decided to take the Hallidays to the theater one evening. Summer stock in Maine was in full swing in those days. Lakewood Theater near Skowhegan was one of the oldest in the land, and had had plays featuring stars such as Humphrey Bogart, Joan Fontaine, and even a Barrymore or two. We took the Hallidays down the coast to a playhouse in Kennebunk to see a popular domestic drama by Somerset Maugham.

It was a lovely summer evening, and as we took our seats we noticed that the house was full and there was a loud buzz of conversation. But as the time went on there was a gradual hush. What was the delay in taking the curtain up? Finally a figure in a tuxedo appeared before the footlights.

"Is there a doctor in the house?"

Andy and I sat firmly in our seats and looked blankly into space.

"*Is there a doctor in the house?*"

I felt Mary nudging me. Mrs. Halliday was eyeing Andy. We both were hoping there was another doctor in the house, but evidently there wasn't.

We stood up, and the people in the rows behind and in front of us turned to watch us edging our way out into the aisle.

"I'm not licensed to practice over here," murmured Andy as we strode toward the stage.

"Moral support," I returned. We followed the man in the tux up some steps and found ourselves in the wings. Our guide turned to us and said he was the manager. Would we come with him onto the stage?

And this is where it became my strangest house call, for we stepped onstage into the elegant front room of an English stately home: grand piano in the corner, grandfather clock, mullioned windows, bowl of flowers on the Chippendale table, two armchairs, and, center stage, a chintz-covered sofa. Our patient reclined on it in a rumpled evening gown. Two other actors—"relatives"?—stood behind the chairs.

"This is Bianca Canby." (She was a well-known Broadway actress.) "She can't go on. Suddenly collapsed."

The manager stood back to allow me to examine her. Andrew joined me. Miss Canby was lying against a cushion, her hair falling over her eyes and her arms splaying out over the back of the sofa.

"How do you feel, Miss Canby?" I asked. I felt as if I were saying a line in the play, the setting was so unreal.

She opened her eyes wide and gazed at me as if being confronted with some strange animal.

Halliday and I leaned forward to catch her reply: "*Perfectly* all right, darling," she said.

Andy met my eyes while I took her pulse. He inclined his head to indicate the need for a quick word on the side. We both went up-stage left.

"She's drunk!" I murmured.

"Squiffy as a newt," Andy concurred. "Nothing more, nothing less."

But what to do and how to do it was the question. Fortunately, at that moment a tubby little man dressed for sailing made an entrance. He apologized and said that he was the company doctor. Was there a problem?

We left him to it and marched back up the aisle to our seats, basking, we thought, in the admiration of the audience who had seen two dedicated doctors responding to the call.

"They ought to be playing 'Rule Britannia,' old boy," Andy said.

"Don't you believe it."

Mary rarely asked about my patients, but in these theatrical circumstances she couldn't resist.

I told her the leading lady was indisposed.

"Serious?"

"Andy said she was as squiffy as a newt."

"Well, I never!" Mary turned to Mrs. Halliday, and I heard her passing on the explanation, concluding in a hoarse whisper: "Tony says the leading lady is squiffy as a newt."

The audience was restless, but as the lights still played on the stage curtains, no one moved. Eventually the theater manager again appeared and apologized for the delay, saying that Miss Canby had been momentarily indisposed, but, in the great tradition of the theater, she insisted that the show must go on.

And go on it did. The curtains parted to reveal the baronial drawing room where I had just done my house call. Two young actors playing nonchalant aristocrats opened the dialogue, their American accents modified with an occasional long *a* to represent the English drawl.

Enter Bianca Canby as the lady of the manor. She crossed to center stage as steady and majestic as Lady Macbeth greeting Duncan for dinner and an overnight. Her speech rang out as clearly as Scarlett's "I'll think about that tomorrow."

Mary turned to me accusingly. "I thought you said she was squiffy as a newt!" she whispered.

It was the first and only time she had questioned my clinical ability. I sat back, hoping to be supported by Andy during the intermission. But when the time came for us to take that break, the man in the seat beside me held me back.

"Pardon me, Doctor, but I spent two years in your country during the war. I couldn't help overhearing. In the States, the expression 'squiffy as a newt' is not appreciated."

"I'm sorry. I meant no offense."

"No—that's O.K. But over here we like to say 'soused to the gills.' Great performance!"

CHAPTER

S O WHY DID I LEAVE GENERAL practice and become a pathologist? It's a question I am still being asked, and the reasons that I had the day I closed my office doors seem to have become increasingly valid as the years roll by.

I take all the blame for desertion under fire. For one thing, I was a poor organizer. I tried to keep my primary office in Albion yet I had to get to the hospital at least once a day, and if I had an obstetric case, I had to remain in the vicinity of Waterville until the patient had been delivered. And it always seemed that while I was anchored to the hospital, Mary would be frantically trying to get me back to see patients who were waiting for me in the office or needing me in their homes.

At the same time, I was trying to do house calls halfway to the coast, covering Liberty, South China, and beyond Unity to Burnham and Clinton. I found myself torn between one patient's need and another's. These house calls could each take over an hour and involve driving forty or fifty miles. After a few of these I'd return exhausted. Financially, they were absurdly unprofitable. Night calls added to the load. This was the picture that was emerging as we approached our third year in Albion.

Our attempts at taking more leisure were usually sabotaged if I stayed within my practice area. Patients would find me at the lake, on the golf course, or at the movies—but I was a doctor, wasn't I?

Dr. Hornberger was sympathetic when I outlined my problems. We had become good friends, and I gave him any surgical case that came my way. It was he who suggested that I take the family away for two weeks.

"And who will look after my practice?" I asked.

"I will."

"But you've never done general practice. Albion has its moments, but it's a bit different from M.A.S.H. in South Korea."

"Try me."

It took nothing to persuade Mary. We'd already had an invitation from Dr. Sharp and his wife to stay with them on the New Jersey shore for two weeks, and she was raring to go. Memories of her Trenton days had suddenly been transformed, and the Garden State had become a place of balm and roses.

I accepted Hornberger's generous offer. Next it was necessary to show him over the office and tell him about the current status of the patients.

When he arrived in Albion he wasn't overly impressed with the office equipment and became diverted by a pair of surgical forceps.

"Jeez, where d'yer get this baby?" he inquired, exercising the blades like an executioner warming up.

"I inherited them from an old practitioner."

"And who did he inherit them from—Washington's surgeon general?"

He inspected the gallon bottles of cough syrup and boxes of various pills and was fascinated with my stock of five hundred phenobarbital pills and load of estrogen tablets. "Got an epidemic of hot flashes, or can't the neighborhood sleep?"

I don't think he paid much attention while I gave brief outlines of various patients' idiosyncrasies. I showed him my notes and he took a tour of the waiting room, pausing before a vase filled with fresh goldenrod from the garden.

"Drumming up the asthma business?"

"No, a flower arrangement to add to the decor."

"Them ain't flowers, buster," he said with a grin.

We left on our vacation. It was a joy from beginning to end and we came back refreshed. Nothing disastrous had overtaken the practice under Hornberger's tillage, although I had forgotten to warn him about the plumber's wife and the electric light. He also had been puzzled by the arthritic patients wanting a change of tablets—"more of the green ones, Doctor"—so had invited them into the back room to choose for themselves. Mrs. Welsome later reported that she had found him unusual but charming.

The vacation gave me a chance to stand back and look at the practice and think of some ways of easing the problems. I told Hornberger that I felt I ought to move the office into Waterville.

"Great idea. You can share mine. I see about three patients a week and the rest of the time I spend trying to write those stories that nobody wants."

So we moved. To our surprise, the community showed little sorrow at our uprooting. "Expect you're bettering yourself," was a constant comment.

But the Waterville move was not a success. I found I still had to run an office in Albion in the evenings. Living near the hospital eased some of the strain, but we found, as we had expected, that we lost some patients. The bank balance entered its phase of decline and fall—and it didn't have far to go.

Then another cloud appeared on the horizon. The era of medical malpractice litigation had begun. Our insurance premium went up like a rocket, and the hospital, fearful of being taken to court at the drop of a hat, started to limit privileges. General practitioners would be restricted in the operating and delivery rooms. General practitioners would no longer deal with wounds or fractures in the emergency room unless supervised. General practitioners must have a specialist in consultation for their hospital admissions. General practitioners could get lost.

Before the year was out it was easy to see the writing on our wall. And beneath that writing, if one looked closely, were words not in Babylonian script but plain English: "If you can't beat them, join them."

I must specialize. But what residency could I afford to take for a minimum of three to five years and still support a family—now with three children?

There is an iron bridge crossing the Messalonskee River at Benton. I once delivered a baby in the middle of it when we failed to make the hospital on time. And it was in that very spot, one night when I was returning from a house call in Unity, that I realized the answer: pathology.

I had liked the field as a medical student and had reached the finals in a medical competition at the London Hospital, when I'd had to do an autopsy and deduce the clinical picture. I enjoyed looking down a microscope.

The following day, after talking to Mary, I went to see Dr. Goodof, the pathologist at Thayer Hospital. He and his wife had made a point of befriending us. Now he listened with a sympathetic ear.

Without a word he reached for his telephone and called Dr. Joseph Porter, chief pathologist at Maine Medical Center in Portland.

After a short conversation he turned to me and said, "There's an opening in two months. It's an excellent residency and pays one thousand a year." I nodded and sat back while my decision was conveyed to Dr. Porter. A thousand a year would just about feed the cat. We had some savings, largely as a result of the Eagle Lake practice, which could supplement Dr. Porter's offer. Perhaps I could do some moonlighting. Perhaps I could see a few patients on the outskirts of Portland. . . .

"He'd like to see you as soon as possible for an interview, so give him a call at his office." Dr. Goodof wrote the number down and gave it to me. "And good luck."

How we journeyed into the world of pathology from Portland to Boston and back again would make a good story—but one for some other time.

More books of interest from
DOWN EAST BOOKS

Tides of the Heart
By Thomas M. Sheehan

Concerns for her declining health lead Miss Worthley, a wealthy spinster, to relax her cynical, condescending attitude toward the people around her. At the heart of the transition is a young encyclopedia salesman, the painful memory of her long-dead lover, and the plight of Staddleford Creek's migrating alewives. A beautifully crafted tale of renewal, rediscovery, and love in the tradition of *Driving Miss Daisy*.

My Love Affair With the State of Maine
By Scotty Mackenzie and Ruth Goode

Take two energetic young professionals fresh from the New York advertising world, drop them into a small Maine town as the new owners of the village store/restaurant/dance hall/soda fountain/guest house/bowling alley, and you are guaranteed some highly entertaining results.

Life List: Remembering the Birds of My Years
By John N. Cole

1998 Small Press Book Award Winner

Life List is much more than a book about birds. It is the unusual biography of a remarkable man whose work has ranged from commercial fishing off Long Island to founding a successful alternative newspaper in Maine.

A Show of Hands: A Maine Mystery
By David A. Crossman

Retired National Security Agent Winston Crisp thought his career of delving into dark, unpleasant secrets was over when he retired to a peaceful Maine island. However, when the body of a young woman is discovered frozen in the ice of an abandoned granite quarry, he just can't stop himself from asking a few questions.

The Day Before Winter
By Elisabeth Ogilvie

The long-awaited new volume in Ogilvie's Bennett's Island series rejoins Joanna Sorensen's family during the Vietnam era. The Sorensens have settled and raised families, but into the peace of island life come two young men trying to shed the traces of past mistakes. The close-knit island must wrestle with difficult questions of family loyalty, ethics, and the good of the community.